CRIME AND CRIME CONTROL

CRIME AND CRIME CONTROL

A GLOBAL VIEW

Edited by Gregg Barak

A World View of Social Issues
Andrew L. Cherry, Series Adviser

Greenwood Press
Westport, Connecticut • London

Library of Congress Cataloging-in-Publication Data

Crime and crime control : a global view / edited by Gregg Barak.
    p. cm.—(A world view of social issues, ISSN 1526–9442)
    Includes bibliographical references and index.
    ISBN 0–313–30681–8 (alk. paper)
    1. Crime prevention—Cross-cultural studies. 2. Criminology—Cross-cultural
studies. I. Barak, Gregg. II. Series.
    HV7431.C686 2000
    364.4—dc21   99–049044

British Library Cataloguing in Publication Data is available.

Library of Congress Catalog Card Number: 99–049044
ISBN: 0–313–30681–8
ISSN: 1526–9442

First published in 2000

Greenwood Press, 88 Post Road West, Westport, CT 06881
An imprint of Greenwood Publishing Group, Inc.
www.greenwood.com

Printed in the United States of America

The paper used in this book complies with the
Permanent Paper Standard issued by the National
Information Standards Organization (Z39.48–1984).

10 9 8 7 6 5 4 3 2 1

CONTENTS

SERIES FOREWORD

Why are child abuse in the family and homelessness social conditions to be endured or at least tolerated in some countries while in other countries they are viewed as social problems that must be reduced or eliminated? What social institutions and other factors affect these behaviors? What historical, political, and social forces influence a society's response to a social condition? In many cases, individuals around the world have the same or similar hopes and problems. However, in most cases we deal with the same social conditions in very dissimilar ways.

The volumes in the Greenwood series A World View of Social Issues examine different social issues and problems that are being faced by individuals and societies around the world. These volumes examine problems of poverty and homelessness, drugs and alcohol addiction, HIV/AIDS, teen pregnancy, crime, women's rights, and a myriad of other issues that affect all of us in one way or another.

Each volume is devoted to one social issue or problem. All volumes follow the same general format. Each volume has up to fifteen chapters that describe how people in different countries perceive and try to cope with a given problem or social issue. The countries chosen represent as many world regions as possible, making it possible to explore how each issue has been recognized and what actions have been taken to alleviate it in a variety of settings.

Each chapter begins with a profile of the country being highlighted and an overview of the impact of the social issue or problem there. Basic policies, legislation, and demographic information related to the social issue are covered. A brief history of the problem helps the reader better understand the political and social responses. Political initiatives and policies are also discussed, as well as social views, customs, and practices related to the problem or social issue. Discussions about how the countries plan to deal with these social problems are also included.

These volumes present a comprehensive and engaging approach for the study of international social conditions and problems. The goal is to provide a convenient framework for readers to examine specific social problems, how they are viewed, and what actions are being taken by different countries around the world.

For example, how is a problem like crime and crime control handled in third world countries? How is substance abuse controlled in industrialized countries? How are poverty and homelessness handled in the poorest countries? How does culture influence the definition and response to domestic violence in different countries? What part does economics play in shaping both the issue of and the response to women's rights? How does a national philosophy impact the definition and response to child abuse? These questions and more will be answered by the volumes in this series.

As we learn more about our counterparts in other countries, they become real to us, and our worldview cannot help but change. We will think of others as we think of those we know. They will be people who get up in the morning and go to work. We will see people who are struggling with relationships, attending religious services, being born, and growing old, and dying.

This series will cover issues that will add to your knowledge about contemporary social society. These volumes will help you to better understand social conditions and social issues in a broader sense, giving you a view of what various problems mean to different people and how these perspectives impact a society's response. You will be able to see how specific social problems are managed by governments and individuals confronting the consequences of these social dilemmas. By studying one problem from various angles, you will be better able to grasp the totality of the situation, while at the same time speculating as to how solutions used in one country could be incorporated in another. Finally, this series will allow you to compare and contrast how these social issues impact individuals in different countries and how the effect is dissimilar or similar to our own experiences.

As series adviser, it is my hope that these volumes, which are unique in the history of publishing, will increase your understanding and appreciation of your counterparts around the world.

Andrew L. Cherry
Series Adviser

ACKNOWLEDGMENTS

I would like to acknowledge the contributors to this volume for their willingness to participate in a comparative project in which they did not necessarily know each other or me. As editor, I have had numerous emails and a fewer number of snail mail communications with the different contributors over a two-year period. Moreover, some of us met one another at comparative sessions that I and William Pridemore arranged at the 12th International Congress on Criminology in Seoul, Republic of Korea, in August 1998 and the annual meetings of the American Society of Criminology in Washington, D.C., in November 1998. Working in this virtual and global context has been a real "eye-opener" and an intellectual enterprise that has substantively altered and enhanced my cultural understanding of the development of crime and crime control over the centuries.

A global venture in public and general education like this one has also involved the contributors' goodwill and necessary understanding of the editing cuts that reduced the original manuscript from approximately 140,000 words to some 90,000 words. More important, this project has involved the contributors' confidence in my editing ability to "rewrite" their contributions not only for the purposes of finding a common voice and narrative but in order to forge a truly comparative study of crime and crime control in the world today. As a result, we have produced a first-of-its-kind comparative volume on the cross-cultural study of crime and justice from a global perspective.

In turn, there are a few others who made this book possible and need to be acknowledged. First and—as it has turned out—foremost, there is Emily

Birch, Acquisitions Editor for Greenwood Press. She was not only able to see the proverbial "trees through the forest" and to help keep my "eyes on the prize" as we whittled down the manuscript to the appropriate size, but also came up with the initial framework for reorganizing the 15 chapters so that they were, in effect, consistent with each other. I would also like to acknowledge the copy editor, Susan E. Badger, for a job well done. Finally, I would like to thank both Eastern Michigan University for a sabbatical leave during Winter semester 1999 and Ian Taylor of Durham University for arranging a lecture circuit for me in the United Kingdom. Together, these allowed me to travel extensively in the United Kingdom and to engage a number of criminologists there who are working with transnational and global concerns. Specifically, conversations with Ian Taylor, Jock Young, and Jim Sheptycki were particularly insightful for this international project.

INTRODUCTION: A COMPARATIVE PERSPECTIVE ON CRIME AND CRIME CONTROL

Gregg Barak

As an academic specialty, the study of comparative, cross-cultural crime and crime control is less than 30 years old. As a subject matter, then, comparative criminology is relatively new and still in its formative years. Not too long ago, Neuman and Berger (1988) were arguing, for example, that comparative crime theories were immature, and a decade earlier, Blazicek and Janeksela (1978: 234) had pronounced that the methods associated with the study of crime control abound with "ambiguity, confusion and misuse of the term 'comparative.' " Nevertheless, for the past decade or more, there has been an increasing number of criminologists who have turned their previously parochial and national gazes on crime and crime control to other nations besides their own.

Today, there are still alternative views, definitions, and theories of, as well as approaches to, comparative crime and crime control. For example, there are globalists who contend that before comparative criminology gets "its house in order," criminologists will have moved on to doing international and transnational criminology (Friday, 1996; Jamieson, South, and Taylor, 1997; Sheptycki, 1998). As the number of comparative studies have grown, however, some clarity of purpose has been established in the field, including the perspective adopted here that comparative criminology involves the study of crime and crime control at the national, international, and transnational levels.

CRIME AND CRIME CONTROL: A GLOBAL VIEW

Up to the present time, an overview of the development of the comparative study of crime and crime control reveals quantitatively based research findings and explanations that can best be described as operating at "macro-levels," or institutional levels, rather than at "microlevels" or individual levels of analysis. In short, comparative work has been more about studying criminality (crime and criminalization) than it has been about the actual studying of criminal behavior. At the present time, qualitative studies of crime and crime control are unique, and conducting, in particular, ethnographic studies of criminals in relationship to the changing social, political, and economic structures should be a part of qualitative studies.

It is our hope that this comparative study contributes to the developing basis of qualitative knowledge on crime and crime control. However, as part of our research design, we did not pursue an ethnographic direction per se. Instead, our desire was to provide, from a global point of view, a succinct and manageable representation of crime and crime control in 15 nation-states. Nevertheless, the contributors to this volume are indigenous to or have lived in the countries about which they write. As a consequence, these authors have brought to their analyses what might be referred to as an "ethnographic sensibility," even though their primary tasks were to supply broad brush strokes on the development of crime and crime control for one particular country.

More specifically, in *Crime and Crime Control: A Global View*, we survey the cross-cultural relationships of crime and crime control for 15 countries or nation-states. As part of our global analysis of crime and crime control, we have grouped these societies into one of three nation-state classifications based on their social, political, and economic integration into the worlds of multinational corporatism and lifestyle consumerism (Waters, 1995). The classification follows the country's name in each chapter.

Developed Nation-States:
Germany
Netherlands
New Zealand
Taiwan
United Kingdom
United States

Developing Nation-States:
Brazil
China
India
Iran
Poland
Russia

INTRODUCTION

Posttraditional Nation-States:

Ghana

Navajo Nation

Nigeria

Most people have little, if any, difficulty distinguishing between the underdeveloped (posttraditional) and the developing or developed nations. When it comes to distinguishing between developed and developing nations, however, some disagreements between people occur depending on which combinations of social, political, and economic factors are emphasized. There are also those who maintain that some nations, such as the independent, oil-rich Middle Eastern ones, fall outside of the core, periphery, and semiperiphery distinctions. Hence, we acknowledge that some theorists might take issue with one or two countries that we have located within the developed or developing categories.

For our analysis, if any of the developmental pieces were missing, including the presence of modern institutions and secularized values, industrialization and urbanization, rapid economic development, and the dissolution of the traditional or repressive social orders, then the middle-level classification of development was used. If all of the pieces were present, then the upper-level classification of development was used. If most of the pieces were missing, then the lower-level classification of development was used.

Historically, cross-cultural research that embodies a large number of countries typically employs national or aggregated data sets, such as the United Nations World Crime Surveys, the Comparative Crime Data File, INTERPOL, Correlates of Crime, 1960–1984, or the Human Relations Area Files (which contain numerous data from different cultures, past and present). Whereas our study of 15 nations sporadically incorporates findings from some of these sources, there has been no systematic undertaking to apply these kinds of data sets to our basic inquiries. For the most comprehensive synthesis of research and data sets on the nature of crime, the operations of national criminal justice systems, and the state of crime prevention from a cross-national perspective, consult the *Global Report on Crime and Justice* compiled by the United Nations Office for Drug Control and Crime Prevention (Newman, 1999). In general, the findings from our 15 nation-state study and those of the United Nations' *Global Report* are quite similar.

Our examination, however, is primarily qualitative and descriptive in nature. Nevertheless, by utilizing those data that were accessible or made available to them during their research expeditions of 1998, our contributors provide an array of empirical—qualitative and quantitative—information on crime and victimization. They do so, however, not as investigators systematically collecting the same material for 15 nation-states but as members of a fragmented team asked to individually conduct, one nation at a time, simultaneous research on crime and crime control.

The primary focus of our nation-state studies has also been localized. In other words, these studies are keenly historical and concerned with telling the developmental stories of crime and crime control for each particular country. In different ways, most of these national studies are comparative in the sense that not only do they explore crime and crime control in two or more historical periods but, at the same time, examine these relationships in terms of their changing political, economic, and social contexts.

These individual analyses of crime and crime control are comparative in two other senses as well. Considering that the contributing authors are generally experts on crime and crime control for two or more nation-states, most of them do make occasional comparisons to other countries that they are familiar with. Moreover, several of the authors compare and contrast their particular nation's crime and crime control with the trends and patterns common to those of the United States, Japan, and nations from Western Europe.

Ideally, it has been my assumption that some kind of integrative macrolevel/microlevel of analysis of crime/criminals is preferable to either/or macroanalyses versus microanalyses. Yet again, our cross-cultural comparative study is predominantly concerned with the historical records and territorial developments of crime and crime control at the macrolevels or institutional levels (e.g., political, economic, and legal) of analysis. At the same time, our comparative analysis moves back and forth between the national and global panoramas, appreciating the importance of locally changing conditions, such as ethnic diversity, population growth, politicalization, urbanity, economic development, marginality, inequality, and so on, on the one hand and the importance of the developing processes and landscapes of integration, globalization, and homogenization on the other hand.

In each of the chapters that follows, the authors have agreed to present reviews of more or less the same essential materials for the purposes of comparative examination. These include for each country: (1) data provided on the trends and rates of crime and victimization; (2) presentations on the historical development of crime and crime control, incorporating a profiling or conceptual framework of the changing demographics, politics, economics, and cultural styles of living and consumption; (3) a discussion on the philosophical issues and responses to crime and on the circumstances concerning legal and policy developments in crime control; and (4) a speculative discussion on the future trends in crime and crime control. Finally, in rewriting and editing the draft manuscript for final publication, it became necessary, for comparative purposes, to superimpose six topical headings across the 15 nation-state chapters:

THEORETICAL ORIENTATIONS TO CRIME AND CRIME CONTROL: MODERNIZATION, WORLD SYSTEM, AND OPPORTUNITY

In the field of comparative criminology, there are essentially three broad perspectives on the development of crime and crime control: modernization, world system, and opportunity. Comparatively speaking, each of these models incorporates various assumptions, concepts, and relationships about "law," "crime," and "social change," and each model proffers a different explanation for the variation in crime and crime control.

First, there are the modernization explanations that have argued that social changes, such as urbanization and industrialization, are associated with changes in crime and victimization patterns. According to these models, the changes in crime and crime control are primarily the products of the internal influences of development, regardless of time and place. Second, there are the world system explanations that have argued that contemporary developing nations are dependent on—and to varying degrees, exploited by—already developed nations. Hence, the changes in crime and crime control in any country, regardless of its developmental status, are primarily the products of external influences, in relationship to a changing political economy. Third, there are the opportunity explanations that have argued that both crime and crime control reflect a mixture of developing material resources and social environments. Thus, changes in the patterns of crime and victimization, over time, are primarily the products of interacting internal and external factors.

Traditionally, the three models used to explain the cross-national differences in such crime rates as homicide and theft, for example, have been viewed as alternative, competing, or overlapping models. In terms of the similarities between models, the opportunity and modernization approaches are both "evolutionary, focus on processes of adaptation, and emphasize industrialization, urbanization, cultural diversity and population growth," whereas the opportunity and world system approaches are more "holistic, materialistic, relational, and emphasize hierarchical or dominance relations" (Neuman and Berger, 1988: 288). Therefore, it may be better to think of these three models as comprising a continuum of comparative explanations on crime and crime control, with world system theory and modernization theory at either end of the continuum and the opportunity theory somewhere in between. At the same time, it may make more sense to think of these models as providing complementary rather than mutually exclusive explanations of crime and crime control. And in the final analysis, it might be that the ultimate value of these theories and other similarly reworked and combined theories may turn out to reside in some kind of synthesis or integrative model of the three.

As approached in this volume, crime and crime control are viewed as products of inequality, poverty, and political oppression that accompany development based on exploitation and dependency (Humphries and Greenberg, 1981; Platt and Takagi, 1981). In the context of capitalist development and class struggle, the various forms and expressions of crime itself are regarded as structural adaptations, where there are essentially two fundamental kinds of crime behaving (Quinney, 1977). First, there are the "crimes of domination" and "crimes of control" methodically committed by capitalist/governing classes and their agents. Second, there are the "crimes of accommodation," "crimes of interpersonal violence," and "crimes of resistance/rebellion" erratically committed by working and subordinate classes and referred to in their totality as "crimes of survival."

Examples of the crimes of domination and control encompass those acts that systematically injure or harm consumers, workers, and the general public, including offenses like antitrust violations, worker-related illnesses and deaths, environmental pollution, organized corruption, abuses of law enforcement, and so forth. Examples of the crimes of survival include offenses like property crimes of theft and illegal entrepreneurial activities involving drug sales, gambling, and prostitution; offenses like murder, assault, rape, and domestic violence; and offenses like political organizing, protests, riots, and strikes. When comparing Quinney's classification of crimes in the context of developing political economies, the former acts can be viewed generally as the product of group and organizational activities engaged in on behalf of the direct or indirect accumulation of capital, whereas the latter acts can be viewed generally as the product of isolated and individual incidents of predation, except when they involve the less common social and collective acts of resistance and rebellion.

GLOBALIZATION AND CRIME AND CRIME CONTROL

As we move into the new millennium, globalization has become a fact of life on earth. We do, indeed, live in the "global village." *Globalization* refers to the interdependency of events and of the actions of people and governments around the world. Globalization appreciates that

1. The effects of the events on one side of the world are likely to ripple all the way around the globe.

2. Calculations of national sovereignty are routinely affected by the interest and needs of 160 other nations.
3. There is no longer a country on the face of this shrunken planet that can go it alone. (Hufstedler, 1980: 8)

More specifically, globalization refers to the worldwide political economies and to the expanding communications-transportation networks that have had the effects not only of reducing the planet in time and space but of creating an excess of opportunities for both capital(ist) and criminal(ist) expansion. The latter appears as innovative and spontaneous forms of "old" and "new" crimes against property and person alike.

For example, the fraudulent and unfair trade practices in commerce, the laundering of unauthorized drug and arms trade profits, the smuggling of illegal immigrants into and out of alien nations, the dumping of toxic wastes and other forms of ecological destruction, the acts of terrorism committed by and against various states, and the behavior of multinationals to move capital to exploit cheap labor all embody the illicit practices of globalization. Other crimes of control and domination engaged in by corrupt police, militia, and other governmental agents, inside and outside of the criminal justice system, also reflect the illicit commodities of international productivity and service delivery. These crimes appear geographical and involve organized networks functioning in local, regional, national, and international markets. The developing contours of some criminality are currently undergoing fundamental changes: [W]ith decreases in barriers of language, communication, information and technology transfer and mobility, and the ever increasing globalization of the economy, there has been a growing trans-national character of organized, financial, sex-related, immigration, and computer crime" (Travis, 1998: 1).

Despite the internationalization of the world economy, we are not arguing that national cultures, economies, and borders are dissolving before our very eyes, nor are we suggesting that "national economies and, therefore, domestic strategies of national economic management are increasingly irrelevant" (Hirst and Thompson, 1996: 1). What we are saying, however, is that the emergence of the Euro on January 1, 1999, as a means of Western Europe "cooperatively" trying to compete with the U.S. dollar and the Japanese yen for alternative places to invest their national currency reserves has all kinds of regional and global implications, not only for the monetary and fiscal policies around the world but also in terms of the various kinds of marginality and crime and crime control.

Finally, we are not implying, as extreme globalists do, that the world economy is dominated by uncontrollable market forces and by transnational corporations that no longer owe any allegiance to the nation-state. In other words, like Hirst and Thompson, it is our belief that these economic developments are more complex and more equivocal than many global analysts believe. The point being that close attention should be devoted to understanding local conditions, domestic strategies, and national policies in relationship to the internationalization of the world economy.

CROSS-NATIONAL CAPITAL, LABOR, CRIME AND CRIME CONTROL

In the context of capitalist development worldwide, the twenty-first century is witness to a highly mobile and international capital. At least since the end of the Cold War in the 1980s, capital has been actively engaged "in a worldwide political offensive in favor of free trade, deregulation, privatization and cuts in social spending" (Early, 1998: 33). By contrast, labor has been fairly quiet, provincial, and regional in its orientation to the global economy. Hence, labor primarily operates "within the framework of a single national-state or, worse yet, one domestic industry, firm, or craft" (34). Unlike capital, labor remains fragmented and disorganized. It finds itself still groping for ways to go beyond traditional forms of nationalism. In short, workers, whether organized or not, have been in retreat, on the defensive, and predominantly absorbed in struggles against the further erosion of their position in the capital-labor schemata of a worldwide swing to "laissez-faire" capitalism.

When it comes to criminality, both criminals and criminal organizations seem to resemble the worlds of business more than they do the worlds of labor and criminal justice/crime control. By analogy, organized criminals, like their counterparts in organized business, may resort to knowledge, wealth, and violence to accomplish their tasks. Tactically speaking, however, both prefer using knowledge and capitalizing on the "information revolution" rather than using force or wealth. For example, Moore and Fields (1996: 3) have observed that criminal organizations "have taken advantage of the information and technological revolution to as great or a greater degree than has government and business, and to a far greater degree than has the criminal justice system." In fact, some "criminal confederations" are using intelligence systems, developing technology, and fine-tuning their criminal techniques on an international scale. On balance, the information and intelligence networks of some crime groups have been superior to those of law enforcement, but these "networks" are still no match for the most powerful multinational corporations.

These changing developments involving capital, labor, crime, and crime control are motivated by three contemporary economic forces that are driving the capital megamergers of the new world order of "global companies." These forces are (1) the demand by money managers for quarterly performance and earnings growth that will propel stock prices upward; (2) the marketplace itself whose logic is swelling demand for companies to integrate their global strategies with global capital markets; and (3) the rush for global market dominance.

In effect, the globalization of capital, labor, crime, and crime control over the last decade of the twentieth century reveals a developing worldwide political economy where capitalist reformers in Mexico or in the former Eastern bloc nations, for example, may have promised prosperity for their nation's workers, but so far, these laborers have been the primary benefactors of austerity, job insecurity, and greater under- and unemployment. Moreover, these workers have also experienced increasing levels of "criminal" victimization. In other parts of the world—developed, developing, and underdeveloped—the same general trends appear: an unparalleled and untrammeled degree of competition in which free trade, cheap labor, and crime are all abundantly available and in great demand.

At the same time, the profits from capitalist expansion and global consumerism are at an all-time high. In addition, with respect to crime control and the integration of criminal justice services, the ideology and practice of the privatization of crime and punishment fit neatly into the political economies of contracting welfare states and deregulating governments. Hence, the still nascent but emerging sectors of the world's criminal justice systems are gradually becoming part and parcel of a private as well as a public apparatus of crime control. Often referred to as "police-industrial" and "penal-service" complexes, these privatized forms of crime control contribute to multinational profits as they simultaneously create new forms of "surveillance" and "corrections" (Nuzum, 1998).

As part of the process of globalization, both the legitimate and illegitimate fields of "criminal enterprise" have been freed-up for the greater exploitation of humankind:

1. The borders that constrained commerce—but also protected companies from the full brunt of competition—are eroding.

2. Governments are retreating from control of the commanding heights of their economies: they are privatizing and deregulating.

3. Barriers to trade and investment are coming down rapidly.

4. Ever-cheaper communications and ever-faster computers, along with the Internet, are facilitating the flow of goods and services, as well as knowledge and information. (Yergin, 1998: 27)

And so it goes: With global competition and the international flow of goods and services, knowledge, and information comes the worldwide growth in crime and crime control. Yet these global developments are not unencumbered by the local experiences of politics, nationalism, and domestic strategies of social change. Hence, it is advocated here that the fully integrative comparative analysis of crime and crime control should take into account both of these sets of relations, especially as they interact with one another.

SOME TENTATIVE CONCLUSIONS

From a global point of view, a negative outcome of the thawing of East/West relations has been the influx of conflict and crime worldwide. During the past decade, one consequence of the end of the Cold War has been the international increase in transnational or border crimes, especially those involving the smuggling of goods and services out from and into various nation-states. For example, as late as the 1980s, the majority of stolen cars in the United States were hot-wired for "joy riding" or for do-mestic "chop shops" to sell the disassembled parts locally. With the breakup of the Soviet Union, the loosening of border controls across Eastern Europe, and the opening up of the "free market" in the early 1990s, the international demand for stolen cars (as operating vehicles) has increased and expanded worldwide. As a result, and in less than a decade, the business of both stealing and protecting cars in the United States, and elsewhere, has been completely transformed (Bradsher, 1999).

As we enter the twenty-first century, the internationalization of markets in all kinds of criminal contraband (i.e., weapons, drugs, sex, alcohol, tobacco, coffee), and the international efforts to combat this activity, is but one illus-tration of the globalization of crime, surveillance, and control. Yet despite the development of transnational crime, the bulk of most crime, violent and prop-erty, individual, organized, corporate, or governmental (state), is usually con-fined within the geographic boundaries of the existing nation-states. While some would like to talk about the nation-state as an obsolete institution, the conclusion drawn here is that while the likes of border crimes and transna-tional efforts of crime control are on the rise, the examination and investiga-tion of crime and crime control should be carried out one nation at a time, since the bulk of criminality is still primarily a domestic affair, although its roots today are both national and global in nature.

Even when dividing 15 countries into differentially classified nation-states as was done in this study, it is still very hard not only to generalize about particular nation-state formations and their relationship to the patterns and trends in crime and crime control but also to provide findings that defini-tively resolve the theoretically raised questions about the similarities and differences in crime and crime control for our developed, posttraditional, and developed nation-states. Having stated these caveats up front, what our examination of 15 countries has revealed is that both crime and crime con-trol are growing and expanding enterprises worldwide. This seems to be true for developed, posttraditional, and developing countries. In general, as found here and in other studies, as nations and inequality develop, crimes against property expand more rapidly than crimes against the person. In

many ways, the expressions of crime and criminality are more uniform between the three types of nations than are the responses to crime or the
expressions of crime control. That is to say, trends in crime within and
between the different kinds of nation-states are more alike than are the
trends in crime control and criminal justice.

For example, within the developed nation-states, while there is a great
deal of "risk analysis," "actuarial examination," and "legal rationalization"
of the criminal justice system, there are not clear-cut directions toward either
"repressive" or "social" justice in general or trends in sentencing and punishment in particular. So, on the one hand, we witness the United States
and the United Kingdom experiencing tougher and longer sentencing
schemes, whereas, on the other hand, Germany and the Netherlands have
resisted such tendencies, keeping their punishment schemes in line with their
more "liberal" practices of the post–World War II generation. Similarly, the
former countries have started privatizing some of their responses to crime,
whereas the latter countries have not. At the same time, all four of these
developed countries have been experimenting with "restorative" forms of
justice and with victim compensation schemes, not to mention other forms
of community law enforcement and corrections, reminiscent of some of the
practices characteristic of posttraditional countries.

In the posttraditional societies like Ghana, the Navajo Nation, or Nigeria,
there have been attempts to balance the values and practices of traditional
and postcolonial forms of law enforcement and adjudication. But the similarities of poverty and gross inequalities in these peripheral societies express
themselves differently in the various forms that their criminality takes. At
least in part, this is a result of each nation's unique economic relationship
with other countries of the core and semiperiphery. Hence, the forms of
crime that are manifested will vary as was revealed by the self-abuse, batter-
ing, alcoholism, and other forms of domestic violence perpetrated among
residents of the Navajo Nation as contrasted with the vast amounts of graft
and corruption engaged in by the politicos and organized crime interests
found in Ghana and Nigeria.

In the developing nations, there is even less uniformity in the expressions
of crime and crime control, as these have varied to the extent that the political, economic, and social institutions have been democratically freed from
autocratic or fundamentalist rule. In contemporary Iran, for example, just
about every kind of nonconformist behavior is a crime, from etiquette and
sin to actual violence against the person and thefts of property. In most of
the developing nation-states, especially those from the former Eastern bloc
nations, criminal epidemics revolve around hard-to-get goods and services.
In other words, in Russia and Poland, the underground economies compete
head-to-head with the above-ground economies, making it a situation where
bribes, corruption, and other felonies and misdemeanors pay better than
legitimate work or no work whatsoever.

In sum, while there do seem to be trends and patterns, if not general laws, for the origins and developments of crime, especially with respect to the production and reproduction of criminal formations, the responses in crime prevention and social control seem to be less uniform across nations. Compared to the crime, crime control is more variable and subject to the perceptions, discourses, philosophies, and cultural attitudes of particular societies. The responses to crime will range, accordingly, to the way in which nations view criminals and think about crime, punishment, and society. In those societies like the United States or the United Kingdom, where criminals are viewed as enemies, they are to be isolated and excluded; in other societies like the Netherlands or the Navajo Nation, where criminals are viewed as vulnerable persons worth saving, they are to be brought back into the community fold.

Taken as a whole, these 15 nation-state stories of crime and crime control suggest that despite the globalization that is occurring, it is far too early to dismiss the nation-states and their domestic sources and resources—political, economic, and cultural—from influencing and shaping the crime and crime control policies of particular countries.

What I think is well discerned from this study is that while the global village is becoming smaller through cyberspace, telecommunications, and rapid transportation, the nation-states of the world are just beginning to become more integrated through a globalization of their economic, political, legal, and social institutions. Moreover, as these countries become increasingly interdependent and experience common social and environmental problems, criminal and noncriminal, it is hoped that the peoples of the world will learn to address the fundamental problems of the Other from a center in which reciprocity and social justice have eventually displaced the avarice, greed, and inequality in the distribution of goods and services within and between the have and have-not nation-states.

REFERENCES

Barak, Gregg (ed.). 1991. *Crimes by the Capitalist State: An Introduction to State Criminality.* Albany: SUNY Press.

Blazicek, D., and G. M. Janeksela. 1978. "Some Comments on Comparative Methodologies in Criminal Justice." *International Journal of Criminology and Penology* 6: 233–45.

Bradsher, Keith. 1999. "For Car Thieves, a Technological Arms Race." *New York Times*, Sunday, March 21, F1.

Early, Steve. 1998. "Slicing the Globaloney: A Review of *Workers in a Lean World: Unions in the International Economy.*" *The Nation* (February 16): 33–35.

Ebbe, Obi (ed.). 1996. *Comparative and International Criminal Justice System: Policing, Judiciary, and Corrections.* Boston: Butterworth-Heinemann.

Frate, Ann A. Del, Uglgesa Zvekic, and Jan J. M. van Duk. 1993. *Understanding Crime: Experience of Crime and Crime Control.* Rome: United Nations Interregional Crime and Justice Research Institute.

Friday, Paul. 1996. "The Need to Integrate Comparative and International Criminal Justice into a Traditional Curriculum." *Journal of Criminal Justice Education* 7: 227–39.

Hirst, Paul, and Grahame Thompson. 1996. *Globalization in Question: The International Economy and the Possibilities of Governance*. Cambridge: Polity Press.

Hufstedler, Shirley M. 1980. "World in Transition." *Change* (May–June): 8–9.

Humphries, Drew, and David Greenberg. 1981. "The Dialectics of Crime Control." In David Greenberg (ed.), *Crime and Capitalism*. Palo Alto, CA: Mayfield, 209–54.

Jamieson, Ruth, Nigel South, and Ian Taylor. 1997. *Economic Liberalisation and Cross-Border Crime: The North American Free Trade Area and Canada's Border with the US*. Salford Papers in Sociology, No. 22, University of Salford, United Kingdom.

Moore, Richter H., and Charles B. Fields. 1996. "Comparative Criminal Justice: Why Study?" In Charles Fields and Richter Moore (eds.), *Comparative Criminal Justice: Traditional and Nontraditional Systems of Law and Control*. Prospects Heights, IL: Waveland Press, 1–14.

Neapolitan, Jerome L. 1997. *Cross-National Crime: A Research Review and Sourcebook*. Westport, CT: Greenwood Press.

Neuman, W. Lawrence, and Ronald J. Berger. 1988. "Competing Perspectives on Cross-National Crime: An Evaluation of Theory and Evidence." *Sociological Quarterly* 29, 2: 281–313.

Newman, Graeme (ed.). 1999. *Global Report on Crime and Justice*. Published for the United Nations Office for Drug Control and Crime Prevention, Centre for International Crime Prevention. New York: Oxford University Press.

Newman, Graeme, Debra Cohen, and Adam C. Bouloukos (eds.). 1995. *International Fact Book of Criminal Justice Systems*. Washington, DC: U.S. Bureau of Justice Statistics.

Nuzum, Marlyce. 1998. "The Commercialization of Justice: Public Good or Private Greed?" *Critical Criminologist* 8, 3 (Summer): 4–7.

Platt, Tony, and Paul Takagi (eds.). 1981. *Crime and Social Justice*. Totowa, NJ: Barnes and Noble.

Quinney, Richard. 1977. *Class, State, and Crime*. New York: Mckay.

Sheptycki, James W. E. 1998. "Policing, Postmodernism and Transnationalization." *British Journal of Criminology* 38, 3 (Summer): 485–503.

Travis, Jeremy. 1998. *NIJ Request for Proposals for Comparative, Cross-National Crime Research Challenge Grants*. U.S. Department of Justice, National Institute of Justice, April.

Walters, Malcolm. 1995. *Globalization*. London: Routledge.

Yergin, Daniel. 1998. "The Age of 'Globality.'" *Newsweek* (May 18): 24–27.

1

BRAZIL

(Developing Nation-State)

Emilio E. Dellasoppa

PROFILE OF BRAZIL

From the point of view of its territory, Brazil is almost a continent: more than 3.3 million square miles. This is also true regarding its structure of social relations, due to the diversity of regional peculiarities. The gentle land, as Brazilians used to see it, is populous as well: more than 157 million inhabitants—78.4 percent urban, 54.2 percent white, 5.1 percent black, 40.1 percent brown, 0.5 percent yellow, and 0.1 percent Native Brazilian (Indian). Most of the population (57.6 percent) is concentrated in the south and southeast regions. According to the Brazilian Bureau of Census, in 1991, two metropolitan areas constituted 17 percent of the Brazilian population: Rio de Janeiro (9, 814, 574) and São Paulo (15, 145, 410) (IBGE, 1998).

From the point of view of its economy, Brazil is also large—typically among the 10 largest economies (e.g., gross domestic product) in the world. The wealth of Brazil, however, is marked by inequality, where, for example, the income of the richest 20 percent of the population is 26 times greater than the income of the poorest 20 percent, according to figures provided by the United Nations in the early 1990s. For context, among those countries with more than 10 million inhabitants in 1991, Brazil had the worst distribution of income. In 1990, 39 million, or 27 percent of the population, were living beneath the poverty line, on a monthly per capita family income of $35. Moreover, figures from the Instituto Brasileiro de Geografia e Estatistica (IBGE, 1997) for 1990 revealed that 32 million children were living with families earning less than half of the minimum wage monthly ($56 at 1998 values).

During the 1980s, Brazil experienced improvements in its political processes and institutions, with the reestablishment of democracy and civil rights after almost two decades of authoritarian military rule. However, the political democratization did not include a social democracy inclusive of welfare improvements for most of the Brazilian population. This period of time was also one of economic stagnation and has been referred to as the "lost decade." Associated with these political and economic changes were increases in the indicators related to violence, such as mortality by external causes such as homicide as well as more general modalities of violent crime.

HISTORICAL PERSPECTIVE ON CRIME AND CRIME CONTROL

A recent historical picture of crime and crime control cannot be separated from the authoritarian regime that was in place. In just a short period of time—encompassing 30 years or so—the pattern of homicide rates in Brazil has changed dramatically. For example, in the municipality of São Paulo, the homicide rate was 4 per 100,000 in 1940 and 5 per 100,000 in 1960. However, between 1960 and 1997, the homicide rate increased from 5 to almost 50 per 100,000 inhabitants.

In the past, homicide in Brazil was mostly due to passionate and individual causes (Coelho, 1980); nowadays it tends to be associated with the settlement of scores between drug gangs, the clandestine activity of the *esquadroes da morte* or *policias mineiras* (death squads) and the *justiceiros* (vigilantes), and the use of deadly force by the Military Police (PM) of several states, particularly Rio de Janeiro and São Paulo (Pinheiro, 1991a, 1991b, 1998). Generally, during this period the development of crime and crime control reflected the emergence and unfolding of complex criminal networks, with entrepreneurial organization and other important connections, nationally and internationally. These groups took over the control of drug trafficking, for example. By similar means, the trade in drugs and heavy weapons, chemical resources, and facilities has also taken on complex patterns involving money laundering and the extensive corruption of state bureaucracies. What Brazilians are now facing, in addition to the individualized crime of the past, is organizational crime on a huge scale that is relatively new and still growing.

PUBLIC PERCEPTION OF CRIME AND CRIME CONTROL

While there has been an increase in indicators of violence, such as mortality rates, number of years lost by violent causes, and homicide rates, these increases are not experienced uniformly and vary by demographic variables, which is also consistent with international trends. Similarly, the kinds of violent incidents that Brazilians are likely to suffer differ widely as to causes, nature, and probability, depending on the region where they live and work. In short, the social distribution of the risk of becoming a victim of a violent attack exemplifies extreme inequality.

Nevertheless, fear and insecurity have increased in all social sectors, from the very poor to the very rich. And since the 1980s there seems to be a consensus in Brazilian public opinion that is critical of the state's role in crime control and prevention. In general, Brazilian perceptions of the state's inability to control crime and its causes have led to public condemnation of the continued absence of a strategic plan in crime prevention and control.

Brazilian citizens are also dissatisfied with the way the police control crime in their areas of residence. In Rio de Janeiro, for instance, 77 percent of the citizens were "dissatisfied" and only 12 percent "satisfied" (United Nations, 1998). Such dissatisfaction is consistent with victimization surveys that reveal very low rates of reporting robbery, theft, sexual incidents, assaults, burglaries, car thefts, and so forth (Kahn, 1997). Most of the victims justified their decision not to report their victimization to authorities of law enforcement by claiming that the police were inefficient, largely impotent, and highly bureaucratic.

Worse yet, there is the public perception that much of the violence in Brazilian society originates at the hands of the state and its agencies of crime control. Specifically, the view that the criminal justice system is corrupt, unreliable, slow, and unfair contributes to the belief that crime control in Brazil is "out of control." It also contributes to such phenomena as vigilantism (*justiceritos*) and death squads and to those organizations of gunmen hired by small shopkeepers or owners of public transportation companies, especially in the peripheries of many Brazilian cities.

CONTEMPORARY CRIME

Issues of contemporary crime in Brazil are closely related to issues of citizenship and to a culture of subordination (Jelin and Hershberg, 1996; Mitchell and Wood, 1997). Crime and crime control cannot be separated from the kind of authoritarian and repressive (violent) society that Brazil was in its recent past. For example, both the use of hired gunmen and the extent to which vigilantism is used to control crime extralegally are cases in point. The hired "death squads" have attempted to control crime ultimately by killing thieves and even groups of homeless children who have refused to pay for transportation or who pose threats to the "public order."

The extent of these "slaughters" (*chacinas*), as they are referred to in Brazil, is well known, and some of the larger and more notorious ones have been denounced abroad. The press (i.e., *Folha de São Paulo*) currently keeps statistics on the number of slaughters in the Metropolitan Area of São Paulo and elsewhere in Brazil. Typically, these multiple killings involve an average of three to four victims per slaughter. For example, from January to November 1995, the São Paulo Metropolitan Region registered 163 homicides in 48 *chacinas*, and in the same period for 1996, there were 162 homicides in 46 *chacinas* (*Folha de São Paulo*, November 30, 1996). In the country as a whole, between 1990 and 1996, there were eight major slaughters involving a combined total of more than 200 deaths.

A picture of the unconventional violence characteristic of Brazil should also include reference to lynching. Revenge through lynching by populations that are the victims of crime and have no hope obtaining justice and redress from the police and the criminal justice system are often viewed as spontaneous acts. In most of these cases, however, there has been a hidden structure organizing the lynching (Martins, 1989; Pinheiro, 1991a). Between 1979 and 1989, there were 272 cases of lynching, half of those since the end of the period of military rule.

In the city of Salvador, in the northeastern state of Bahia, there were 26 cases of lynching in 1988, 82 in 1989, and 112 in 1990. In the first three months of 1991, there were 53, which meant one every three days (Pinheiro, 1991a). Lynching and associated violence persist in many places. In July 1993, in Olaria, a neighborhood of Rio de Janeiro, three teenagers, suspected of being robbers but later found to be innocent, were persecuted by a mob and beaten to death for two and one-half hours. As it was noted in the local media (*Veja*, July 14, 1993), the mob was instigated by four employees of a *bicheiro* ("syndicate") who controlled the illegal lottery (*jogo do bicho*) in the area. In fact, there was a pact of silence in Olaria: " 'Whoever talks dies' was the *bicheiro*'s order."

As for the more conventional forms of crime and violence, they, too, seem to be epidemic. Take the case of firearms in the commission of homicides. According to a United Nations (1997) report, Brazil is the world leader in homicides committed with a firearm, with a rate of 25.8 per 100,000 inhabitants. The same report also indicated that the profile of the Brazilian criminal of today was now younger, with less education and a tendency to commit more serious crimes than criminals of the past. They were also more prone to reoffend and not to resocialize, compared with earlier offenders, both before and after the authoritarian regime.

In studies of change in deaths by violent causes and by homicide, using Brazilian census data for 1980 and 1991, Bercovich, Dellasoppa, and Arriaga (1997a) found that the number of years of life lost by external causes for Brazil and for all regions of the country increased between 1980 and 1991. These increases were higher in the Metropolitan Areas of Rio de Janeiro and São Paulo. Of the two, the highest increase was for the Rio de Janeiro Metropolitan Area, where the figure more than doubled. The increasing number of lost years of life due to external causes is basically a male problem. The female loss of life by external causes was/is almost nonexistent and has remained virtually unchanged during this period. The patterns for women in the regions of Brazil are also very similar to international standards.

In a breakdown of the changing proportion of deaths by external causes and age groups of males in 1980 and 1991 due to transportation accidents, homicides, and other causes, there was a strong rise in the proportion of deaths by homicide for all the age groups but especially for the younger ones. In other words, there was a sharp *scissors effect* between the homicides and the transportation deaths when plotted against the age groups. Hence, the problem of homicide was/is not only a male problem but also a young male problem—once again conforming to international patterns.

Similarly, when it came to the increases in homicides committed with firearms between 1980 and 1991, there was a rise for all age groups. However, the more intense increases were for the first two age groups, 15 to 24 and 25 to 34. As firearms are readily obtained and are almost free from state control, the Brazilian pattern of homicide by weapons used approaches the patterns of the United States, with almost two thirds of homicides committed with a firearm.

More generally, the 1990s has witnessed a crisis in three areas of criminality that has had an impact on the ability of the criminal justice system to respond to serious crime. These areas include (1) the rapid rise in urban violent crime; (2) the development and specialization in such forms of organized crime as drug trafficking, firearms smuggling, and the wholesale corruption of law enforcement and judicial officials; and (3) the common occurrences of human rights violations, involving torture, use of lethal force, and slaughters. The third group of offenses have been committed mainly by police officers and other hired gunmen.

CONTEMPORARY CRIME CONTROL

Like Brazilian crime, crime control in Brazil is still related to the version of democracy that followed the rule of the military dictatorship—the "delegative democracy" that was established after the regime became a social basis for strongly conservative and even authoritarian practices. Hence, the formal and informal responses to crime (and crime control) present in the daily life of Brazilian society today can be traced to the customs of an earlier repressive regime that prevailed for some two decades.

Police

Brazil has a small number of national policemen, the Federal Police, who are dispersed throughout a huge territorial area. These law enforcement personnel deal with everything ranging from immigration to drug trafficking. The majority of police, however, are employed on a state-to-state basis and are divided into two kinds of organizations: Policia Militar (PM, Military

Police) and Policia Civil (PC, Civil Police). The PM is in charge of patrolling, order control, and summary arrests. They also address transit control and vehicle documentation. The Civil Police consist of Delegacias de Policia (DPs, Police Departments), each run by a *delegado* (station chief) who must be a university graduate in law. The Civil Police also oversee the Brazilian Judicial Police, who are in charge of investigations, including conducting interrogations, gathering evidence, and preparing an *inquerito* (indictment) that is sent to the courts for the prosecution.

Estimates for the State of Rio de Janeiro and for the State of São Paulo are 1 patroling policeman per 1,200 and 3,000 inhabitants, respectively. Comparatively, these are very low number; for example, in England the ratio is about 1 per 460 inhabitants (Collier, 1997). In terms of the expenditures for public law enforcement and private security in Rio de Janeiro, in 1997, the total estimated expenses came to almost $6.5 billion (Diniz, 1998). Nevertheless, criminality has outgrown the capacity of the PCs to control it. The inefficiency and the corruptibility of the police, as well as publicized cases of police wrongdoing, make not only for a poor showing in law enforcement but for a poor public image as well.

The Brazilian Judicial Police were developed and deployed to compensate for the poor methods used by, and lack of criminal investigation carried out by, some 1,500 personnel doing crime investigative work. The PC's Judicial Police are specifically involved in the investigative process and collection of evidence. However, their impact is limited, as there are still obstacles and difficulties encountered in trying to register occurrences of crime at the local police precinct levels. Problems range from police authorities with "bad attitudes" to even the use of intimidation and other pressures not to register complaints, especially if the person trying to report the incident is poor or marginal.

In sum, what is investigated or not is usually arbitrarily decided. Even in those extreme cases with known victims and corpses—when the law makes their investigations mandatory—the actual inquiry procedure is anything but certain. Inquiries, when they are realized, are frequently conducted in a negligent manner. Once initiated, many investigations languish as witnesses are unqualified and material proofs often undeveloped. For example, ballistics tests are rarely employed by those doing investigations involving firearms.

In addition, the police precincts in Rio de Janeiro and throughout Brazil are used as prisons. Because there is a shortage of bed space to maintain the number of persons sentenced to the prison system, in 1998 there were more than 7,000 convicted inmates jailed in the 104 precincts of the State of Rio de Janeiro alone. These precincts are also extremely overcrowded, as they have exceeded their original capacity of 3,500 for housing accused suspects. Conditions in these "prison" precincts are a real hell where prisoners share extreme temperatures (more than 122 degrees Fahrenheit in some cells during the summer months); cramped, unhealthy quarters (sharing space with cell mates who may have AIDS, other sexually transmitted diseases, and tuberculosis); and a dangerous environment where escapes are frequent occurrences, sometimes with the complicity of the precinct personnel, who either make deals with or are extorted by prisoners, gangs, or family members.

Aside from the array of problems associated with police work, personnel are poorly paid. For example, the average salary of a beginning detective in São Paulo or Rio de Janeiro at the beginning of 1999 was under $250 per month—about the same as a beginning primary school teacher, not much more than a bus driver. These problems and a host of others have contributed to a less-than-professional police presence in Brazil.

At the marginal ends of that police culture are the extralegal methods of punishment and justice that are often administered in the form of a death penalty through the police use of deadly force. These "sanctioned" forms of violence against the criminal are, in practice, an expression of the common wisdom that "thieves must die." These beliefs are shared by criminal justice functionaries as well as by large sections of the population, irrespective of social status. This is perhaps one of the perverse results of the failure of the criminal justice system on Brazilian society. It feeds a cynicism and repressive apparatus of formal and informal social control. As one consequence of this pessimism, a fundamental belief in an alternative crime control that looks beyond enforcement and corrections to the justice system's role as an integral part of education, prevention, and treatment is currently unthinkable in Brazil.

In context, then, the inefficiency of the criminal justice system, the extremely low proportion of sentenced prisoners (as shown in the next section), and the corruption of the Civil Police contribute to deviance and violence of various kinds, including punishments that go outside the law, such as police use of deadly force. In effect, since there is no formal punishment or justice, there is no point in making arrests. Instead, the resolution of conflicts is often accomplished through the use of "unofficial" violence.

Punishment

Impunity, fragility, and corruption surround both the judicial and penal-correctional apparatuses. Impunity, believed to be a Brazilian characteristic, is marked by extreme resilience, even in those cases where the pressures of civil society lead to some kind of punishment. The resilience of impunity can be detected at the highest political and economic spheres of society, including the extremely limited consequences of the impeachment of former President Fernando Collor De Melo.

However, the resilience of impunity also applies to ordinary crime and criminals, such as drug trafficking, *jogo do bicho* (a type of illegal lottery), and allegations of mass murder committed by the police. For example, in the case of several murders in the State of Rio de Janeiro, trial and punishment procedures typically followed at an extremely slow pace. And even after severe sentences were pronounced, the results were dubious or mixed.

Impunity is the consequence of the failure of the judiciary system as it interacts with processes of collusion that are a constant presence in Brazil today. A research study on 290 cases out of a total of 622 homicides of children and teenagers in São Paulo revealed that after all of the criminal prosecutions, only 17 percent were sent to prison (Castro, 1996). The extremely low proportion of sentenced prisoners is a primary measure of the inefficiency of the criminal justice system. It also speaks to the weaknesses in criminal prosecution in Brazil.

Another distinguishing feature of Brazilian crime control is its fragility. Along with impunity, the fragility results in low proportions of sentenced prisoners. Specifically, of the total number of 4,274 prisoners prosecuted for crimes against the person in 1992, 33 percent were sentenced to prison. In the case of crimes against property, the proportion of sentenced offenders was even smaller, only 28 percent (Adorno, 1992). The same situation is found throughout the states of the Brazilian federation.

Since the 1970s, along with the impunity and fragility of the judiciary system and closely related to it has been the increased importance of corruption. This is a consequence of the development of drug trafficking, which offered opportunities for high profits in drugs, in arms trafficking, and in money laundering. Extortion of drug traders by policemen has become a common situation, to the point that among the Civil Police of Rio de Janeiro there was a so-called *banda podre* (rotten gang) that made high profits from extortion and other serious offenses.

Corruption exists not only within the police but also in the judiciary system and in almost all the bureaucratic agencies of government. The expression *montar um esquema* (to set up an organization dedicated to crime and/or corruption) is part of a common language that is synonymous with corruption. In the decade of the 1990s, then, lynching, slaughtering, police use of deadly force, and the impunity and fragility of Brazilian criminal justice converge so as to unite the Military Police and the people in a shared view of the uselessness of the Civilian Police and the judicial system.

Despite the uselessness of civilian policing and adjudication, the imprisonment rate in Brazil more than doubled between 1985 and 1997, from less than 40 to more than 100 prisoners per 100,000 population. As noted earlier, most of the prisoners are young; 58 percent were less than 30 years old. Blacks are noticeably overrepresented in prison statistics; for example, in 1991 they made up 16 percent of the prison population at Casa de Detencao in the city of São Paulo, whereas they accounted for only 5 percent of the population there.

FUTURE OF CRIME AND CRIME CONTROL

Brazil is changing its economy in a profound and painful way as social inequalities remain and crime lingers. Nevertheless, "fixing" crime and crime control seems to be at the end of the political agenda. Hence, the future of crime and crime control looks bleak and dismal. Brazilian prisons, despite lax enforcement and adjudication, will remain overcrowded, and penal populations are likely to grow. Meanwhile, in the near future crime control through education, prevention, and treatment will remain out of the criminal justice picture.

Furthermore, as Brazil's current financial problems and recession suggest a rise in criminality, and as the limited use of sentencing alternatives (only 2 percent) to imprisonment continue to reinforce punitive responses to crime, the existing social relations of crime and punishment become further entrenched in Brazilian society. So in the future, as in the contemporary past of the last two decades, impunity and fragility of the judiciary system, combined with corruption and a penal law with severe punishments rarely enforced, will reproduce a criminal justice system in Brazil that continues to inadequately address the social problems of crime while it overcrowds its prisons with poor and illiterate people. The time for radically different criminal justice policies in Brazil is way overdue.

REFERENCES

Adorno, S. 1992. "Criminal Violence in Modern Brazilian Society: The Case of the State of São Paulo." Paper presented at the International Conference on Social Changes, Crime, and Police, Budapest, Hungary, June 1–4.

———. 1998. "O gerenciamento público da violência urbana: a justiça em ação." In P. S. Pinheiro et al., *São Paulo sem medo: um diagnóstico da violência urbana*. Rio de Janeiro: Garamond.

Araújo, J. M. Jr. (org.). 1991. *Sistema Penal para o Terceiro Milênio*. Rio de Janeiro: Revan.

Arriaga, E. 1984. "Measuring and Explaining the Change of Life Expectancies." *Demography* 21(1): 83–96.

———. 1996a. "Los Años de Vida Perdidos: Su Utilización para Medir el Nivel y el Cambio de la Mortalidad." *Notas de Población*. XXIV, 63: 7–38. Santiago, Chile: Centro Latinoamericano de Demografía.

———. 1996b. "Comentarios sobre algunos Indices Para Medir el Nivel y el Cambio de la Mortalidad. In *Estudios Demográficos y Urbanos* 11, 1: 5–30. Mexico: El Colegio de Mexico.

Barak, G. 1998. "An Integrative Approach to the Globalization of Crime and Crime Control." Paper presented at the International Congress on Criminology. Seoul, Korea, August 24–29, 1998. Mimeo.

Becker, G. 1986. "Crime and Punishment: An Economic Approach." *Journal of Political Economy* 76 (March-April): 169–217.

Benjamin, C. 1998. *Hélio Luz, um Xerife de Esquerda.* Rio de Janeiro: Relume-Dumará.

Bercovich, A., and Madeira, F. 1992. "Demographic Discontinuities in Brazil and in the State of São Paulo." Paper presented at the XXIInd General Population Conference, Session 21, Population in the XXIst Century: Demographic Prospects. Montreal. August 24–September 1, 1993.

Bercovich, A., Dellasoppa E. E., and Arriaga, E. 1997a. "Violence, Civil Rights and Demography in Brazil: The Case of the Metropolitan Area of Rio de Janeiro." Paper presented at the 1997 Annual Meeting, Population Association of America (PAA). Session 7: The Demography of Violence. Washington, March 27–29, 1997.

———. 1997b. "Violence as a Public Health Problem: Socializing Adolescents in the 1980's in Rio de Janeiro." Paper presented at IUSSP IIIrd General Conference, Beijing, China. October 11–17 1997.

———. 1998. "J'adjuste, mais je ne corrige pas: Jovens, violência e demografia no Brasil. Algumas reflexões a partir dos indicatores de violencia." In *Jovens acontecendo na trilha das politicas públicas.* Brazil: Comissão Nacional de População e Desenvolvimento (CNPD), vol. I: 293–362.

Bicudo, Hélio. 1996. "Violência, desemprego e polícia." *Folha de São Paulo* (April 11): 1–3.

Blumstein, A. 1994. "Youth Violence, Firearms and Illicit Drug Markets" (Working Paper). Pittsburgh: Carnegie Mellon University, The Heinz School.

Bryson, John M. 1984. "The Policy Process and Organizational Form." *Policy Studies Journal* 12, 3 (March).

Castro, M.M.P. de. 1996. "Vidas sem valor: Um estudo sobre os homicídios de crianças e adolescentes e a atuação das instituições de segurança e justiça." Ph.D. dissertation, University of São Paulo, Brazil.

Coelho, E. C. 1978. "A Criminalidade da Marginalidade." *Revista de Administração Pública, Rio de Janeiro,* 12, 2 (April–June): 139–161.

———. 1980. "Sobre sociólogos, pobreza e crime." *Dados, Rio de Janeiro* 23, 3: 377–83.

Collier, P. 1997. "Performance Measurement, Financial Constraint and Behavioural Control: Conflict and Consequences in the Management of a Police Force—An Institutional/Social Model." Paper presented at the Fifth Interdisciplinary Perspectives on Accounting Conference, Hume Hall, University of Manchester, United Kingdom.

Dellasoppa, E. E. 1991. "Reflexões sobre a violência, autoridade e autoritarismo." *Revista USP,* no 9 (Março-Maio).

———. 1995a. "Estrutura de Relações Sociaise e Interação: Relações Colusivna Sociedade Brasileira ou a Lógica das Restrições Estabilizantes." Mimeo.

———. 1995b. "Violência, Estrutura de Relações Sociais e Interação: Relações de Conluio na Sociedade Brasileira." *Estudos IUPERJ,* No. 91 (Agosto): 41–54.

———. 1997. "Funkin' Rio: Music, Violence, and the Socialization of the Young Wave." Paper presented at the ISA Research Committee 41 (Sociology of Population) Workshop on Population. Beijing, October 11.

Desgualdo, M. A. 1998. *Folha de São Paulo* (24 de Março) 3–6.

Diniz, C. N. 1998. "Gestão da informação e sistema de informações políciais em uma Delegacia da Policia Civile do etado do Rio De Janeir, FGV." Master's thesis, Escola Brasileira de Administração Pública.

Dunham, R. G., and G. P. Alpert. 1993. *Critical Issues in Policing*. Prospect Heights, IL: Waveland.

Fernandes, N. et al. 1997. "R\$ 2 bilhões, o preço do mercado do medo no Rio." *Jornal do Brasil, Rio de Janeiro* (6 de julho): 1–16.

Freund, J. 1979. "La Violence et ses Rapports avec la Ville et les Communautés." *Violence et Transgression*. Paris: Anthropos, 35–59.

Gold, R. 1970. "Urban Violence and Contemporary Defensive Cities." *Journal of the American Institute of Planners* 36, 3 (May).

Heilborn, M. L. 1997. "O Traçado da Vida: Gênero e Idade em Dois Bairros Populares do Rio de Janeiro." In F. R. Madeira (org.), *Quem Mandou Nascer Mulher? Estudos sobre Crianças e Adolescentes Pobres no Brasil*. Rio de Janeiro: Rosa dos Tempos.

IBGE (Instituto Brasileiro de Geografia e Estatistica). 1997. *Censo demografico 1940–1991* (Demographic census 1940–1991). Rio De Janeiro: Author.

———. 1998. *Brazil in Figures*. Rio de Janeiro: Author.

Jelin, E., and E. Hershberg. 1996. *Constructing Democracy: Human Rights, Citizenship and Society in Latin America*. Boulder, CO: Westview Press.

Kahn, T. 1997. *Sistema penitenciário. Mudanças de perfil dos anos 50 aos 90. Revista ILANUD*, no. 6. United Nations, São Paulo.

Katz, J. 1988. *Seductions of Crime*. New York: Basic Books.

Lengruber, J. (org). 1996. *Alternativas à Pena de Prisão*. Vol. II. Governo do Estado do Rio de Janeiro. Secretaria de Estado de Justiça. Rio de Janeiro.

Luz, H. 1995a. "Hélio Luz à Queima-roupa." *Entrevista, Revista da Folha* 4, 181 (8 de Outubro).

———. 1995b. "O Tira-teima." *Entrevista, Veja Rio* 5, 34 (Agosto).

———. 1996. "A Polícia foi Criada para ser Corrupta." *Entrevista, O Globo* (24 de março).

Machado da Silva, L. A. 1991. "Violência Urbana: Representação de uma Ordem Social." Encontro Anual da ANPOCS. Caxambú. October 15–18.

Madeira, F., and A. Bercovich. 1992. "A Onda Jovem e seu Impacto na População Econômicamente Ativa Masculina em São Paulo." In *Planejamento e Políticas Públicas*. Brasília: IPEA.

Martins, J. de S. 1989. "Linchamentos: A vida por um fio." *Travessia. Revista do Migrante* (São Paulo, Centro de Estudos Migratorios) 2, 4 (March–August): 21–27.

Mercy J. A., M. L. Rosenberg, K. E. Powell, C. V. Broome, and W. L. Roper. 1993. "Public Health Policy For Preventing Violence." *Health Aff.* (Winter): 7–29.

Mitchell, M. J., and C. H. Wood. 1997. "Ironies of Citizenship: Skin Color, Police Brutality and the Challenge to Democracy in Brazil." Mimeo copy of paper to be published in *Social Forces*, forthcoming.

Mortara, G. 1946. *Tábuas de Mortalidade e Sobrevivência Brasileiras*. Distrito Federal e Município de São Paulo. Rio de Janeiro: IBGE.

O'Donnell, G. 1994. "Delegative Democracy." *Journal of Democracy* 5, 1.

Padgett, T. 1998. "Criminal Cops. Cop Crisis. Report on Region's Abusive Police." *Time* (Latin American Edition) (August 24).

Paixão, A. L. 1988. "Crime, Controle Social e Consolidação da Democracia: As Metáforas da Cidadania." In F. W. Reis and G. O'Donnell (eds.), *Democracia no Brasil: Dilemas e Perspectivas.* São Paulo: Vértice. 168–199.

Pinheiro, P. S. 1991a. "Democracia, direitos hamanos e desenvolvimento econômico e social: Obstáculos e resistências: O caso do Brasil." Paper presented at the Seminário Latinoamericano de Expertos em Direitos Humanos, Democracia, Desenvolvimento Econômico e Social, Santiago, Chile.

———. 1991b. "Violência fatal: Conflitos policiais em São Paulo (81–89)." *Revista USP*, no. 9 (March–May): 95–112.

———. 1998. *São Paulo sem medo: Um diagnostico da violencia urbana.* Rio de Janeiro: Garamond.

Reiss, J. A., and A. J. Roth (eds.). 1993. *Understanding and Preventing Violence.* Washington, DC: National Academy Press.

Riches, D. (ed.). 1986. *The Anthropology of Violence.* Oxford: Basil Blackwell.

Robert, P. 1990. "Ordres Publics, Ordres Privés." Paper Presented at the International Colloquium: Urban Violence, Public Order and Social Control. São Paulo, *USP* (19–21 março).

Silva, J. da, and M. Malin. 1994. "A Polícia é a nossa cara." *Jornal do Brasil* (4 de Novembro): 11.

Soares, L. E. 1994. "Polícia, drogas e democracia: lições americanas." *Jornal do Brasil* (10 de Novembro): 12.

United Nations (UNICRI). 1995. "Criminal Victimisation in the Developing World" (by Ugljesa Zvekic and Anna Alvazzi del Frate). Rome, March 1995.

———. 1997. "Report of the United Nations Expert Group Meeting on Information Gathering and Analysis of Firearm Regulation." Vienna International Centre Vienna, Austria, 10–14 February 1997.

———. 1998. "UN Report on Human Development." New York.

2

CHINA

(Developing Nation-State)

Mark S. Gaylord

PROFILE OF CHINA

China is a vast country, stretching 3,100 miles from east to west and 3,400 miles from north to south. Its population, the world's largest, is estimated to be at least 1.2 billion. Because of its complex topography, however, China's population density varies greatly over its nearly 3.7 million square miles, with the sharpest contrast found between the eastern half of the country, which has the highest density, and the sparsely populated west and northwest regions. About 20 percent of the population is urban.

China comprises 56 ethnic groups, but the Han Chinese form the great homogeneous mass (about 94 percent) of the population. The minority (non-Han) peoples live primarily in the west and northwest regions. The size and form of the administrative structure of the Chinese state reflect this diversity. The country is divided up into provinces, prefectures, municipalities, counties, and a range of smaller administrative units. In order to cope with ethnic and national differences, there are also "autonomous regions," such as Inner Mongolia and Tibet. Many of these regions contain peoples that previous Chinese states have colonized through military conquest (Brewer et al., 1988).

China is a communist republic. The Chinese Communist Party (CCP) dominates society, controlling all major governmental, economic, and cultural institutions. The country's policy-making power rests with the seven-member Politburo Standing Committee, which is elected by the CCP's

Central Committee, a body of 210 full and 138 alternate members. Many major party officials occupy high-level positions in government.

The National People's Congress (NPC) is the highest organ of state power in the People's Republic of China (PRC). This legislative body, with more than 2,900 members, is elected to five-year terms by legislatures from the provinces, autonomous regions, municipalities, and the People's Liberation Army (PLA). It normally holds one session each year. The NPC appoints a Standing Committee to be its permanent body and elects a president to serve as China's titular head of state. On the recommendation of the CCP's Central Committee, the NPC also elects a premier, who, in turn, advises the NPC on the appointment of the State Council, China's executive body. The State Council is composed of the premier, vice premiers, the auditor-general, the secretary-general, and about 50 heads of ministries and commissions. All governmental actions must be consistent with policy guidelines established by the CCP. Since the late 1970s, the CCP's leadership has sought to increase the government's role in the decision-making process (*People's Republic of China Yearbook 1995/96*, 1997).

During the Cultural Revolution (1966–1976), the social movement launched to revitalize China's flagging revolutionary values stressed ideology and political instruction, but now it encourages students to acquire scientific and technical knowledge and develop professional skills. Nevertheless, the CCP still rigidly controls the nation's television, radio, and press, using them to mobilize support for party policies. *Renmin Ribao* (People's Daily), the official newspaper of the CCP's Central Committee, has characterized the news media as the "loyal eyes, ears, and tongue" of the Party's leadership (*Encyclopaedia Brittanica*, 1991: 230).

The PRC has a developing economy that is still mainly government owned. The All-China Federation of Trade Unions, comprising more than 400,000 member trade unions, is government controlled. Similarly, all national banking is state controlled, but a limited number of foreign banks are allowed to operate in China. Development remains centrally controlled through five-year plans. As a result of a series of economic reforms following Deng Xiaoping's return to power in the mid-1970s, China's gross national product more than doubled in the 1980s. Its economy is now the world's third largest, exceeded only by those of the United States and Japan.

HISTORICAL PERSPECTIVE ON CRIME AND CRIME CONTROL

China's cultural heritage includes an organized crime tradition that dates back over 200 years. It is now believed that the first Triad secret society, the Tiandihui (Heaven and Earth Society), was founded at the Goddess of Mercy Temple in Fujian province in 1761 (Cai, 1964; Zhang, 1980). The rapid population growth and resultant severe economic dislocation during the early Qing period forced those who had lost their livelihoods working the land to migrate from their indigenous communities in order to earn a living. In southeast China, one of the strategies for those displaced from their villages was to create organizations of their own for self-protection. The Tiandihui expanded with the migratory patterns of China's lower classes; as new arrivals came into contact with the most marginalized residents of their host communities, the Tiandihui gradually became part of the social fabric of more settled communities. The Tiandihui also became a vehicle for such activities as robbery, feuding, and rebellion (Murray, 1993).

A century later, before Sun Yat-sen established the Chinese Republic in 1912, he appealed to secret societies to help him. He traveled the world, visiting Chinese communities and asking for their help in toppling the Manchu regime (Ma, 1990). To encourage their financial and organizational aid, Sun praised the alleged "nationalistic, anti-Manchu origins" of secret societies, hoping to rally the latent patriotism of North American and Southeast Asian societies, which historically had been rather more like mutual aid societies than "cabals of revels-in-waiting" (Ownby, 1993: 6). Later, in his bid to control China, Sun's successor, Chiang Kai-shek (like Sun, a Triad member), repeatedly turned to secret societies, which by then had become deeply involved in prostitution, gambling, and the opium trade (McCoy, 1992). In fact, because of Chiang's heavy reliance on his Triad allies, they often served as generals, soldiers, spies, businessmen, and hired thugs in his Kuomintang (KMT), or Chinese Nationalist Army (Dubro and Kaplan, 1986).

By the beginning of the twentieth century, the opium trade, which had been inflicted on China by the British, had fallen into the hands of the Chinese underworld following what Seagrave (1985: 331) calls Britain's "moralistic turnabout." After the Shanghai Opium Commission of 1909 and the International Opium Conference at The Hague in 1911–1912, China's suppression of domestic opium cultivation led gradually to a shift in consumption to imported morphine and heroin from Europe and to the centralization of Shanghai's Triads, notably the Green Gang, over China's now-illicit opiates trade (McCoy, 1992).

By 1923, Shanghai drug syndicates were importing over 10 tons of heroin annually from Japan and Europe to meet the growing demand (United Nations, 1953). In the early 1930s, with Japanese laboratories in north China producing large quantities of narcotics and a network of Russian and Greek smugglers living in Shanghai, China began supplying America's illegal market, by then the world's second largest. In fact, during this time Chiang's Nationalist government had an alliance that protected the narcotics network from the regime's highly publicized (but largely symbolic) anti-opium campaign of the 1930s. For example, the head of the government's Opium Suppression Bureau was an active member of the Green Gang (McCoy, 1992).

Table 2.1
Crime Rates in the PRC, 1950–1995 (criminal cases per 100,000 population)

1950	93	1961	35	1977	58.00	1988	77.41
1951	59	1962	62	1978	55.30	1989	181.49[2]
1952	42	1963	36	1979	64.80	1990	200.90
1953	50	1964	35	1980	76.30	1991	209.44
1954	65	1965	33	1981	89.37	1992	138.60[3]
1955	37 (53)	1966–1972	40–60[1]	1982	74.02	1993	140.30
1956	23 (29)	1972	46	1983	59.81	1994	142.83
1957	58 (46)	1973	60	1984	49.91	1995	144.04
1958	120 (32)	1974	57	1985	52.06		
1959	35 (30)	1975	52	1986	51.91		
1960	33	1976	53	1987	54.12		

1. The estimate for 1966–1972 is based on a range of statistics reported in China's criminological literature. The Cultural Revolution saw a breakdown in the public security system. No national-level crime statistics exist from this period, only rough estimates derived from local data. Details on how this estimate was constructed are described in material published by the Ministry of Public Security, which based its estimates on "typical examples" from selected areas.
2. The sudden increase in 1989 was due mainly to changes in the criteria used to define criminal cases.
3. The apparent fall in crime rates beginning in 1992 is entirely due to changes in the criteria used to define criminal cases, in particular cases of theft. Comparable crime rates went up 5 percent from 1991 to 1992. With a reported increase in crime of 2.41 percent from 1991 to 1995, and allowance made for annual population increase, the likely approximate figure for 1995 comparable to the standard used before 1992 would be about 222 cases per 100,000. Disregarding redefinitions, the crime rate has shown a steady increase since 1984–1985. In Interpol statistics, the overall crime rate is reported slightly lower: 124.38 for 1992 and 127.75 for 1993.

Source: Bakken, 1999.

Crime and Crime Control under Mao

Although Mao Tse-tung, the Chinese Communist Party chairman, praised and wooed the secret societies before 1949, after the communists came to power, Mao moved quickly to crush what he correctly saw as a potential source of opposition to his new government (Seagrave, 1985). Hundreds of leaders from the Yi Guan Dao (Way of Basic Unity) and the Ge Lao Hi (Society of Brothers and Elders), in particular, were imprisoned (Hood, 1992). Many others were summarily executed by the simple expedient of a bullet to the back of the head.

Aside from the political criminals and criminality, following the 1949 revolution, crime rates fell sharply until 1957 (see Table 2.1). In 1956, for example, the overall crime rate was a mere 23 cases per 100,000 population (Xin, 1991). In 1957, however, crime began to increase rapidly as a consequence of the Anti-Rights movement, the yearlong crackdown on intellectuals and other critics of CCP policy. Political arrests caused the overall crime rate to rise to 58 per 100,000 that year. The next year, "counter-revolutionary crime" accounted for nearly 46 percent of all cases (Cao, 1988). When such arrests are discounted, however, the 1958 rate is still about 65 cases per 100,000, a jump in nonpolitical crime that may have resulted in part from the economic and social disruptions of Mao's ill-conceived Great Leap Forward (1958–1960).

The 1950s were a decade of national consolidation. The communists abolished all Nationalist laws and judicial organizations and moved to construct socialist agencies of law enforcement. The new government faced severe problems, however. Sabotage, dissent, and resistance were daily occurrences in the cities, the KMT's former strongholds. In the countryside there were riots and peasant disturbances in reaction to central government efforts to impose a uniform tax system. Also, it was not long before the Korean War (1951) gave hope to diehard supporters of the Nationalists that communist rule might collapse. During this period, it was difficult to develop any systemwide police policies as police had to act quickly in crisis situations, and they were often assisted by the militia and, at times, by the People's Liberation Army (Brewer et al., 1988).

One of the new government's major goals was the destruction and prohibition of privately owned enterprises and their businesses. The frequently violent, draconian process to accomplish this goal lasted from 1953 to 1956 (Yang, 1991). From that point onward, average citizens were not allowed a private life exempt from the scrutiny of officialdom. In the towns, the Party controlled all jobs. In the countryside, it bought all produce and owned all land. Individuals were bound to their *danwei* (work units), which allocated housing, education, and health care. By these means, and by the savage punishment of resisters, the Party elite controlled the masses ("The Road from Tiananmen," 1994).

Simultaneously, and in the face of the UN trade embargo with China associated with the Korean War, the PRC moved toward a closer relationship with the Soviet Union. For China's criminal justice system, this led to an increasing emphasis on specialists within the police, procuracy, and the courts. Nevertheless, the CCP continued to play a dominant role in the administration of justice, often superseding the police and overwhelming every aspect of judicial decision making.

Although China's overall crime rates remained low throughout the Cultural Revolution, the decade of 1966 to 1976 witnessed a public order shattered by large-scale, regime-sponsored attacks on public figures, institutions, and party factions deemed hostile toward the Maoist line. While there was no outbreak of ordinary criminal activities, ideological criminality was allegedly bountiful. As a consequence, industrial production was crippled, and schools and universities were closed. Throughout this period the police became secondary to the PLA as an enforcement agency. In the south, the police lost control of Guangzhou (Canton) to the Red Guards, Mao's young ideological supporters. Hundreds of political deaths were reported during this period.

PUBLIC PERCEPTION OF CRIME AND CRIME CONTROL

Older Chinese citizens still remember the mid-1950s as a "Golden Age," a period when Party officials and ordinary citizens alike were honest and united (Bakken, 1993). Those Chinese who can recall the Cultural Revolution remember that it involved a basic redefinition of the concept of crime. They also recall the politicalization of law enforcement, the spying, and the subordination of criminal justice to the politics of "law and order."

During this period, thousands of police were purged for not following the "correct" political line. As a result, many police chose simply to keep a low profile and to act only under direction from the new revolutionary mass organizations. In many places, people still recall whole units of secret police acting on orders from leftist political factions to infiltrate universities, factories, and other areas of unrest in order to act as a focus for demonstrations and other activities against Mao's rightist opponents (Brewer et al., 1988).

Today, Chinese people are aware of and perceive a high degree of political and economic corruption involving Party and government officials at every level. What began in the early 1980s as a handful of private entrepreneurs and petty crooks operating at the margins of society has evolved into a complicated web of quasi-legal and illegal associations. The Chinese refer to these practices as *hei shehui* (black society). By design, *hei shehui* is hidden from view, obscured by secrecy, corrupt officials, and the hopelessly blurred distinction between private and public sectors.

Black society is an all-encompassing term. It includes small bands of highwaymen to international heroin syndicates; from gang-controlled cigarette stands on urban street corners to nationwide publishing networks operating outside the state-run monopoly; from local sects rooted in feudalistic superstition to secret societies with thousands of members. As China's state sector has become progressively hollowed out from corruption and mismanagement, a parallel universe has simultaneously expanded to fill the void left by the diminishing influence of central authority. The problem, in fact, has become so acute and so widely known by the public that, in 1993, the Ministry of Public Security was moved to issue a list of "10 No-Nos" for police officials. For example: no selling of protection services to dance halls, massage parlors, and smuggling rings; no tipping off crooks about police raids in advance; no helping oneself to food or merchandise from shop owners without paying. As one disgusted factory manager complained, "Next thing you know, you'll have to remind the police 'no killing, no stealing' " (quoted in Kuhn, 1994).

So common and so public is the state of corruption in contemporary

China that a new lexicon of corruption had cropped up in the Chinese popular press by the mid-1990s. It included such terms as "pocket-swapping," in which public assets are transferred to private control, or "sign-flipping," whereby a government agency transforms itself into a private consultancy by merely changing its name and then parlaying its clout into fees (Kaye, 1993). In the view of some Chinese, however, corruption, greed, and disorder are an acceptable price to pay for economic and social liberation. According to a lawyer in Beijin: "When the economy grows, crime will grow with it" (quoted in Hornick, 1993).

CONTEMPORARY CRIME

Urbanization has increased rapidly in China over the past two decades. At the same time, China has industrialized at a fast pace. Following the dissolution of the commune system in the early 1980s, China's farmers saw their productivity and income rise swiftly. As a result, many of the country's peasants were no longer needed on farms. To absorb some of this mobile labor, new employment opportunities developed in rapidly expanding, labor-intensive light industries and in private and collective enterprises in rural areas. In short, after a long and turbulent hiatus, China has resumed its historic transformation from a rural agricultural society to an urban industrial one.

In the 1980s, the People's Republic of China experienced a sharp rise in crime as well as an increase in the fear of crime within the general population (Curran and Cook, 1993). The statistics on violent crime highlight a marked rise in the general crime rate from 1984 onward. Between 1981 and 1989, for example, homicides reported by the Ministry of Public Security rose from 9,576 to 19,590. In September 1983, the NPC sanctioned a "severe strike" (*yanda*) campaign against street crime.

During the campaign, capital punishment was used extensively, and parts of the criminal code were amended to facilitate easier arrests, detentions, and prosecutions. Sentences for "targeted crimes" were increased dramatically and trial procedures streamlined. Yet the overall crime rate of the late 1980s demonstrates that this brutal campaign did not achieve any long-term effects. From a rate of 49.91 per 100,000 population in 1984, it rose to 77.41 in 1988 (see Table 2.1). After 1989 the stress on public order and crime prevention intensified even more. This effort, paradoxically, also may explain some of the dramatic increase in China's crime rate from that point onward (Bakken, 1993).

It is probably fair to say that the accuracy of China's police statistics is neither significantly worse nor better than those of other developing countries, and given their under-reported official counts of crime, like most nations East and West, by severalfold, as acknowledged by Wang Fang in 1988, the Minister of Public Security (Dutton and Lee, 1993), the question

Table 2.2
Crime by 14- to 25-Year-Olds as a Percentage of Total Crime, 1952–1993

1952	20.2%	1966–1974	40–50%	1984	63.3%	1991	65.0%
1955	22.0%	1975	37.0%	1985	71.3%	1992	65.0%
1956	18.0%	1979	47.6%	1986	72.5%	1993	65.0%
1957	32.3%	1980	61.2%	1987	74.4%		
1961	30.0%	1981	64.0%	1988	75.7%		
1964	30.0%	1982	65.9%	1989	74.1%		
1965	35.0%	1983	67.0%	1990	69.7%		

Source: Bakken, 1999.

still remains, Why did crime increase in China in the 1980s? There are a number of possible explanations for this, but two major ones stand out. The first is based, perhaps universally, on the observation that criminal behavior is, to a large extent, youthful behavior. The second is based, also perhaps universally, on the modernization (or "convergence") theory of criminality.

Hirschi and Gottfredson (1983) have reviewed crime data from England, Wales, France, and the United States over the past 150 years and have found that the conventional index crime, *always and everywhere*, increases with age, peaks in the teenage and early adulthood years, and then declines. In the 1980s, in China, the age group 14 to 25 increased rapidly, rising to a peak of 282 million in 1987. Simultaneously, crime committed by those aged 14 to 25 grew rapidly relative to the total amount of crime (see Table 2.2).

Dutton (1992) believes the decline in the average age of China's criminals can be traced to the beginning of the Cultural Revolution. In 1965, youth crime in many big and medium-sized cities accounted for 30 percent of all crime. By 1975 the figure was 60 percent. At its peak, in the 1980s, youth crime reached a "plague-like" 80 percent of total crime in some cities (Dutton, 1992: 207).

By the early 1990s this age group began to decline relative to China's total population, as the "baby-boomers" of the Cultural Revolution entered their late twenties. The criminal statistics reflect these trends; for example, after 1990, the percentage of crime committed by those aged 14 to 25 as a percentage of total crime declined to pre-1982 levels (see Table 2.2). However, Bakken (1999) believes the apparent decline after 1991 is due entirely to changes in the criteria used to define various crimes rather than to an actual decline in crime (see Table 2.1).

Finally, the age theory may not actually be describing the changing relativity of crime and youthful behavior in China. In the early and mid-1950s, crime committed by youth was *under*represented in China's official crime statistics. That is to say, youth aged 14 to 25 committed *fewer* crimes than adults in both absolute as well as relative terms. If these statistics are valid (always a pertinent question, particularly when addressed to historical material), then this finding casts serious doubt on the alleged universality of the theory that conventional criminal behavior, "always and everywhere," peaks among those in their late teens and early twenties (Bakken, 1993).

The modernization theory of crime is based on the view that urbanization and industrialization inevitably increase the potential for nonconformity, and thus crime, by expanding personal freedom and opportunities for achievement. Developing societies, it is claimed, will experience a rising level of crime as a result of the loosening of the traditional mechanisms of informal social control and the increased opportunities for crime attendant with the growing affluence (Shelley, 1981). Crime, therefore, is said to be a social cost that must be paid by any society wishing to follow the path of modernization. Crimes in China, however, by the mid-1990s had already declined and leveled off as modernization and urbanization were still only "taking off."

Even after the sharp increases recorded since 1987, China has little crime by international standards. Based on data collected by Interpol, for example, China ranked merely 111th out of 113 countries surveyed between 1985 and 1988. In comparison to China, a group of Western countries in this survey has an average crime rate nearly *140 times higher* during the same period (Bakken, 1993). All and all, opinions vary about the size of the crime problem in China. Most agree, however, that official statistics on crime in China present only a partial, and therefore, misleading, picture of the extent of crime in the post-Mao era. The all-prevalent organized crime, for example, is not included in these official crime statistics of China. In other words, to develop a fuller understanding and appreciation of crime in contemporary China, one has to incorporate the study of organized crime and official corruption into the analysis as well (Gaylord and Levine, 1997).

Organized Crime

For nearly 30 years, organized crime in China had appeared to have disappeared, submerged along with other institutions of the earlier era. Following the historic Third Plenum of the Eleventh Central Committee of the CCP, in December 1978, China moved to modernize its economy, including the key decisions to "open up to the outside world" (*kaifang*) and to create a "socialist market economy." For some two decades now, China has been engaged in a pell-mell transition marked by sharp social and ideological conflicts. Furthermore, economic development has widened the income gap between city and countryside; witnessed the emergence of thousands of "economic gangs" (*jingji banghui*), secret societies, and other criminal organizations; and spawned official corruption on a massive scale.

China's ongoing economic transition has been dramatically successful, but increased productivity has displaced millions of workers (Wong, 1994). Conservative estimates indicate that 260 million of China's nearly 900 million peasants, the world's largest rural population, are no longer needed on farms (Kuhn and Kaye, 1994). As many as 100 million of these expendable workers are on the road in search of jobs in towns and cities. In the coastal provinces, farm jobs that remain are being filled by desperately poor peasants from China's interior, willing to work for next to nothing. The pressure of unemployment and personal debt, combined with abuse from venal officials, makes daily life increasingly difficult for growing numbers of Chinese. According to Li Sunmao, a criminal investigator in China's Public Security Bureau, the pressure of such massive rural migration is largely to blame for the growing numbers of new recruits to organized crime groups. In the richer cities, 70 to 80 percent of arrested criminals are now peasants from the countryside (Beck, 1997).

The opening of China's economy, together with the penetration into the mainland by Hong Kong, Macanese and Taiwanese criminals, has seen some astounding figures come to light. Experts estimate the annual number of new recruits to organized crime groups in China has grown from 100,000 in 1986 to more than half a million in 1994 (Beck, 1997). Today the country faces highway bandits, kidnapping gangs, tomb-robbing gangs, tax receipt–forging syndicates (subject to the death penalty under a law passed in 1995), and even "vampire gangs" who bleed their victims and sell the blood to hospitals. The existence of crime groups such as these has led some observers to compare the current situation in China to that which occurred in Russia in the wake of the breakup of the Soviet Union. Others have suggested that much of the corruption, speculation, and disregard for the law that China faces in its headlong rush to development is similar to that confronted by the United States in the late nineteenth-century heyday of robber-baron capitalism (Hornick, 1993).

In China today, contemporary organized crime patterns involve members of business, politics, and law enforcement and not simply members of criminal society. In Shanghai, for example, the PLA is in business with the Public Security Bureau, which has connections to fixers who have paid off Party officials, who in turn know the right people in various ministries, and so on and so forth. In China these reciprocal exchange relationships are denoted by the term *quanxi*. And in the scheme of things, *The Economist* ("City of Glitter and Ghosts," 1995) had argued that in China of the mid-1990s money and *quanxi* trump the law.

What began in the early 1980s as a handful of private entrepreneurs and petty crooks operating at the margins of society has now evolved into a complicated web of quasi-legal and illegal associations that implicate Party and government officials at every level. The problem has become so acute that crimes thought to have disappeared following the communist revolution—drug use, prostitution, the sale of women and children—not only have reappeared but are now widespread. According to Chinese officials, the number of "major criminal cases" has increased 10-fold in the past decade, growing 40 percent per year since 1985.

For example, in Tengzhou, a mid-sized city in Shandong province, officials mobilized 1,000 public security personnel who, over a two-month period in 1991, "broke up 54 human-trafficking rings, captured 165 members and 22 chiefs, and exposed nine bases of operation," according to a provincial radio report. More than 1,000 women and children who had been sold into bondage were rescued. It is also reported that such organizations also have networks stretching across several provinces (Hood, 1992). In addition to crime, populist uprisings against unpopular government officials and policies are also on the increase (Zweig, 1989; Chiang, 1994; Li and O'Brien, 1996). At the same time, China's hinterland is sorely beset by arbitrary tax levies, brigandage, local warlordism, and internecine feuds (Kaye, 1994).

Official Corruption

As with Leninist systems elsewhere, corruption has been a perennial problem in the PRC (Meaney, 1991). Since the early 1950s, the Chinese government has experimented with numerous systems of control: internal administrative audits, separate control commissions, discipline inspection bureaus, and mass campaigns (Findlay and Chiu, 1989). All to no avail. The problem is that the Leninist systems structurally generate clientelism and networks of personal ties, while at the same time making them politically illegitimate. Control over appointments and promotions within the bloated administration bureaucracies of these systems make the Party an efficient vehicle for distributing patronage and exchanging favors. Patronage allows such officials as Party secretaries and cadres to form power bases and networks of personal ties (Meaney, 1991).

Although corruption is not a new phenomenon in the PRC, its current vast scale represents a major change from the past. Until recently, Baum (1994) argues, the extent of corruption in China was limited by the relatively small financial rewards and relatively high social and political costs involved. Under Mao, where corruption did exist, it tended to be rather localized and limited in scale; much of it involved cadres extorting "donations" of various kinds, including money, consumer goods, and sexual favors from members of their work units. In the more permissive, "to get rich is glorious" environment of postreform China, however, the cost-benefit calculus has changed dramatically; now there is a manifold increase in both the *incentive* to engage in corruption (in the forms of substantially greater economic payoffs and diminished ideological restraints) and the *opportunity* to do so (presented by the gap between a newly decentralized, weakened state economic apparatus and a newly strengthened, semiautonomous cadre corps).

CONTEMPORARY CRIME CONTROL

In general, law enforcement is poorly prepared and underfinanced, if not inept, in its efforts to combat organized crime and corruption. In any case, in late 1988, the Chinese government launched a highly publicized crackdown on companies engaged in official corruption, tax evasion, and currency manipulation. *Renmin Ribao* published two commentaries (1988a, 1988b) that called on authorities to "resolutely punish 'speculating officials' " (Zhu, 1991). Other newspapers reported that "such transactions lead to . . . exploitation of consumers," and that "only by removing these tumors from the national economy can the [economic] reform benefit the state and the people" (Zhu, 1991).

Over the next several months, the campaign struck mainly at smaller, politically less well-connected companies. But on July 28, 1989, following the violent military suppression of unarmed students and workers in Tiananmen Square, the Political Bureau adopted a remarkable resolution calling for action against China's largest corporations (*Renmin Ribao*, 1989a). On September 5, the State Council issued an order to close 11 types of corporations, including those that had been established under the leadership of the Central Committee (*Renmin Ribao*, 1989b). Others were punished by administrative measures. By the end of 1989, over 103,000 companies run by the Central Committee, the PLA, local governments, and CCP committees had been closed. Within the Party, the campaign reportedly netted more than 325,000 offenders in its first 18 months of operation. In 1990, an additional 256,000 members had received lesser degrees of Party discipline.

But while the crackdown briefly struck fear within local cadres, the higher ranks of the Party, with few exceptions, were left largely unscathed. Faced with a major challenge to its legitimacy, the state reacted by launching a widely publicized, *but carefully targeted*, crackdown on official corruption and other forms of economic crime. Official newspapers occasionally railed against the "big monkeys," but, as in the past, those occupying the top rungs of the political ladder were able to avoid judicial scrutiny of their misdeeds. Moreover, in the first half of 1992, for example, indictments were handed down in less than one third of the 48,000 cases of lower-level cadre corruption that were officially investigated, whereas from 1988 to the spring of 1993, merely five provincial- and ministerial-level cadres were convicted of economic crimes (Baum, 1994).

Outside the arenas of organized crime and official corruption, the incarceration or imprisonment rates have been estimated to be about 166 prisoners per 100,000 population (Seymour and Anderson, 1997), which is not particularly high by international standards. In Taiwan, for example, the rate is 187; in Singapore, 210; and in the world, 105. Nationwide, there appear to be about 2 million prisoners confined in China's prisons and jails. Esti-

mates also vary as to the percentage of political prisoners, but most observers, including former political prisoners, place the percentage at less than 1
percent (Seymour and Anderson, 1997).

FUTURE OF CRIME AND CRIME CONTROL

Many criminologists believe a rising overall crime rate and a relatively high
proportion of property to personal crime are indices of the transition from
developing to developed country status. Judged by these standards, China
falls into the category of a developing nation in view of its low overall crime
rate. In terms of its high rate of juvenile delinquency, however, China is
similar to the developed countries. To complicate matters further, in the
1980s China had a remarkably low proportion of drug-related crime even
compared to developing countries, but in recent years the proportion has
risen so sharply that it now approaches the level of the developed world
(Bakken, 1999). At the same time, its organized crimes and corruptions are
similar to other postsocialist developing market economies (i.e., Russia, Poland). In terms of its overall crime profile, China is thus a mixed case of
developed and developing nation.

Today China is a nation on the rise. After nearly three decades of numbing
austerity and perpetual class struggle under Mao's rule, Deng Xiaoping's
market-oriented reforms were like a tonic to an exhausted nation. China's
economy rose almost immediately from its lethargy and began to grow at
an unprecedented rate. Nevertheless, social change on such a vast scale was
unlikely to be entirely smooth sailing. Reform brought many benefits to the
Chinese people, but its partial, discontinuous form was responsible for a
number of worrying features as well, including rampant urban inflation, massive unemployment within the state-owned enterprise sector, and rising
crime. The effects proved to be fertile ground for the reemergence of ret-
rograde social forms thought to have vanished from modern China.

Ample evidence suggests that organized crime groups were quick to adapt
to the fast-changing economic and political environment, whereas law enforcement organizations at all levels were ill-equipped and poorly prepared
to meet these challenges. By the late 1980s, the Chinese state faced a crisis
of legitimacy. After living nearly four decades with the fundamental security
that was provided by the old system, the challenges and uncertainties of the
new one were deeply disturbing to millions of ordinary Chinese. An important structural cause of the crisis was the resurgence of the very class
divisions that the communists has promised to eradicate in 1949.

By the mid-1980s, to be rich was "glorious," to be idealistic was passé.
Income gaps visibly widened between rich and poor in the cities as nearly
three decades of Maoist-style egalitarianism were swept away by the forces
of reform. Well-documented businessmen and cadres thrived, whereas ordinary workers felt increasingly disenfranchised. Even more stark than urban

income stratification, however, was the steadily worsening terms of trade between cities and countryside, bringing the income gap between the two to a ratio of about 4 to 1 (Kaye, 1993).

Finally, families living on fixed incomes (still the vast majority in China) have found themselves falling hopelessly behind the cost of living and inflation. Public opinion polls as far back as the 1980s began registering a downturn in popular enthusiasm for reform (Bonavia, 1986). By the end of the decade, China's cities experienced major social unrest as double-digit rates of inflation led to growing levels of frustration, alienation, envy (or what the Chinese call "red-eye disease"), and anger. Not much has changed in the 1990s. In conclusion, the numerous contradictions inherent in China's "market socialism" have been responsible for much of the nation's turmoil in recent years. Until these contradictions are resolved, economic gangs, official corruption, and "black society" can be expected to thrive in the space between the market and the plan.

REFERENCES

Bakken, Borge. 1993. "Crime, Juvenile Delinquency and Deterrence Policy in China." *Australian Journal of Chinese Affairs* 30: 29–58.
——. 1999. *The Exemplary Society.* Oxford: Oxford University Press.
Baum, Richard. 1994. *Burying Mao: Chinese Politics in the Age of Deng Xiaoping.* Princeton, NJ: Princeton University Press.
Beck, Simon. 1997. "Jitters on Chinese Crime." *South China Morning Post,* April 17.
Bonavia, David. 1986. "Problems at the Plenum." *Far Eastern Economic Review* (October 16).
Brewer, John D., Adrian Guelke, Ian Hume, Edward Moxon-Browne, and Rick Wilford. 1988. *The Police, Public Order and the State.* New York: St. Martin's Press.
Cai, Shaoqing. 1964. "Guany Tiandihui de giyuan wenti" (On the question of the origin of the Heaven and Earth Society). *Beijing daxue xuebao* 1: 53–64.
Cao, Manzhi. 1988. *Zhongguo gingshaonian fanzuixue* (The criminology of Chinese juvenile delinquency). Beijing: Qunzhong chubanshe.
Chiang, Chen-chang. 1994. "A Study of Social Conflict in Rural Mainland China." *Issues and Studies* 30, 3: 35–50.
"City of Glitter and Ghosts." 1995. *The Economist* (December 24–January 6).
Curran, Daniel J., and Sandra Cook. 1993. "Growing Fears, Rising Crime: Juveniles and China's Justice System." *Crime and Delinquency* 39, 3: 296–315.
Dubro, Alec, and David E. Kaplan. 1986. *Yakuza.* New York: Addison-Wesley.
Dutton, Michael. 1992. "A Mass-Line without Politics: Community Policing and Economic Reform." In Andrew Watson (ed.), *Economic Reform and Social Change in China.* London: Routledge.
Dutton, Michael, and Lee Tianfu. 1993. "Missing the Target? Policing Strategies in the Period of Economic Reform." *Crime and Delinquency* 39, 3: 316–36.
Encyclopaedia Brittanica. 1991. 15th ed. S. v. "China."

Findlay, Mark, and Thomas Chiu Chor-wing. 1989. "Sugar Coated Bullets: Corruption and the New Economic Order in China." *Contemporary Crises* 13: 145–61.

Gaylord, Mark S., and Paul Levine. 1997. "The Criminalization of Official Profiteering: Lawmaking in the People's Republic of China." *International Journal of the Sociology of Law* 25: 117–34.

Hirschi, Travis, and Michael Gottfredson. 1983. "Age and the Explanation of Crime." *American Journal of Sociology* 89: 552–84.

Hood, Marlowe. 1992. "China's Secret Crime Wave." *Sunday Morning Post* (Hong Kong), May 31.

Hornick, Richard. 1993. "Limits of Progress." *Time* (May 10).

Kaye, Lincoln. 1993. "Rotten to the Core." *Far Eastern Economic Review* (September 16).

———. 1994. "Disorder under Heaven." *Far Eastern Economic Review* (June 9).

Kuhn, Anthony. 1994. "Cops and Robbers." *Far Eastern Economic Review* (June 9).

Kuhn, Anthony, and Lincoln Kaye. 1994. "Bursting at the Seams." *Far Eastern Review* (March 10).

Li, Lianjiang, and Kevin J. O'Brien. 1996. "Villagers and Popular Resistance in Contemporary China." *Modern China* 22, 1: 22–61.

Ma, L. Eve Armentrout. 1990. *Revolutionaries, Monarchists, and Chinatowns: Chinese Politics in the Americas and the 1911 Revolution.* Honolulu: University of Hawaii Press.

McCoy, Alfred W. 1992. "Heroin as a Global Commodity: A History of Southeast Asia's Opium Trade." In Alfred W. McCoy and Alan A. Block (eds.), *War on Drugs: Studies in the Failure of U.S. Narcotics Policy.* Boulder, CO: Westview Press.

Meaney, Connie Squires. 1991. "Market Reform and Disintegrative Corruption in Urban China." In Richard Baum (ed.), *Reform and Reaction in Post-Mao China.* London: Routledge.

Murray, Dian. 1993. "Migration, Protection and Racketeering: The Spread of the Tiandihui within China." In David Ownby and Mary Somers Heidhues (eds.), *"Secret Societies" Reconsidered: Perspectives on the Social History of Modern South China and Southeast Asia.* Armonk, NY: M. E. Sharpe.

Ownby, David. 1993. "Secret Societies Reconsidered." In David Ownby and Mary Somers Heidhues (eds.), *"Secret Societies" Reconsidered: Perspectives on the Social History of Modern South China and Southeast Asia.* Armonk, NY: M. E. Sharpe.

People's Republic of China Yearbook 1995/96. 1997. "Structure of the State." Hong Kong: N.C.N. Limited.

Renmin Ribao. 1988a. September 3.

———. 1988b. October 26.

———. 1989a. July 29.

———. 1989b. September 6.

"The Road from Tiananmen." 1994. *The Economist* (June 4).

Seagrave, Sterling. 1985. *The Soong Dynasty.* London: Sigwick and Jackson.

Seymour, James D., and Richard Anderson. 1997. *New Ghosts, Old Ghosts: Prisons and Labor Reform Camps in China.* Armonk, NY: M. E. Sharpe.

Shelley, Louise I. 1981. *Crime and Modernization: The Impact of Industrialization and Urbanization on Crime.* Carbondale, IL: Southern Illinois University Press.

United Nations. 1953. Department of Social Relation's *Bulletin on Narcotics* 5, 2 (April–June): 49.

Wong, Linda. 1994. "China's Urban Migrants: The Public Policy Challenge." *Pacific Affairs* 67, 3: 335–55.

Xin, Ming. 1991. *Fanzui xue* (Criminology). Chongqing: Chongqing chubanshe.

Yang, Cheng. 1991. "Corporate Crime under a Changing Socialist Economic System." Paper presented at the annual meeting of the American Society of Criminology, San Francisco, November 8–11.

Zhang, Jifa. 1980. "Cong guoli gugong bowuyuan diacang Qingdai dang'an tan Tiandihui de yuanliu" (A discussion of the origins of the Heaven and Earth based on Qing archives held in the National Palace Museum). *Gugong jikan* 14, 4: 63–91.

Zhu, Su-li. 1991. "Economic Structure and the Crime of Speculation." Paper presented at the Joint Meeting of the Law and Society Association and the Research Committee on the Sociology of Law, Amsterdam, June 26–29.

Zweig, David. 1989. "Struggling Over Land in China: Peasant Resistance after Collectivism, 1966–1986." In Forrest Colburn (ed.), *Everyday Forms of Peasant Resistance.* Armonk, NY: M. E. Sharpe.

3

GERMANY

(Developed Nation-State)

Hans-Joerg Albrecht and Raymond Teske

PROFILE OF GERMANY

After reunification of the former German Democratic Republic and the former Federal Republic of Germany in 1990, the size of the population at the end of the 1990s was slightly over 80 million, including some 8 million foreign nationals, as well as 3 million ethnic Germans from the former Soviet Union. The political system of Germany is federal in nature and consists of 16 states. The division of legislative and administrative powers between the federal level and the state level is laid down in the German Constitution, which gives the Federal Parliament a strong position in legislation. On the other hand, implementation of laws and law enforcement is entrusted almost completely to the states, which gives them a strong position in justice administration. Hence, in spite of uniform administrative rules that have been issued to serve as guidelines for criminal administration, differences in law enforcement practices remain prevalent and are sometimes the expression of significant differences in crime control policies between states, such as in the area of drug control, prosecution, and selective enforcement (Aulinger, 1997).

HISTORICAL PERSPECTIVE ON CRIME AND CRIME CONTROL

Police recorded crime figures demonstrate an upward trend in the 1950s, 1960s, and 1970s for West Germany.[1] Crime rates, then, reveal a rather flat line in the 1980s and resume their upward trend in the 1990s. However, in the mid 1990s the increase levels off, and a modest decrease in the overall crime rate can be noted. It is property crimes that explain most of the increase that can be observed throughout the last four decades. While in the 1960s and 1970s the focus was primarily on phenomena such as mass crimes, during the 1980s and 1990s it was essentially on illicit drugs, violence, sexual abuse, and organized/transnational crime, as well as on serious economic and environmental crime.

Major reforms in sentencing and the system of criminal penalties date back to the end of the 1960s and 1970s when German criminal law underwent profound changes, driven primarily by concerns for offender prevention and rehabilitation. Criminal law reforms in 1969 and 1975 brought about a complete revision of the system of criminal sanctions (Albrecht, 1980, 1997d). As regards the relationship between imprisonment, the suspended prison sentence, and the fine, legislation was introduced ordering that fines should typically have priority over short-term imprisonment (e.g., less than six months). The rationale to limit or reduce the use of short-term imprisonment was based on the idea that it could not be effective with respect to the longer-range goals of rehabilitation. Moreover, short-term imprisonment was believed to open up the possibility of offenders experiencing the corrupting effects of the prison environment. According to these legal reforms, first-time offenders and offenders having committed crimes of a nonserious nature were to be the main target groups of criminal fines. Longer prison sentences were to concentrate on repeat offenders of serious crimes. Located in between imprisonment and fines there emerged the suspended prison sentence.

During the 1970s and 1980s, the once powerful belief in rehabilitation and prevention, and its potential for guiding sentencing, as well as the trust in the feasibility of establishing precisely the risk of recidivism, faded away. In addition, criminal policy turned its attention away from both traditional crimes and the type of marginal offenders that were better suited for the rehabilitative approach. Economic crimes, organized crime, and drug trafficking became the main targets of policy making and criminal law reform in the late 1980s and during the 1990s.

The types of offenses and offenders associated with these new phenomena also brought about the need to reconsider sentencing goals and sentencing theory. With these changes the focus of sentencing theory shifted from individualization toward equity and from individual prevention toward general prevention. The present crisis of rehabilitation provokes the question of how the choice between fines, suspended prison sentences, and immediate imprisonment should be made and how consistency in sentencing can be established.

When looking at sentencing practices over the last three decades, several long-term trends can be observed. The absolute number of offenders convicted and sentenced is rather stable during the 1970s and 1980s (oscillating around 700,000 per year and equaling approximately 1,300 criminal convictions per 100,000 population). During the mid-1990s the figure increased to some 760,000 (i.e., 1996: 763,690). Stability was also due to the successful implementation of diversion or nonprosecution policies cutting off steadily increasing numbers of suspects. The rates of sentenced offenders among the German population has actually decreased over the past couple of decades. In 1975, there were 1,342 sentenced German offenders per 100,000 German nationals. By 1996, the rate was 1,076 per 100,000. However, the increase in the numbers sentenced during the 1990s was accounted for by the rapidly growing proportion of foreign offenders.

In short, evidence from German prison statistics reveal that imprisonment rates for German nationals is still on the retreat, whereas the overall increase in prison populations can be explained by the tremendous (and ongoing) increase in the number of foreign nationals entering the prison system (Albrecht, 1997b). The data displayed in Table 3.1 demonstrate that there are two processes going on in the German prison system. The first is a long-term trend with a steady increase in the proportion of foreign nationals among the prison population at large, certainly a reflection of the corresponding trends in immigration. The second is a more recent trend, set off around 1990 with the abolition of border controls between the East and West of Europe, leading to immediate and significant increases in the share of young foreign nationals in the prison population. Around the mid-1990s this trend seems to have leveled off.

The use of prison sentences, both immediate and suspended, has remained stable since the beginning of the 1970s with a proportion of around 16 to 18 percent of all criminal sentences. The rate of unconditional prison sentences declined until the end of the 1980s. In absolute numbers, they varied between 30,000 and 40,000 per year; for example, in 1996, they were 36,874 or 5 percent of all criminal penalties. The use of suspended prison sentences increased steadily until the end of the 1980s. In 1996, they accounted for 70 percent of all prison sentences and 12 percent of all criminal penalties. The share of fines increased sharply at the end of the 1960s and has remained stable, amounting to some 82 to 84 percent of all sentences during the last two decades. Again, in 1996, they represented 83.8 percent of all sentences.

The consequence of the distribution of criminal penalties outlined above was, on the one hand, a rather high average period of imprisonment compared to other European countries (e.g., approximately six months compared to an average of around two months in the Netherlands). On the other hand, the rate of offenders receiving unconditional prison sentences was rather low in Germany.

Overall, during the 1980s and 1990s, there was no uniform development in sentencing practice. In the case of most traditional crime, for example,

Table 3.1
Age Patterns of Sentenced Foreign Prison Populations in Germany (percent
of total prison population) between 1971 and 1997

	14–17	18–20	21–24	25–30	31–40	41–50	51–60	>60
1971	2.3	3.2	4.3	3.2	2.9	5.3	4.6	3.0
1972	3.8	3.3	5.5	4.3	3.4	4.9	5.5	3.4
1973	3.9	4.3	6.3	5.1	3.8	5.2	6.6	2.2
1974	3.3	4.6	6.1	6.4	4.6	5.7	7.8	3.4
1975	4.9	4.3	6.3	7.3	4.7	5.5	8.4	2.7
1976								
1977								
1978	6.3	4.1	4.9	7.0	6.5	5.6	8.8	4.6
1979								
1980								
1981	11.9	6.9	7.0	8.1	9.6	6.9	8.9	5.5
1982								
1983	19.2	8.9	7.7	10.4	11.0	8.3	8.3	7.3
1984								
1985	17.9	10.0	8.7	10.0	11.1	8.0	7.6	7.1
1986								
1987								
1988	28.6	16.6	11.9	10.5	10.9	8.5	8.1	6.8
1989	34.9	17.9	13.4	12.3	11.6	9.0	8.4	9.6
1990	35.5	22.5	14.4	13.5	13.0	9.9	8.4	10.2
1991								
1992	43.4	30.9	18.9	17.4	14.1	12.5	9.0	11.2
1993	34.7	34.6	25.7	19.5	15.8	13.5	10.3	11.5
1994	35.1	35.4	31.3	22.9	18.0	15.2	11.5	9.4
1995	31.9	33.0	33.6	25.3	20.2	15.2	10.5	10.2
1997	30.6	30.2	39.3	29.6	22.6	16.7	10.4	10.5
Ratio								
1971/1997	1:13	1:9	1:9	1:9	1:8	1:3	1:2	1:3

traffic offenses, property crimes, robbery, and assault, prosecutors' offices
and the courts tended to pursue diversionary policies. They also pursued
sentencing policies favoring fines and prison sentences near the minimum
allowed in offense statutes. In the case of simple theft, approximately 9 out
of 10 offenders were fined. A corresponding rate could be found in assault
cases and vandalism. Serious property offenses and drug offenses involving
simple possession also resulted in large proportions of fines. On the other
hand, the sentencing practices for other offenses, such as violent sexual offenses (especially rape and child sexual abuse) and drug trafficking, became
more severe at the end of the 1970s and the beginning of the 1980s
(Schöch, 1992). The length of prison sentences increased significantly, with

prison sentences of more than five years doubling between 1978 and 1983. Taken together, by 1998 a dynamic upward trend in incarceration revealed imprisonment rates above 100 per 100,000 and, thus, a return to the level of the early 1960s, prior to criminal law reform.

PUBLIC PERCEPTION OF CRIME AND CRIME CONTROL

Penal politics as expressed in criminal legislation in the 1990s clearly reflect the conditions of a pluralistic society where uniform perceptions of threats to social order can no longer be expected. What we observe is a trend toward differentiation in the threats to public safety and social stability. The outcome of such differentiation results in something that might be labeled "popularistic" criminal justice policy.

Main threats to social order today are seen in the spread of organized crime and related problems such as undermining the social fabric through its potential for corrupting the values of conventional society. Trafficking of illicit drugs, uncontrolled immigration, and extremist groups have been highlighted. What some of these threats have in common is: Like organized crime and the mafia, they are viewed as coming from "outside" the community and serve as "convenient enemies." Among the traditional threats to social order, we see that poverty and unemployment have been spreading. Also posing threats are the spread of mass media and new information technology. Last, but not least, many families are regarded as incapable of raising their young to become law-abiding and orderly citizens. The dysfunctional family ranks high on the agenda of threats.

Partially, the threat and safety debate transforms into a debate on values as the organized crime debate shows. Those who maintain that organized crime poses threats to social order argue that it is the conventional society itself, or large parts of it, that are supporting organized criminal activities by expressing demands for drugs, gambling, pornography, and other vices. According to these perspectives, it is the loss of values that produces individuals who can so easily be corrupted into "black markets" (or hidden economies). The basic critique, then, is not addressing organized crime but the society and social policies at large, which are viewed as having contributed to those social conditions that, in turn, provide fertile ground for all types of organized crime.

On the other hand, the discourse on what the focus should be regarding penal politics has also demonstrated what has been put aside in the 1990s. It is evident that the new concern for rational, organized, and serious crime goes hand-in-hand with a policy of retreating from the responsibility for the control of most small-scale crimes. By the 1990s, for example, these crime control responsibilities were being reassigned to the private area and to the community, under the direction of the state Ministries of the Interior.

Fear of crime and the mass media are often linked to public perceptions and feelings of insecurity. As measured by victim surveys that began focusing questions on the effects of social and economic transition in the early 1990s, a marked increase in the fear of crime was associated with rapid changes in crime rates in former East Germany. Even though the victimization rates were similar for both East and West Germany, the fear of crime, at least temporarily, registered twice as high in former East Germany as in former West Germany. Eventually though, by 1995, the fear of crime had leveled off or even declined slightly in East Germany (Boers, 1996).

More important, international comparative victimization research has pointed out that perceptions of the risk of becoming a crime victim and fear of crime measures are to some degree independent from rates of actual experiences with victimization (as well as from the rates of police recorded crime). The absence of a positive relationship between experiences with victimization and insecurity measures is usually explained, in part, by the trivial and petty nature of the bulk of victimizing events that are reported in surveys. In part, the absence is also explained by the role of the media and the overrepresentation of violence and other exceptional crimes in all types of media. However, it is still not understood how insecurity and crime in the media are intertwined; yet the implicit and explicit relationships seem to somehow be related to policies of crime and crime control.

CONTEMPORARY CRIME

Related to immigration from reunification as well as from the tearing down of the Iron Curtain in general, youth and hate violence became public and criminological concerns around 1990. When police recorded assaults and street robbery among children and juveniles began to increase rapidly around 1990, youth and hate violence became concerns of the public and researchers alike. Although not quantitatively significant phenomena, hate violence and hate crimes in general triggered deep interest. Disproportionately committed by juveniles and young adults, those vulnerable to such crimes are typically immigrants and ethnic Germans from the former Soviet Union (Willems, 1993; Albrecht, 1994; Mansel and Hurrelmann, 1998).

Drug trafficking, abuse, and related crime are also topical issues of research and public affect (Rautenberg, 1998). With respect to use of illicit drugs, young people from former East Germany did not catch up during the 1990s in terms of incidence and prevalence. In 1993, 25 percent of West Germans yet only 6 percent of 16- to 29-year-old East Germans reported to have ever used cannabis products. In 1997, 193,558 drug offenses (302 per 100,000) were registered by police in former West Germany, whereas in former East Germany 11,541 drug offenses (72 per 100,000) were counted (Bundeskriminalamt, 1998: 218).

The issue of foreigners' crime has attracted policy and research attention since the 1960s when "guest workers" were recruited in large numbers in countries from southern Europe in order to respond to labor shortages in the West German economy. However, it was in the 1990s that the issues of immigration and crime became of paramount importance for policy in general and during election campaigns in particular. The available data on foreign minorities and police recorded crime should be interpreted as displaying different trends. The opening of the borders after the breakdown of communist regimes in the east of Europe has given rise to a sharp increase in property offenses. These are mainly of a petty nature and are committed by short-term migrants consisting of tourists and/or asylum seekers. The wealth on display, for example, in department stores in near-border cities has clearly served (and still serves) as an important pull factor.

Foreigners' crime has been underlined by the huge increase in shoplifting figures that was experienced in some cities in the eastern part of Germany, near the border of Eastern European countries (Ahlf, 1994). For example, in the city of Berlin the shoplifting figures jumped between 1989 and 1990, from some 36,000 cases to more than 60,000 cases (Landeskriminalamt Berlin, 1994). This type of foreigners' crime may be understood as "migration crime" associated with short-term individual migration, illegal immigration, restrictions on legal employment, and poverty more generally.

Furthermore, huge "black markets" in the east of Europe have popped up, resulting in a growing demand for all types of those goods that have not been available or produced in sufficient quantities in Eastern European countries (i.e., cars, computers, communication technology). Although foreign nationals have been involved in these activities, for the most part, those involved have not belonged to populations settling in Germany. In fact, these types of serious property crimes concern cross-border (or transnational) crime linked with "black market" economies. Of course, immigrant youth and other groups coming from resident foreign populations heavily contribute to all types of ordinary criminal offenses. Finally, these markets and shadow economies in Germany, especially drug ones, have continued to provoke the need for a supply that has been provided by various ethnic and foreign groups (e.g., South American groups in the case of cocaine; North Africans and Black Africans, Kurdish, and Arab groups in the case of heroin and cannabis). Like conventional markets, illegal markets today reveal international networks necessitating participation of residents from various countries either on the supply side or on the demand side.

Criminal policy debates and criminal law reform of late have been increasingly driven by the topic of organized crime. Empirical research and police data, however, have not kept pace with developments in criminal policy. Since 1991 when police data on organized crime first became available in Germany, the official picture of such activities has not been spectacular. In 1996 a total of 8,384 suspects and 47,916 offenses were allocated to organized crime (Bundeskriminalamt, 1997). In relation to the total of 6.5

million offenses that came to the attention of the police in 1996, including 2.2 million suspects, organized crime is only about 8 percent of all registered offenses and 4 percent of suspects.

The problems with measuring and identifying organized crime have been clearly demonstrated in the field of money laundering where the legitimate and illegitimate workings of "taking care of business" intersect. Such problems have also been evident in the fields of environmental and economic crime. Among those developments in the field of organized and rational crime that need to be studied, for example, are the transitions of an underworld bound to new forms of economic, environmental, and white-collar crimes, which make them difficult to distinguish from their legal counterparts.

CONTEMPORARY CRIME CONTROL

The development of contemporary criminal justice policy is without, or defies, some kind of uniform trend. Rather, several trends or tendencies make up the overall approach to crime control. Basically, a three-tier approach to crime control emerged in the 1990s, with soft approaches adopted toward the juvenile offender and small-scale criminals (in particular in the field of traditional property and personal crimes), with firm approaches aimed at the rational and organized offender, and with tough and incapacitating approaches focused on the individual, dangerous offender. Victim policies developed along very similar lines. For example, mediation and compensation schemes developed as part of the soft approaches adopted toward juveniles and small-scale criminal offenders. Better protection of victims, then, has been sought in the trial stage in cases of serious violent and sexual offenses. The latter goal was expressed in a new piece of legislation amending procedural law through the introduction of closed-circuit TV as a means to protect vulnerable witnesses (Bundesministerium der Justiz, 1998). As regards law reform triggered by the issue of organized crime, policies have developed around the anonymous witness and witness protection programs that, in general, are aimed at more efficient prosecution of criminal networks.

Decision Making in the Criminal Justice System

Since the mid-1970s, the discretionary powers of the public prosecutor to dismiss criminal cases were extended considerably. For example, section 153a of the German Procedural Code authorized the public prosecutor to dismiss a case of minor guilt if the offender complied with (punitive) conditions determined by the public prosecutor (i.e., fine, community service, compensation). In March 1993, another law went into force that was essentially justified on the basis of economic problems created by German reunification. As rebuilding the justice system in former East Germany consumed a lot of resources, the need was felt to streamline criminal procedures further in order to be able to reduce costs significantly. Criticism has arisen that with these extensions the balance of powers has been seriously affected, the principle of due process has been threatened, and a marginalization of the role of the judge in sentencing has occurred. But it seems evident that budget concerns have outweighed legitimate interests in keeping up proper lines between the public prosecutors' task of investigating criminal cases and indicting criminal suspects, on the one hand, and the judges' task of imposing criminal punishment, on the other hand.

Besides the option of nonprosecution, the public prosecutor has the choice between two procedures in bringing the case to court. One procedure involves indictment with the consequence of a regular criminal trial. The other simplified procedure consists of mere written proceedings. If the public prosecutor concludes that the case is not complicated in terms of proving guilt and that a fine is a sufficient punishment, a penal order may then be suggested to the judge where, besides the indictment, the public prosecutor proposes a fine as a means of punishment. If the judge agrees, then a penal order is mailed to the suspect, who may appeal the order within a period of two weeks and request a trial. In the case of ordinary crimes that in principle could be brought to court (approximately 1.3 million cases per year), almost 40 percent are dismissed, another 21 percent are dealt with in simplified procedures, and just 17 percent are carried forward to trial. For 1996, these data revealed that most cases were resolved in a less formal manner and short of trial.

Major changes in the course of trial proceedings have also been introduced, not through legislation but through developments in custom or practice. The acceptance of these procedures is very close to the "plea bargaining" associated with the Anglo-Saxon criminal justice systems (Weigend, 1992). Faced with complex economic cases and the extensive right to move for the collection of evidence during trial, court etiquette has developed a system that, in German doctrine, is called "agreement." The core of such agreements lies in an exchange agreed upon between the public prosecutor and the court, on the one hand, and the defense council, on the other hand. The agreement is predicated on a confession that makes further proceedings unnecessary and the promise of the court to mitigate punishment.

The Supreme Court as well as the Constitutional Court have ruled that such agreements, although not explicitly a part of German criminal procedural law, can, in principle, be reached if certain conditions are fulfilled. There is strong opposition voiced in the academic field against such agreements. However, it is obvious that the justice system feels a potent need for such agreements in order to reduce the burden placed upon them by complex cases.

Sentencing

Each offense in the German Criminal Code carries its own penalty range. The range of penalties is defined with a minimum and a maximum penalty. With "day fines" the sentencing decision is broken down into two steps (Albrecht, 1980). First, the number of day fines, reflecting the seriousness of the offense, has to be determined. The minimum day fine is 5 days, and the maximum is 360 days. Second, the size of a 1-day fine unit (which may vary between DM2 and DM10,000, or $1.30 and $6,700) must be adjusted according to the daily net income of the offender. In other words, an offender is sentenced to a specific number of days of imprisonment, which is then assessed as a day fine of an equal number of days based on net income. If the offender cannot, or will not, pay the fine, then the offender serves the equivalent number of days in prison.

Actual imprisonment is the second main penalty where a statutory minimum has been set at one month and the statutory maximum at 15 years. Life-term imprisonment essentially is restricted to murder. With a 1992 criminal law amendment, a financial penalty was introduced that may be imposed if the offender is sentenced to imprisonment of 2 years or more. The fine itself may amount to the total value of the offender's property and assets.

Sentencing options available in German criminal law also differ according to age. Criminal law classifies individuals into four categories according to age. Under the age of 14, no criminal culpability exists, but only child welfare laws apply. A particular system of juvenile criminal justice deals with juvenile offenders (14–17 years) and is based upon the Youth Court Law, in force since 1923. Young adult offenders (18–20 years) are presumed to be adults and therefore fully responsible in cases of criminal offending (Albrecht, 1997c). However, under certain conditions as defined in section 105 of the Youth Court Law, young adults may be prosecuted, adjudicated, and sentenced as if they had been juveniles when committing the crime.

The difference between juvenile and adult criminal justice concerns sentencing goals. That is to say, the definitions of juvenile and adult crimes do not vary. Unlike the United States, for example, where "status offenses" for minors exist, the same set of criminal offense statutes apply to juveniles as well as to adults. Rehabilitation has been established as the exclusive goal for juvenile offenders under the Youth Court Law. Proportionality of punishment in relationship to the guilt of the offender and the seriousness of the offense is required by the basic statute on criminal sentencing, section 46 of the German Criminal Code.

Besides criminal penalties of fines and imprisonment, the use of which is strictly bound to the goal of "proportionality" and individual guilt, German adult criminal law also allows for another set of "measures" of rehabilitation and security, not dependent on personal guilt but solely dependent on the degree of dangerousness exhibited by a criminal offender and the corresponding need for preventing a relapse into serious crime. This bifurcated approach was based on the assumption that punishment that is strictly proportional to the harm committed and the degree of culpability may not be sufficient to respond to dangerous offenders who are likely to recommit very serious offenses. So under very restrictive conditions, at the time of sentencing, a criminal court may impose on addicted offenders, in addition to the actual criminal punishment, further detention in a detoxification and treatment center for a maximum of up to two years; on mentally ill offenders an indeterminate detention in a psychiatric facility; or on dangerous offenders an additional incapacitative sentence.

When it comes to the application of the penal sanction, German criminal law provides for a two-step procedure in sentencing (Albrecht, 1997d). The first step requires a decision on the severity of punishment, which must be proportionate with the individual level of guilt and the seriousness of the offense. Rehabilitation and deterrence according to mainstream legal doctrine may be pursued only within a narrowly specified range of penalties deemed to be consistent with the principle of proportionality. The second step requires a decision on the type of penalty, in terms of whether punishment should be imposed as a day fine, as a suspended prison sentence, or as a sentence of immediate imprisonment. In this decision, considerations of individual and general prevention (deterrence) play the decisive role. It should be pointed out that such policies have not been without their problems. For example, the problem of how proportionality can be established and how control of proportionality by superior courts can be exerted has not been resolved (Albrecht, 1997a). And although German adult criminal law was heavily influenced during the 1950s and 1960s by the ideal of rehabilitation, it never allowed for indeterminate sentencing.

While alternatives in the 1960s and 1970s were heavily influenced by the goal of rehabilitation (and the aim of reducing stigmatization and labeling coming with criminal sanctions), the 1980s and 1990s have been preoccupied with cost-benefit considerations and safety. This has led to the search for restrictive sentences that can be served in the community, such as house arrest and electronic monitoring, but that are also intended to provide tight supervision at a minimum cost. In effect, electronic monitoring has replaced the community bound sanctions of the 1960s and 1970s that were directed toward rehabilitation and reintegration of criminal offenders.

New technologies in implementing criminal penalties concern electronic tagging. Although electronic monitoring has been used as a criminal sanction in the United States since the mid-1980s, European countries until the early 1990s were rather reluctant to add electronic controls to their systems of sanctions. By the 1990s, electronic monitoring had indeed entered the European crime policy arena (Bishop, 1995). England and Wales, Sweden, and the Netherlands were among the first to discuss the introduction of electronic monitoring as an alternative penalty to pretrial detention. Later, in several German states (i.e., Hessen, Berlin, Hamburg), electronic monitoring was proposed as an alternative penalty to short-term imprisonment. In terms of the actual number of sanctioned offenders who will participate in some kind of electronic monitoring, it is thought that such penalties will not be of a significant number to play much of a role in penal dispositions.

Nevertheless, attention has been paid to the role of technology and commerce in pushing criminal sanctions such as electronic monitoring, especially in the context of overcrowded and costly prisons. The current attraction of electronic monitoring is apparently due not only to the heavy concern for the costs in the criminal justice systems but to the potential to symbolize a cost-benefit consciousness and modernity. Finally, the appeal of electronic monitoring for politicians has been to symbolize their concerns for tough crime control and supervision.

Pretrial detention contributes heavily to current capacity problems in the prison system. In 1997, approximately 30 percent of the average daily number of 71,000 prisoners in Germany had been held in detention prior to trial. Court statistics revealed that out of approximately 1 million offenders adjudicated in 1996, some 4 percent had been for a time detained prior to their trial. Another problem associated with pretrial detention concerns the phenomenon that a substantial proportion of those offenders doing time in pretrial detention will not be sentenced to imprisonment; rather, will be sentenced to suspended prison sentences or fined. From those 38,000 offenders detained prior to their criminal trials in 1996, some 31 percent received suspended prison sentences; another 11 percent were fined.

Critics suggest in this respect that criminal courts sometimes use pretrial detention for punishment purposes (Schöch, 1997). In detention prior to trial, the share of foreigners is especially marked. Foreign nationals, for example, make up approximately two thirds of all pretrial detainees. Moreover, repressive policies toward drug markets where supply, to a large extent, is organized by ethnic and foreign minorities seem to contribute heavily to increasing rates of imprisonment among particular foreign minorities. In addition, pretrial detention may be regarded as part of the response to migrating groups and cross-border crime, as well as a backup to policies of expulsion (Albrecht, 1997b).

Victims

In the 1980s and 1990s, emphasis was placed upon the implementation of victim policies, in particular victim-offender mediation, victim restitution, and victim protection during trial. Early surveys revealed that the victim plays a central role in determining the input to the justice system.

Although most of the research devoted to the analysis of the victim's role as gatekeeper of the criminal justice system is based either on the crime measurement approach or on coping strategies, we notice a shift in research orientations and an attempt to go beyond the mere functional properties of reporting behavior toward the question of which goals the victims pursue when reporting a criminal event to police (Rosellen, 1980; Kury, Teske, and Wurger, 1999). The findings on reporting motives have shown that victims of crime are rather interested in the police as a crisis intervention agency and that immediate conflict settlement and immediate restitution fall among the most prominent motives for reporting criminal events.

Another issue that has emerged in recent years refers to the position of the victim in criminal proceedings and evaluation of policy aimed at improving the victim's position (Kaiser, 1992; Kilchling, 1995). Critics argue that the crime victim has been marginalized in the criminal law and that the criminal justice system does not respond to the victim's most urgent needs. Rather, the system is preoccupied with punishing the offender. Evaluation of legislative efforts to improve the victim's position in criminal proceedings and to provide better opportunities to put forward financial and other interests and demands shows that, despite official encouragement, courts are still rather reluctant to handle civil law problems within the framework of criminal justice (Albrecht, 1990; Kury, Kaiser, and Teske, 1994).

Victim-offender reconciliation, available as a disposition in juvenile criminal law for a long time, was recently introduced in the adult criminal law as an expressly stated mitigating factor in sentencing (section 46a, German Criminal Code). New legislation has also introduced protective devices for the child or juvenile victim of sexual abuse and rape, who, for example, may be allowed to communicate through closed-circuit television and video conversations of interviews and so on (Bundesministerium der Justiz, 1998).

Finally, victim policies have also become a part of legislation related to organized crime. Anonymous witness and witness protection programs, on the one hand, aim at the protection of the individual victim of crime and, on the other hand, focus essentially on making the investigation and prosecution of organized crimes more efficient.

Investigation and Surveillance

The introduction of new investigative techniques was justified mainly by law enforcement problems in the field of organized crime (Gropp, 1993). First, a search procedure based on electronic information reduction techniques has to be mentioned (sections 98a–c, Criminal Procedural Code). Modern societies produce enormous amounts of information on individuals in various public and private sectors. Credit card companies, telephone companies, social service administrations, housing agencies, and many more collect data from their clients. New provisions empower police and public prosecutors to search these information systems by using certain matching techniques in order to filter out smaller groups of individuals who, in principle, fit into "profiles" established for certain groups of offenders (e.g., drug traffickers). Critics argue here that the principle of proportionality might be violated, as with such techniques, the privacy of a large number of citizens may be infringed upon. In addition, it is argued that these practices involve large numbers of innocent citizens falling under the scope of police investigations and public prosecutions.

New surveillance technologies were admitted through the 1993 law amendment to sections 100c–d of the Criminal Procedural Code, which allowed for the electronic and video-based surveillance of suspects without their knowledge. With these new provisions the police may follow up on suspects with the help of video cameras as well as other electronic equipment in order to record, visually and acoustically, communication in which suspects are engaged. Another new investigative technique is "undercover policing," also introduced in the 1993 amendment. With undercover policing a bundle of legal problems have arisen that can be summarized under the topics of "deception" and "covered methods."

An undercover agent, according to German criminal procedural law, is a police officer who has adopted a "legend" and thus changed his or her identity. False documents and a false name should—according to the official reasoning—allow an undercover agent to penetrate gangs and organized criminal networks in order to produce evidence that otherwise (and with traditional methods) would not be obtainable. The undercover agent is empowered to approach other people, enter premises under disguise, and deceive others regarding his or her true identity. The basic reason for introducing such methods of investigation lies in the conception of organized crime, which is seen to create serious obstacles for traditional methods of investigation.

What comes up as legal problems is the circumvention or neutralization of basic rights of suspects, among them the right to remain silent as well as the right not to be obliged to support investigative authorities in producing evidence against himself or herself. Furthermore, the right to remain silent also applies to certain categories of relatives who are not obliged to give testimony. The legislature, therefore, has restricted the use of undercover agents to cases of serious crimes and has tried to limit such investigative techniques to cases where traditional investigative techniques presumably would not be successful.

In addition, a dislocation of powers from the judiciary to the investigative authorities has been observed. Pre- or post facto control of the use of undercover policing through the judiciary has been reduced to exceptional cases. What we find here is also clear evidence that this type of pretrial investigation is seen to be merely an executive task. Consequently, the investigative strategies allowed through undercover policing have set further limits on the implementation of the principle of legality. Undercover policing is based on discretion, and with this, it is up to the investigative authorities to choose among the crimes which ones should be subject to undercover policing.

What is not regulated in the amendments of 1993 is the role and deployment of so-called whistle-blowers or private informants during pretrial investigations. Such informants have been heavily used as far back as the 1970s, essentially for the very same reasons that triggered legislation on undercover policing. There are two techniques applied with private informants. First, private informants usually are used to provoke crimes. So, for example, a regular method is "buy and bust" techniques in drug markets: A private informant approaches another person and asks him or her to sell illegal drugs. When drugs and money are passed over, the police, having observed the transaction, may then interfere and arrest the trafficker.

Second, private informants are used to trigger information from suspects (or other people likely to refuse to cooperate with police) in terms of confessions or other information leading to evidence. However, the statutes regulating undercover policing may not be applied to private informants. Heavy criticism has been raised regarding the Supreme Court's decisions that authorize these types of investigative activities, which are viewed as creating conflicts with basic procedural and other rights. Perhaps most important among them is the right to remain silent.

Finally, other newly introduced techniques concern the so-called search-net investigation as well as "police observation." With a search-net all information electronically or otherwise collected during customs/passport controls at airports or borders or during traffic or other police controls may be used and/or turned over as data files that can then be screened for individual persons or groups of persons. With police observation, information on suspects or persons assumed to have contacts with a suspect can be collected routinely during police controls to facilitate location of a suspect.

FUTURE OF CRIME AND CRIME CONTROL

What has happened so far in the reform of criminal procedural law in the Federal Republic of Germany might best be understood from a theory of modernization. On the one hand, the changes in criminal law, as well as social changes affecting crime patterns, have led crime control into the control and investigation of phenomena that belong to hidden economies. Hidden economies or "black markets," such as the drug market, essentially differ from traditional fields of crime control as they involve so-called victimless crime. Information on drug offenses can be collected only if police adopt proactive strategies of policing. On the other hand, legislation in basic criminal law during this century increasingly adopted the concept of endangering offenses that focus on the risk associated with certain types of behavior, no longer emphasizing the results of human behavior (as was done with traditional offense types such as assault, theft, and murder).

With endangering offenses, criminal law was then extended into very complex subsystems of society such as the economic system and the natural environment. With all of this, investigative activities moved away from repression and toward prevention. The traditional role of criminal investigation was no longer, if ever, successful in dealing with victimless crime. Therefore, a certain demand for modernization and adaptation in investigation and procedure was triggered by changes in the larger society as well as in basic criminal law and crime policies. With the introduction of the new investigative methods, trial procedures adjusted accordingly. However, the traditional structure of the criminal procedure, the concept of defendants' rights, and the customary balance of power as expressed in the relationship between police, public prosecutor, defense counsel, and the judiciary have been deeply affected during this process.

In the future, modern criminal justice most probably will be headed toward further simplification and the goal of speeding up trials, as well as reducing the costs associated with traditional rules of criminal procedure. We may also assume that the preventive approach will continue to prevail. On the other hand, crime victims' concerns will continue to receive support, although the consideration of crime victims will be weaker as there are no powerful interest groups pressing toward victims' rights.

The future of criminal policy seems to be influenced heavily by the rhetoric on organized crime. The concept of organized crime, indeed, is very influential in crime policy as it refers to the rational offender, to the *homo economicus*, to whom economic theories of punishment may be applied. While during the 1960s and 1970s criminal policy was based on the concept of the maladapted or desocialized offender, the 1990s presented the rational cost-calculating offender who behaves like any other businessman weighing the benefits and costs of different options of behavior. Most probably, this model of the criminal offender will not only affect criminal law and sentencing decisions, but it will have just as significant an effect on prison regimes. The model of the rational offender might also contribute to putting more weight on the efficiency model of criminal law as opposed to the justice model or to proportionality. This fits with arguments in policy debates stressing the need for amendments and reform in order to make criminal law more efficient.

Increasing rationalization occurs as a response to new risks in modern society. Penal politics in the 1990s have affected criminal procedure. This points toward a shift in power toward the executive branches of the criminal justice system and particularly toward law enforcement. Within the procedural field, the emphasis of investigation is put on the presuspicion field. Then criminal policies in regard to criminal procedures are aimed at reducing costs through simplification as well as diminishing the opportunities to appeal. Finally, the discourse surrounding crime and crime control is preoccupied with the concept of internal safety as well as with organized crime as the main threat to that safety.

NOTE

1. All police recorded crimes in this chapter refer only to West Germany through 1991. Beginning in 1992, police data refers to both West and East. All other data such as convictions, sentencing, and imprisonment refer only to the West as information systems for the East do not exist yet.

REFERENCES

Ahlf, E. H. 1994. "Ausländerkriminalität in der Bundesrepublik Deutschland nach Öffnung der Grenzen." *Zeitschrift fur Ausländerrecht,* 132–38.

Albrecht, H. J. 1980. *Strafzumessung und Vollstreckung bei Geldsstragen—unter besonderer Berücksichtigung des Tagessatzsystems.* Berlin: Duncker & Humblot.

———. 1990. "Kriminologische Aspekte der Wiedergutmachung: Theoretische Grundlagen und Empirishche Befunde." In A. Eser, G. Kaiser, and K. Madlener (eds.), *Neue Wege der Wiedergutmachung im Stragrecht.* Freiburg: Max-Planck-Institut, 43–72.

———. 1994. *Strafzumessung bei schwerer Kriminalität: Eine Vergleichende Theoretishce und Empirische Studie zur Herstelung und Darstellung des Strafmasses.* Berlin: Duncker & Humblot.

———. 1997a. "Dangerous Criminal Offenders in the German Criminal Justice System." *Federal Sentencing Reporter* 10, 3: 69–73.

———. 1997b. "Ethnic Minorities, Crime and Criminal Justice in Germany." In M. Tonry (ed.), *Crime and Justice: A Review of Research.* Chicago: University of Chicago Press, 21: 31–99.

———. 1997c. "Juvenile Crime and Juvenile Law in the Federal Republic of Germany." In J. Winterdyk (ed.), *Juvenile Justice Systems: International Perspectives.* Toronto: Canadian Scholars' Press, 233–70.

———. 1997d. "Sentencing and Punishment in Germany." In M. Tonry and K. Hatlestad (eds.), *Sentencing Reform in Overcrowded Times: A Comparative Perspective.* New York: Oxford University Press, 101–7.

Albrecht, H. J., and W. Schädler (eds.). 1986. *Community Service, Gemeinnützige Arbeit, Dienstverlening, Travail d'Interêt Général.* Freiburg: Max-Planck-Institut.

Arnold, H. 1984. "Verbrechensangst und/oder Furcht vor Viktmisierung—Folgen von Viktmisierung." In H. J. Albrecht and U. Sieber (eds.). *Zwanzig Jahre Südwestdeutsche Kriminologische Kolloquien.* Freiburg: Max-Planck-Institut, 185–236.

———. 1986. "Kriminelle Viktimisierung und ihre Korrelate." *Zeitschrift für die Gesamte Strafrechtswissenschaft* 98: 1014–1058.

———. 1991. "Fear of Crime and Its Relationship to Directly and Indirectly Experienced Victimization: A Binational Comparison of Models." In K. Sessar and H. J. Kerner (eds.), *Developments in Crime and Crime Control.* New York, Springer, 87–125.

Aulinger, S. 1997. *Rechtsgleichheit und Rechtswirklichkeit bei der Strafverfolgung von Drogenkonsumenten: Die Anwendung von Sec 31a BtMG im Kontext anderer Einstellungsvorschriften.* Baden-Baden: Nomos.

Bishop, N. 1995. "Le controle intensif par surveillance electronique: Un substitut suedois a l'emprisonnement." *Bulletin d'Information Penologique* 19–20: 8–9.

Boers, K. 1991. *Kriminalitätsfurcht. Über den Entstehungszusammenhang und die Folgen eines sozialen problems.* Centaurus: Pfaffenweiler.

———. 1996. "Sozialer Umbruch und Kriminalität in Deutschland." *Monatsschrift für Kriminologie* 79: 314–337.

Böttger, A., and Ch. Pfeiffer. 1994. "Der Lauschangriff in den USA und in Deutschland." *Zeitschrift für Rechtspolitik*, 7–17.

Bundeskriminalamt. 1993. *Lagebild Organisierte Kriminalität. Bundesrepublik Deutschland 1992.* Wiesbaden: BKA.

———. 1997. *Lagebild Organisierte Kriminalität: Bundesrepublik Deutschland 1996.* Wiesbaden: BKA.

———. 1956–1998. *Polizeiliche Kriminalstatistik.* Wiesbaden: BKA.

Bundesministerium der Justiz. 1998. *Gesert zur Bekämpfung von Sexualdelikten und anderen Gefährlichen Straftaten.* Koblenz: Verlag.

Busse, D. et al. 1996. *Belastungserleben von Kindern in Hauptverhandlungen.* Bonn: Forum.

Chilton, R., R. Teske, and H. Arnold. 1994. "Race, Crime, and Ethnicity: German and Non-German Suspects 1960–1990." In D. F. Hawkins (ed.), *Ethnicity, Race, and Crime.* Albany: Suny Press, 323–40.

Flade, A. 1996. "Zur öffentlichen Sicherheit in den ostdeutschen Großsiedlungen." *Monatsschrift für Kriminologie* 79: 114–24.

Fromm, H. 1998. "Finanzermittlungen—Ein Herzstück der OK-Bekämpfung?" *Kriminalistik* 52: 463–69.

Garland, D. 1996. "The Limits of the Sovereign State. Strategies of Crime Control in Contemporary Society." *BritJCrim* 36: 445–71.

Gropp, W. 1993. "Besondere Ermittlungsmaßnahmen zur Bekämpfung der Organisierten Kriminalitat." *Zeitschrift für die Gesamte Strafrechtswissenschaft* 105: 405–29.

Heinz, W., and R. Storz. 1992. *Diversion im Jugendstrafverfahren der Bundesrepublik Deutschland.* Bonn: Forum-Verlag.

Heitmeyer, W. et al. 1995. *Gewalt. Schattenseiten der Individualisierung bei Jugendlichen aus unterschiedlichen sozialen Milieus.* Weinheim, München: Juventa.

Hoch, H. 1994. *Die Rechtswirklichkeit des Umweltstrafrechts aus der Sicht von Umweltverwaltung und Strafverfolgung.* Freiburg: Max-Planck-Institut.

Kaiser, G. 1990. *Befinden sich die strafrechtlichen Maßregeln in der Krise?* Heidelberg: C. F. Müller.

Kaiser, M. 1992. *Die Stellung des Verletzten im Strafverfahren.* Freiburg: Max-Planck-Institut.

Kanduc, Z. 1995. "Crime in Slovenia: A Criminological Analysis." *European Journal on Crime Policy and Research* 3: 64–72.

Kerner, H. J., and O. Kästner. 1986. *Gemeinnützige Arbeit in der Strafrechtspflege*. Bonn: Deutsche Bewährungshilfe.

Kilchling, M. 1995. *Opferinteressen und Strafverfolgung*. Freiburg: Max-Planck-Institut.

Kinzig, J. 1996. *Die Sicherungsverwahrung auf dem Prüfstand*. Freiburg: Max-Planck-Institut.

Kury, H. (ed.). 1997. *Konzepte kommunaler Kriminalitätsprävention*. Freiburg: Max-Planck-Institut.

Kury, H., M. Kaiser, and R. Teske. 1994. "The Position of the Victim in Criminal Procedure: Results of a German Study." *International Review of Victimology* 3: 66–81.

Kury, H., R. Teske, and M. Würger. 1999. "Reporting of Crime to the Police in the Federal Republic of Germany: A Comparison of the Old and New Lands." *Justice Quarterly* 16.

Kürzinger, J. 1978. *Private Strafanzeige und polizeiliche Reaktion*. Berlin: Duncker & Humblot.

Landeskriminalamt Berlin. 1994. *Polizeiliche Kriminalstatistik Berlin: Ausländerkriminalitat 1993*. Berlin: Landeskriminalamt.

Lindenberg, M. 1997. *Ware Strafe, elektronische Überwachung und die Kommerzialisierung strafrechtlicher Kontrolle*. München: Beck.

Lutterer, W., and H. Hoch. 1997. *Rechtliche Steuerung im Umweltbereich*. Freiburg: Max-Planck-Institut.

Mansel, J., and K. Hurrelmann. 1998. "Aggressives und Delinquentes Verhalten Jugendlicher im Zeitvergleich: Befunde der Dunkelfeldforschung' aus den Jahren 1988, 1990, 1996." *Kölner Zeitschrift für Soziologie und Sozialpsychologie* 50: 78–109.

Oswald, K. 1997. *Die Implementation gesetzlicher Maßnahmen zur Bekämpfung der Geldwäsche in der Bundesrepublik Deutschland*. Freiburg: Max-Planck-Institut.

Palidda, S. (ed.). 1996. *Délit d'immigration* (Immigrant Delinquency). Bruxelles: European Union.

Pfeiffer, Ch. 1997. *Täter-Opfer-Ausgleich im Allgemeinen Strafrecht*. Baden-Baden: Nomos.

Pfeiffer, Ch. et al. 1998. *Ausgrenzung, Gewalt und Kriminalität im Leben junger Menschen*. Hannover: DVJJ.

Pitsela, A. 1986. *Straffälligkeit und kriminelle Viktimisierung ausländischer Minderheiten in der BRD*. Freiburg: Max-Planck-Institut.

Rautenberg, M. 1998. *Zusammenhänge Zwishchen Devianzbereitschaft, Kriminellem Verhalten und DrogenmiBbrauch*. Baden-Baden: Nomos.

Reuband, K. H. 1992. "*Objektive und subjektive Bdrohung durch Kriminalität*. Ein Vergleich der Kriminalitätsfurchtn der Bundesrepublik Deutschland und den USA 1965–1990." *Kölner Zeitschrift für Soziologie und Sozialpsychologie* 44: 341–53.

Rosellen, R. 1980. "Private Verbrechenskontrolle—Eine Empirische Untersuchung zur Anzeigeerstattund." In Guenther Kaiser (ed.), *Forschungsgruppe Kriminologie*. Freiburg: Max-Planck-Institut, 93–112.

Scherp, D. 1998. "Lagebild Geldwäschebekämpfung. Eine Zwischenbilanz zur Gesetzesänderung vom Mai 1998." *Kriminalistik* 52: 458–62.

Schöch, H. 1992. *Empfehlen sich Änderungen und Ergänzungen bei den Stragrecht-lichen Sanktionen ohne Freitsentzug?* Munich: Beck.

———. 1995. "Die Entdeckung der Verbrechensfurcht und die Erkundung der Vor-stellungen und Erwartungen der Geschädigten als Forschungsgegenstand." In Bundesministerium der Justiz (ed.), *Das Jugendkriminalrecht als Erfüllungs-gehilfe gesellschaftlicher Erwartungen?* Bonn: Forum, 68–82.

———. 1997. *Der Einfluss der Strafverteidigung auf den Verlauf der Untersuchung-shaft.* Munich: Beck.

Sessar, K. 1981. *Rechtliche und soziale Prozesse einer Definition der Tötungskriminali-tät.* Freiburg: Max-Planck-Institut.

Statistisches Bundesamt Wiesbaden. 1997. "Staatsanwaltschaften 1996." Wiesbaden: 14–15.

Steffen, W., E. Elsner, and G. Stern. 1998. *Kinder-und Jugendkriminalität in Mün-chen.* München: Landeskriminalamt.

Stephan, E. 1976. *Die Stuttgarter Opferbefragung.* Wiesbaden: Bundeskriminalamt.

Sutterer, P., Th. Karger. 1994. "Self-Reported Juvenile Delinquency in Mannheim, Germany." In J. Junger-Tas et al. (eds.), *Delinquent Behavior Among Young People in the Western World.* New York: Kugler Publications, 156–185.

Tonry, M. (ed.). 1997. *Ethnicity, Crime, and Immigration: Comparative and Cross-National Perspectives.* Chicago: University of Chicago Press.

Vahle, J. 1998. "Ein Koloß auf tönernen Füßen. Anmerkungen zur (Neu-) Regelung des sogenannten Großen Lauschangriffs." *Kriminalistik* 52: 378–81.

Walmsley, R. 1996. *Prison Systems in Central and Eastern European Countries: Prog-ress, Problems and the International Standards.* Helsinki: HEUNI.

Weigend, Th. 1984. "The Bare Bones of Criminal Justice: The Simplification of the Criminal Process." In HEUNI (ed.), *Effective, Rational and Humane Crim-inal Justice.* Helsinki: HEUNI, 233–39.

———. 1992. *Absprachen im Ausländischen Strafverfahren.* Freiburg: Max-Planck-Institut.

Welp, J. 1994. "Kriminalpolitik in der Krise. Der SPD-Entwurf eines Zweiten Ge-setzes zur Bekämpfung der Organisierten Kriminalität." *Strafverteidiger* 161–68.

Werle, G. 1991. "Aufbau oder Abbau des Rechtsstaats?" *Juristen-Zeitung* 46: 789–97.

Willems, H. 1993. *Fremdenfeindliche Gewalt: Einstellungen, Täter, Konflikteskala-tion.* Opladen: Leske & Budrich.

4

GHANA

(Posttraditional Nation-State)

Obi N. Ignatius Ebbe and Chris Abotchie

PROFILE OF GHANA

Ghana was known as Gold Coast until 1957, when it ceased to be a British dependency. After 207 years of British tutelage (from the British Royal African Company administration, 1750–1842, to British direct control of the territory, 1843–1957), the English legal system permeated every aspect of social, political, and economic life of the Ghanaian people (Ellis, 1971; Kaplan et al., 1971; Goldschmidt, 1981). Between 1843 and 1925, a British governor and the all-European executive and legislative councils made laws for the people of Ghana.

Contemporary Ghana is a parliamentary democracy with an elected executive president as the head of State. Unlike Nigeria and the United States, Ghana is not a federation. Instead, Ghana has a centralized system of government with local divisions of 11 regions. When Gold Coast became the independent state of Ghana on March 6, 1957, the independence constitution created a National Assembly as the main lawmaking body for the country. The National Assembly replaced the colonial legislative assembly. Today, there is only one legislature in the country: the president and the National Assembly. Regional leaders report to the central government in Accra.

Ghana is also a capitalist democracy. However, its traditional concept of communalism, extended family responsibility, and social cohesion still form the bedrock of the social structure. An estimated 51 percent of Ghanaians are economically active. The gross domestic product grew at 5.1 percent in

1997. This was 0.4 percent lower than the targeted growth rate but not far lower than the 5.2 percent achieved in 1996. The inflation rate has continued to decline. In 1997, an inflation rate of 20 percent was achieved, compared with 32.7 percent in 1996.

The rate of unemployment at the end of 1997 was 20 percent. And up to 70 percent of the workforce is in the rural areas, with agricultural self-employment accounting for over 60 percent of all employment, and most of them are subsistence farmers. On the whole, the informal (agricultural and nonagricultural) sector represents about 80 percent of all employment, with 20 percent males and 8 percent in wage employment. The services sector has recorded the highest rate of growth under the nation's Economic Readjustment Program and is the single largest source of employment (18 percent).

HISTORICAL PERSPECTIVE ON CRIME AND CRIME CONTROL

Following the English legal system and normative standards, the colonial governor and his two councils made the laws for Ghana. In 1853 an ordinance created courts to handle criminal and civil issues (Ellis, 1971; Kaplan et al., 1971). In 1892 a criminal code, which was drafted in 1877, based on English criminal code and common law tradition and adopted in St. Lucia, was introduced into Ghanaian society (Daniels, 1964; Rubin and Murray, 1966).

The Republic of Ghana inherited the English common law tradition, the principle of stare decisis. The independence constitution provides for the prerogative writs including that of habeas corpus and independence of the judiciary. The court structure and general legal procedures are, for the most part, English legal procedures. The informal criminal justice system, however, has survived both the colonial and postindependence administrations. During the colonial era, the colonial governors allowed traditional chiefs and rulers to administer justice based on African customary laws as long as the laws were not in violation of English laws and values (Danguah, 1928; Daniels, 1964; Harvey, 1966).

After the abolition of the slave trade in 1807, policemen were deployed by the colonial authorities to guard the forts and castles along the coast and to ensure that the orders banning the slave trade were obeyed. The colonial police also attended the Magistrate's and Judicial Assessor's Courts and guarded prisoners as they worked. They were employed in the prisons as wardens and also performed the duties of the sheriff. The colonial police, in addition, served summonses on people in the remote areas of the country for serious crimes and acted as messengers between the district commissioner and the chiefs or as escorts for European companies' valuable goods in transit. The colonial police wore duck uniforms with goatees, forage caps, and half boots. They carried muskets with bayonets with the usual cross belt of the period. The mere sight of the red coat was more than enough to quiet incipient riots between town companies, even in places far from the seat of colonial government (Gillespie, 1955).

The traditional, precolonial measures of crime control persisted in Ghana in spite of the introduction of a formalized British colonial police force. With the Ordinance of 1894, the Gold Coast Constabulary, which had been at work in the coastal districts of the country, was split into the Gold Coast Police Force and the Gold Coast Regiment. In 1902, the Force assumed the two main branches of Escort and General Police constituted by illiterate and literate personnel, respectively. The marine police were established in 1916 but disbanded after 25 years. In 1952, there was the establishment of women police to deal with women criminals and juvenile offenders.

The traditional ("precolonial") mechanisms of crime control fall into three categories, namely, control at the private or lineage level, control by the chief and his court at the public level, and control through magico-religious processes.

The Private (Lineage) Control Mechanism

The lineage is a corporate group, a collection of families recruited patri-lineally or matrilineally, as the kinship system is a combination of the two. It is the smallest political unit in traditional Ghana, with reference to the maintenance of law and order. Each family under this kinship system lives in its own compound house, which is often but not always enclosed by a fence. Presiding over the group of families that form the lineage is the head (known in Akan as *abusua panyin*). This head is usually the most senior surviving male member and oversees the families under his jurisdiction (whether near his home or a distance aways). The duty of the head is to interpret the code of behavior to his people and to educate them on the sanctions. When violations occur, the head is under the obligation of the moral code to enforce the penalties to the letter.

The traditional sanctions are both sacred and secular. The most severe penalty is expulsion from the lineage, which entails both spiritual and secular consequences. In the spiritual domain, expulsion means the loss of rights and privileges in the ancestral cult, the loss of protection from the ancestors both here on earth and in the Land of the Dead, and the loss of rights to reincarnation. In the secular domain, expulsion means the loss of economic, political, and other social privileges derived from lineage membership. As the most extreme penalty, expulsion from the lineage is invoked against the most serious transgressions only, such as culpable homicide or incest. For lesser offenses, a number of secular sanctions may be invoked, such as the loss of rights to land use, the imposition of fines or special duties, denial of support in times of financial need, ostracism, and a variety of other punitive measures considered commensurate with the offense.

The Public Control Mechanism

Violations of public delicts are dealt with by the traditional ruler, the chief. The chief in Ghana is a person who hails from a royal lineage and has been duly selected and installed as a chief or a queen mother according to tradition. The traditional (precolonial) functions of the chief included military, religious, judicial, administrative, legislative, economic, and cultural duties. The most important perhaps of these functions is the judicial, involving the settlement of disputes and reconciliation. Since crimes are considered offenses not only against people but also against the gods, settlements are between individuals as well as between individuals and the gods (Assimeng, 1981).

The chief's court is constituted by the council of elders (the heads of clans) with the chief as president. As part of his crime prevention measures, the chief relies on his councillors to interpret the customary laws to their people. Additionally, the chief also employs the services of a "town crier" (popularly known as the *gong beater*) who moves from one strategic location in the village to another, publicly announcing to the people state policies based on decisions taken by the Traditional Council and also public summonses and other important messages. Usually these policy decisions or decrees concern town security or social welfare and may be proclaimed either as behests prohibiting or enjoining specific activities or as reminders to the public concerning customary laws.

For example, when a number of deaths in the area have been attributed to evil magic, or when the rate of burglaries or thefts has been on the rise, the chief and his council would order an announcement reminding the public of the traditional mechanisms available to the town for dealing with the culprits. These include trial by order, public disgrace (shaming), exile, or execution. By acting through his councillors and the town crier to educate the public on the existing and freshly enacted customary laws, the chief and his council can be understood to be socializing their people to the norms and the values of their town, to which they are then expected to conform.

The customary laws prescribe specific sanctions to be imposed by the chief's court on violators. The imposition of sanctions by the chief's court would suggest the existence of a formal judicial procedure, which in the modern criminal justice system would require codified laws and rules of procedure; but this was not the case in the traditional judicial system. The quasi-procedural system of trying cases that existed was based on oral traditions expressed in proverbs, aphorisms, axioms, and examples, which Apter (1963: 82) called *proverb law*.

There is no regular court house, and the proceedings of the court may be held in the chief's sitting room, in a public shed that acts as a town hall or a public reception room, or under a shady tree. Witnesses are required to swear an oath calling on the ancestral spirits and the local gods to strike them dead if they tell a lie. In matters of a very grave nature such as homicide, adultery, incest, or the violation of a serious taboo, the oath swearing is preceded by an egg-smashing ritual requiring that an egg be tossed into the air (by the chief or his linguist) before the witness swears the oath. The egg-smashing ritual is believed to compel the ancestral spirits and the gods to act with dispatch if a witness tells a lie or conceals important evidence.

The guilty person is punished for acts of omission committed not only willfully but also by accident. The types of punishment range from fines to the death penalty. Crimes such as murder perpetrated through physical means or through evil magic are considered serious enough to justify total banishment or capital punishment. The incestuous, adulterers, and violators of taboos are required to perform specific purification rituals in addition to the payment of appropriate fines. Punishments imposed for crimes attributed to accident are regarded as the necessary atonement to remove the *blot of sin* from the culprit and his lineage.

The Magicoreligious Control Mechanism

Because traditional Ghanaians believe that crimes are acts despicable to the gods, magicoreligious beliefs and practices naturally play a significant part in the control of crimes. Supernatural forces are believed to be invisibly in interaction, on a daily basis, with the living and are therefore not only able to see every act but also to read every human thought. Hence, no crime escapes their notice. And since supernatural sanctions (which are often in the form of sudden death or inexplicable illness) are believed inescapable once a violation of the moral code has occurred, the potential criminal in the traditional society cannot but take cognizance of the awe-inspiring omniscience of the supernatural forces and the inescapability of their actions.

The fear of these sanctions becomes an impenetrable barrier in the potential criminal's mind and has a great deterrent effect. The notion of inescapability is thus the bedrock upon which the crime control mechanism of the traditional Ghanaian society was constructed. Victimization in traditional Ghana was also explained by rational choice and environmental variables. Given the effectively deterrent belief in the supernatural, the decision to commit a crime was heavily determined by the rewards expected from committing the particular offense and the efforts required in the execution of the action.

The magical procedures for the treatment of crimes in traditional Ghanaian society were broadly in the realm of *divination*—the act of seeking to know hidden things and the future by magical means. The divining modalities include oracle consultation, trial by ordeal, and hexing. Ultimately, these oracles communicate uncanny revelations relevant to the crime under investigation, often giving close descriptions of the culprit and sometimes disclosing his or her name. Invariably the suspects are made aware that they have been identified by an oracle and should make restitution or face spiritual sanctions. The fear of the known consequences, and particularly the awe-inspiring notion of collective responsibility, compels the identified culprits or their kinsmen to make restitution.

PUBLIC PERCEPTION OF CRIME AND CRIME CONTROL

The notion of what constitutes crime in traditional Ghana is aptly expressed in the definitions of *crime* in simple societies that offend strong and definite dispositions of the "collective consciousness" and that evoke punishment as a consequence (Durkheim, 1951). Traditional Ghanaians consider criminal conduct socially harmful and morally blameworthy. Any such conduct is an affront to the gods. The traditional cosmology of Ghanaian society is constructed upon a belief in a pantheon of omnipresent, omniscient, benevolent supernatural forces regarded as the source of justice and fair play, who hold the power of life and death over men.

These "benevolent" forces are believed to be the embodiment of virtue and are supervisory over a code of morals, the precepts of which are similar to the Jewish Ten Commandments. Additionally, there are various other forms of deviance, such as incest, rape, assault, the invocation of a curse upon a neighbor or upon the chief, and the violation of tribal taboos. Together these constitute the sins and crimes of traditional Ghanaian society. More specifically, crime within the modern (secular) criminal justice system in Ghana is conceived generally as an intentional act, committed or omitted in violation of a law commanding or forbidding it and to which is attached statutory penalties such as death, imprisonment, fines, removal from office, or disqualification to hold and enjoy any office of trust, honor, or profit in the society. Finally, contemporary public perceptions are of high waves of crime and increasing crime.

Besides the benevolent supernatural forces, malevolent forces are also believed to exist. Thus, with respect to the cause of crime, traditional Ghanaian philosophy finds expression in the theories of *diabolical possession* and the *free moral agent*. When a person committed a serious offense such as homicide, incest, or rape, he or she was believed to have acted under some evil influence. Viewed as an instrument or venue through which certain crimes were committed, the offender became anathema, a curse, a taboo, which must be expurgated.

Based on this concept of crime, the approach to punishment is either to exorcise the devil or exile or execute the wrongdoer. Punishment is inflicted in order to remove the stain of impurity from society or to prevent a supernatural being from wreaking vengeance on the social group. Not all crimes, however, are blamed on demonic possession. Offenses like stealing or adultery are regarded as the willful acts of free moral agents who deserve to be punished by society for acts of voluntary perversity.

Some offenses proscribed under the traditional moral standards are considered to be sufficiently serious enough to merit the intervention of the community. Hence, victims of such offenses should not be left to seek redress all by themselves. Ghanaians, in other words, recognize a distinction between private and public wrongs based on the degree of gravity of each offense. This degree is determined by the nature of the offense, such as culpable homicide, robbery, or adultery, or by the frequency with which less serious crimes such as falsehood, indebtedness, or filial disobedience are repeated. Such culprits who have been heedless of counsel and warnings or have repeated offenses more than three times risk being sold into slavery.

The indignation shown by traditional Ghanaians against the violation of the laws of public delicts reflects, on the one hand, their moral disapproval of the violation of the victim's human rights and, on the other hand, their intense apprehension about the supernatural consequences for the culprit or his social group. Victims of crime, therefore, count on the support of the public in their pursuit of the traditional processes in seeking redress, either through the public control mechanism, by lodging complaints at the chief's court, or through magicoreligious mechanisms, by lodging complaints at the shrine of a traditional god.

The endorsement given by the traditional Ghana society to the right of the victim to seek redress through these processes makes it incumbent on members of the society to take adequate measures to prevent wrongdoing, since the consequences are abhorrent once the traditional mechanism of justice has been invoked. For example, under the notion of collective responsibility, the penalty for crime, whether supernaturally visited or secularly imposed, threatens the group as a whole and not the offender alone. Penalties imposed by the secular authorities, that is, by the chief and his court, such as fines and the restitution of stolen goods are born by the lineage if the offender is unable to provide the compensation. Although the lineage is innocent of the crime, it is compelled by the social obligation to redeem its good name and necessarily pays up. Families have recognized these actions as proper and have submitted to them, "for they are expected to stand by and assist and defend all its members, whether right or wrong" (Nassau, 1940: 156).

In the event of failure or refusal by the offender or his group to make restitution or redeem the penalty, the victim's lineage considers itself left with no other alternative than to seek redress through the traditional gods. This spells disaster for the offender's group collectively, because the traditional gods are believed to strike at random, sometimes sparing the culprit and killing innocent members of the group. Collective responsibility thus hangs like the sword of Damocles over the lineage group and compels its members to "police" the behavior of each other.

CONTEMPORARY CRIME

Based on police records, offenses of all types have increased in Ghana over the past two decades. The crimes are mostly youth crimes and are related to high unemployment rates and to youth overrepresentation in those rates. Rising crime rates are regarded as part of the rapid rate of postcolonial urbanization and the euphoria that followed the achievement of independence.

The police crime statistics show a phenomenal increase in the crime rate between 1960 (barely three years after independence) and 1970. The total number of crimes recorded during this period rose from 58,302 in 1960 to 99,649 in 1970, a 71 percent increase. This gives a mean annual growth rate of approximately 6 percent (Nortey, 1983). While the total number of crimes reported in 1970 was 99,649, 20 years later it rose to 120,933, a 21.4 percent increase (see Table 4.1). However, the number of murders, armed robberies, and rapes reported to the police during 1989–1991 varied up and down by regions of Ghana (see Table 4.2).

The rates of crime based on offenses known to the police in 1997 reveal low and high variability by crime. The most frequently reported crimes were assault, followed by stealing, with threatening a distant third (see Table 4.3). That assault is number one is not surprising because throughout Africa, south of the Sahara, a simple assault is a common means of resolving serious provocations, and simple assault usually does not reach the attention of the courts. As in South Africa, illegal gold mining is a serious crime in Ghana. For the most part, Ghana does not have a domestic illegal drug problem. Most of the illegal drug cases have involved international traffickers.

Postcolonial and independent Ghana has experienced rising crime rates, due in part to an increasing state of anomie (Durkheim, 1964) and competition in conspicuous consumption that, first and foremost, involves elites and then trickles down throughout Ghanaian society. The competition and the absence of limitations have continued to exert considerable pressure on status aspirants in contemporary Ghana to adopt a variety of deviant responses, particularly involving economic crimes to obtain money to attain greater social honors. The conditions of anomie, then, apply to the predominance of white-collar and other economic crimes in Ghana during the postcolonial period.

CONTEMPORARY CRIME CONTROL

The process of making laws in Ghana today is quite different from that of Nigeria and the United States, as Ghana does not have an upper chamber

Table 4.1
Number of Crimes Reported, 1989-1991

Crimes Reported	1989	1990	Percentage (+00−)	1990	1991	Percentage
Murder	239	275	15.06 INCR.	275	282	2.54 INCR.
Attempted Murder	9	10	11.11 INCR.	10	7	−30.00 DECR.
Manslaughter	19	19	0.0	19	9	−52.63 DECR.
Threatening	5,980	8,937	49.45 INCR.	8,937	9,753	9.13 INCR.
Causing Harm	2,825	1,367	−51.61 DECR.	1,367	1,350	−1.24 DECR.
Armed Robbery	144	112	−22.22 DECR.	112	196	75.00 INCR.
Stealing	41,056	38,532	−6.15 DECR.	38,532	40,254	4.47 INCR.
Fraud by False Pretenses	7,825	7,466	−4.59 DECR.	7,466	9,650	29.24 INCR.
Unlawful Entry	774	658	−14.99 DECR.	658	415	36.93 INCR.
Assault	42,974	51,060	18.82 INCR.	51,060	55,664	9.02 INCR.
Causing Damage	2,821	3,705	31.34 INCR.	3,705	4,341	17.16 INCR.
Dishonestly Receiving	66	91	37.88 INCR.	91	181	98.90 INCR.
Abortion	127	154	21.26 INCR.	154	183	18.83 INCR.
Rape	274	375	37.86 INCR.	375	408	8.08 INCR.
Possession of Dangerous Drugs	95	191	101.05 INCR.	191	163	14.66 INCR.
Possession of Marijuana	542	546	0.74 INCR.	546	607	11.17 INCR.
Abduction	53	99	86.79 INCR.	99	147	48.48 INCR.
Extortion	3	7	133.33 INCR.	7	13	85.17 INCR.
Forgery	18	35	94.44 INCR.	35	43	22.86 INCR.
Smuggling	660	6	−99.09 DECR.	6	297	4,850.00 INCR.
Possession of Cocaine	—	3	0.0	3	7	133.33 INCR.
Possession of Heroin	—	15	0.0	15	20	33.33 INCR.
Counterfeiting	—	2	0.0	2	2	0.0 INCR.
All Other Offenses	9,966	10,958	9.5 INCR.	10,958	10,383	5.25 INCR.
TOTAL NUMBER OF OFFENSES REPORTED	116,471	120,933	3.83%	120,933	134,375	11.12%

Source: Annual Report of the Ghana Police Crime Data Service Bureau, 1989-1991.

Table 4.2
Number of Murders, Armed Robberies, and Rapes Reported to the Police, by Region, 1989–1991

		MURDER			
REGION	*1989*	*1990*	*Percent*	*1990*	*1991*	*Percent*
Accra Region	28	32	14.29 Incr.	32	25	−21.87 Decr.
Ashanti Region	55	59	7.27 Incr.	59	64	8.47 Incr.
Eastern Region	26	37	42.31 Incr.	37	25	−32.43 Decr.
Western Region	20	26	30.00 Incr.	26	49	88.46 Incr.
Central Region	18	18	—	18	21	16.67 Incr.
Brong Ahafo Region	31	35	12.9 Incr.	35	25	−28.57 Decr.
Upper West Region	4	6	50.00 Incr.	6	7	16.67 Incr.
Tema Region	4	6	50.00 Incr.	6	8	33.33 Incr.
TOTAL	186	219	17.7%	219	224	2.3%

		ARMED ROBBERY			
REGION	*1989*	*1990*	*Percent*	*1990*	*1991*	*Percent*
Accra Region	20	42	110.00 Incr.	42	52	23.81 Incr.
Eastern Region	—	4	100.00 Incr.	4	11	175.00 Incr.
Western Region	3	8	160.00 Incr.	8	6	−25.00 Decr.
Tema Region	6	7	16.67 Incr.	7	7	—
Ashanti Region	20	42	110.00 Incr.	42	39	−7.14 Decr.
C.I.D. Headquarters	—	—	—	—	62	—
TOTAL	49	101	106.1%	101	177	34.7%

		RAPE			
REGION	*1989*	*1990*	*Percent*	*1990*	*1991*	*Percent*
Accra Region	67	89	32.84 Incr.	89	99	11.23 Incr.
Ashanti Region	56	86	83.33 Incr.	66	35	−23.25 Decr.
Eastern Region	36	66	83.33 Incr.	66	35	−46.97 Decr.
Central Region	19	26	36.84 Incr.	26	29	11.54 Incr.
Brong Ahafo Region	15	23	55.33 Incr.	23	34	47.82 Incr.
Volta Region	27	32	18.52 Incr.	32	47	46.87 Incr.
Northern Region	2	3	50.00 Incr.	3	9	200.00 Incr.
Tema Region	16	29	81.25 Incr.	29	36	24.14 Incr.
Upper West Region	1	2	50.00 Incr.	2	1	−50.00 Decr.
Upper East Region					4	100.00 Incr.
TOTAL	239	356	49.0%	356	360	1.12%

Note: There are cases of murder, armed robbery, and rape for which the region of occurrence was not reported by Regional Police Headquarters to the Ghana Police Services Headquarters. Such cases were left out by the police in the above computations.
Source: Ghana Police Crime Data Service Bureau, 1989–1991.

like the Senate. In Ghana a bill is introduced in the National Assembly. After the bill has passed three readings on the floor, it is submitted to the president for his assent. For a bill to be an act of Parliament, and therefore the law of Ghana, it requires the president's assent. Like the American pres-

Table 4.3
Rates of Crime Based on Offenses Known to the Police, 1997

Types of Crimes Reported	Number of Crimes Reported	Percentages of Cases Solved	Crimes per 100,000
Murder	483	94%	2.6
Attempted Murder	33	100%	0.2
Manslaughter	154	100%	0.8
Threatening	15,637	100%	82.7
Causing Harm	3,085	88%	16.3
Armed Robbery	169	62%	0.9
Stealing	52,099	43%	275.7
Fraud by False Pretenses	11,063	89%	58.5
Unlawful Entry	1,180	92%	6.2
Assault	79,728	94%	421.8
Causing Damage (Vandalism)	8,366	61%	44.3
Dishonest Receiving	138	100%	0.7
Abortion	165	79%	0.9
Rape and Other Sex Crimes	770	84%	4.1
Possession of Dangerous Drugs (Cocaine/Heroin)	39	88%	0.2
Possession of Marijuana	471	92%	2.5
Abduction	382	85%	2.0
Extortion	1	100%	0.00
Forgery	120		0.6
Smuggling	250	56%	1.3
Child Stealing	5	60%	0.03
Counterfeiting	17	76%	0.09
Illegal Mining of Gold	65	58%	0.3

Total Number of Crimes Reported: 174,420
Population: 18,900,000
Source: United Nations Development Plan, 1997.

ident, a Ghanaian president has the right to veto. Like Nigeria and Kenya, the Ghana Independence Parliament amended the colonial laws to suit the norms, beliefs, and standards of the Ghanaian people, including revocation of English laws that were antithetical to the cherished values of the Ghanaian people.

Theoretically, Ghana has an adversarial system of criminal justice. In other words, the offender is presumed innocent until proven guilty. In practice, however, it is an inquisitorial approach. Part of the reason why countries such as Ghana, Nigeria, and Kenya have the adversarial system in their criminal code but practice the inquisitorial approach is because the offenders who are brought to the attention of the police are accompanied by the persons who caught them. In effect, the element of suspicion is eliminated.

The offender is already presumed guilty by the complainant and the police officer who received the evidence (a static law enforcement system). The true adversarial system in Ghana ended with the eclipse of the colonial criminal court procedure.

Today, as Ghanaians themselves are the operators of the entire English-based judicial system and government, traditional chiefs and elders are allowed to try criminal matters in the rural villages. A chief's or an elder's court may dispose of felonies such as aggravated assault, robbery, burglary, stealing, and so forth without drawing a penalty from the government, even when such crimes are beyond his powers. The informal criminal justice system is more appreciated by the people than the English-based criminal justice system, which has many loopholes for the offender to escape paying for his or her crime.

The criminal justice system is also centralized. The government controls the police, all courts including the judges of the courts, and the prisons. The chief justice of the supreme court, the inspector general of police, and the director of prisons are all appointed and removed from office by the government to serve the whole country.

Basically, all the functions performed by the colonial police with regard to the maintenance of law and order, the prevention and detection of crimes, and the apprehension and prosecution of offenders remained the same for the postindependence force, with the exception of the role played by the police in the prisons, which has now been taken over by prison officers. It is important to emphasize that the traditional societies of Ghana, as outlined earlier, have persisted and operate side by side with the modern criminal justice system in postcolonial Ghana.

Significantly, there has been a numerical expansion and improvement of the efficiency of the police throughout the country as a result of the rising crime rates brought about by the rapid rate of postcolonial urbanization and the euphoria that followed the achievement of independence. To correspond with the rise in crime, in other words, a rise in the strength of the police force occurred as there was a great expansion in the number of police posts and stations throughout the country. For example, between 1960 and 1970, the strength of the police force increased from 6,212 to 16,358, an increase of 163 percent.

Apart from increasing the numerical strength and modernizing the Ghana police (in terms of their acquisition of modern, faster patrol vehicles and electronic communication facilities), the contemporary official policy for crime control consists of a partnership approach involving the individual, the community, local government, the judiciary, the prison service, and the central government as constituent players. The role of the individual is increasingly being focused toward situational-environmental crime prevention where part of the responsibility for the anticipation, recognition, and appraisal of a crime risk and the initiation of action to remove or reduce it devolves on the individual. This becomes a practical reality through his or her deployment of security hardware or target hardening devices such as intruder alarms in houses and cars, hiring of private security personnel, and the use of guard dogs.

Community involvement in crime prevention in Ghana has found expression in the formation of neighborhood watch groups in some communities. The main problem with neighborhood watch schemes, as noted in most reviews, is that the groups tend to dissipate as soon as the crime problem for which they have been established disappears. Alternatively, in communities in which crimes do not occur very frequently, the watchers shortly get tired of looking out for potential criminals. The ultimate decline of interest has proven to be an obstacle to the proliferation of watch groups in Ghana as a useful means of intelligence gathering for the police.

At the local government level, the newly established District Assemblies have been constitutionally empowered to cooperate with the local security agencies to ensure security and justice at the local levels. The Assemblies meet regularly to identify and prioritize local security needs in consultation with the people and then initiate programs to raise funds for the implementation of decisions. The role of the judiciary in crime control has often been criticized by the police based on the fact that some criminals are let off with ridiculously lenient sentences. The police in Ghana would like to see the courts inflict more severe penalties on convicted offenders than the states. However, with the introduction of special tribunals, both the police and the public appear generally satisfied with the current penal system, as the tribunals have achieved the reputation of handing out severe penalties to offenders.

Ghana has a Prison Service that runs maximum and medium security prisons located in the regional capitals of the country. Additionally, there is a Borstal Institute in the national capital, Accra, for juvenile offenders, run by the Prison Service, and an Industrial School for boys and girls, under the Department of Social Welfare, for the purposes of treatment and rehabilitation of these young offenders. At both the adult prisons and juvenile correctional institutions, the main emphasis is on the safe custody of inmates and their training in vocational skills.

Apart from coordinating the activities of institutions under the criminal justice system, the central government of Ghana plays a role in social crime prevention through the creation of job opportunities to reduce the level of unemployment and associated crimes, and in the redistribution of wealth through occasional adjustments in the incomes of workers. The governmental role has, however, been far from adequate. Unemployment is still quite high, and public service workers are generally dissatisfied with their incomes. Unemployment and dissatisfaction have largely been responsible for the high incidence of bribery, corruption, and embezzlement of state funds in the public services.

FUTURE OF CRIME AND CRIME CONTROL

Given current trends, the volume of crimes will increase in Ghana, especially in the urban areas. The key factor in the reduction of criminality will rest with the ability of the government to direct the economy toward the creation of jobs, to reduce inflation, and to adjust the wages and salaries of workers to reflect the existing levels of inflation. But this is a tall order, the redemption of which is largely dependent on international economic trends. This is so because as a predominantly primary commodity exporter, the foreign exchange earned by the country from its exports is determined by the prices the buyers are willing to pay. In the interim, the government should concentrate on rural development, with emphasis on agriculture, the distribution of electric power, and rural industrialization. This will minimize the rural-urban exodus and reduce the impact of overurbanization in the country, competition for scarce jobs, congestion, homelessness, prostitution, delinquency, and other crimes that go with congested urban areas of economic inequality.

Additionally, the government must invest more money in technical education and other forms of vocational education than ever before. Furthermore, incentives should be given to potential foreign investors to invest in Ghana through building small-scale industries, since Ghana has shown some evidence of a stable political structure, unlike most of its neighbors. Finally, given the high incidence of official corruption, including police corruption and organized crime in the country, the government should resort to a strategic law enforcement system by establishing a paramilitary law enforcement agency trained to monitor the police and track down corrupt government officials and criminal businesses. Substantially increased employment opportunities in Ghana will go a long way toward reducing the rates of crime against both property and person in Ghana.

REFERENCES

Annual Report. 1992. *Ghana Police Crime Data Service Bureau (1989–1991)*.

Apter, D.E.K. 1963. *Ghana in Transition*. New York: Atheneum.

Assimeng, M. 1981. *Social Structure of Ghana*. Tema: Ghana Publishing Corporation.

Danguah, J. B. 1928. *Gold Coast: Akan Laws and Customs and the Akim Abuakwa Constitution*. London: George Routledge & Sons.

Daniels, W. Ekow. 1964. *The Common Law in West Africa*. London: Butterworth.

Durkheim, Émile. 1951. *Suicide: Study in Sociology*. New York: Free Press.

———. 1964. *The Division of Labor in Society*. New York: Free Press.

Ellis, A. B. 1971. *A History of Gold Coast West Africa*. London: Curzon Press.

Gillespie, W. H. 1955. *The Gold Coast Police, 1844–1938*. Accra: Ghana Government Printer.

Goldschmidt, Jenny E. 1981. *National and Indigenous Constitutional Law in Ghana*. Accra: Ghana Publishing Corporation.

Harvey, William B. 1966. *Laws and Social Change in Ghana*. Princeton, NJ: Princeton University Press.

Kaplan, Irving, J. L. McLaughlin, B. J. Martin, P. W. Moeller, H. D. Nelson, and D. P. Whitaker (eds.). 1971. *Area Handbook for Ghana*. Washington, DC: U.S. Government Printing Office.

Nassau, R. H. 1940. *Fetishism in West Africa*. London: Duckworth.

Nortey, D.N.A. 1983. "Crime Trends in Ghana." In E. H. Johnson (ed.), *International Handbook of Contemporary Developments in Criminology*. Westport, CT: Greenwood Press.

Rubin, Leslie, and Pauli Murray. 1966. *The Constitution and Government of Ghana*. 2nd ed. London: Sweet.

United Nations Development Plan. 1997. *Ghana Human Resources Development Report*. Accra: Ghana Publishing Company.

5

INDIA

(Developing Nation-State)

S. George Vincentnathan

PROFILE OF INDIA

India is a diverse nation of many cultures, peoples, religions, languages, and political parties. During most of South Asian history, India was ruled by local kings, invading Muslim rulers, the French, the Portuguese, and the British. The British, however, were able to gradually extend and maintain control over most of India by around 1849. Except for the partition of Pakistan from India, political and geographical amalgamation that the British created continued after Indian independence in 1947.

Despite problems connected with Indian national unity and identity, there are also some cultural threads that bind the people together. The recurring fusion and partition of the kingdoms in the past have led to the sharing of certain religious beliefs, ideas, and customs that have come to be part of what is known as Hinduism and the Indian way of life. Similarly, languages deriving their roots from Sanskrit and Tamil, the ancient languages of India that have written literature dating back 6,000 years, have provided some links.

During the last 50 years since independence, India has made slow but steady changes. Education, growth in economy, population mobility, governmental leadership, and media influences have helped somewhat to integrate the nation and shape a national identity that goes beyond traditional, regional, and local identities. However, the nation is also divided by religious fundamentalism, partisan politics, and continuing historical differences based on culture, language, and regionalism, which could become less influential as India becomes more democratic and proceeds into the twenty-first century.

India is about one third the size of the United States and has a population of nearly 1 billion. It is also the largest democracy in the world, with a parliamentary form of government, vibrant political parties, and active public participation. Often between 60 to 90 percent of eligible citizens vote in elections. Cultural, religious, social, and political differences have led to a coalition form of government, without any single party having a stronghold in the governance of the country. The present Bharatiya Janata Party is a good example of coalition rule. It did not have strong backing to fully implement much of its Hindu fundamentalist agenda (Ganguly, 1996a).

Economically, India is a developing country. However, it is the tenth most industrialized nation in the world in its overall industrial production. Its intellectual human resources, if properly managed, could make India a leader in technological and scientific research. India is already the second largest manufacturer of computer software, next to the United States. Successful nuclear test explosions conducted recently placed India in the exclusive category of nuclear superpowers. These nuclear tests have evoked both national pride and at the same time fear for the future.

India has a well-educated middle class pushing the country to heights that were unimagined before. Currently, there are over 250 million people who have the ability to read and converse in English. On the other hand, in 1995 the adult illiteracy rate averaged 48 percent: males, 34.5, and females, 62.3 percent (Europa Publications Limited, 1997: 1598). Moreover, India still has over 36 percent of its people living in utter poverty (Ward, 1997: 37). There are widespread unemployment and inequalities in income and wealth. Such inequalities are not only common now but are increasing and will continue to increase and haunt the nation for many years to come. These may have serious consequences for the social order, as they may precipitate general social upheavals, riots, and crime as well. Recently, group movements, protests, and riots have become very common on the Indian scene. Riots that have emerged suddenly also have disappeared suddenly, without often achieving the targeted objectives.

HISTORICAL PERSPECTIVE ON CRIME AND CRIME CONTROL

The Indian culture and society, through Hinduism and its caste system, have provided for centuries the values and goals that have engendered social contentment and the normative standards that have kept most from taking daring ventures to commit crime. Under Hinduism, individuals are not thought of as independent entities endowed with powers of their own to carve out a place for themselves different from and superior to that of others. Unlike people in Western societies, who learn to prize and pursue separate individual identities and rights at any cost, people in India have historically been molded into powerless beings subjected to groups and societal controls. An individual has been positioned as an integral part of a larger whole, which has been divided into hierarchically arranged castes with clearly defined statuses and roles. In order of rank the four caste categories, or *varnas*, that constituted the society were: *Brahmins* (priests), *Ksatriyas* (warriors, rulers, and landowners), *Vaisyas* (merchants), and *Shudras* (craftsmen and laborers). The *Panchamas* (menial workers and scavengers) formed a lower, "polluted" category beneath the four *varnas*. They are now referred to as untouchables, or *dalits*.

Individuals of each caste were expected to perform the allotted occupational roles as their duty (*dharma*), believed to result from deeds in previous births (*karma*). Everyone was taught to perform their role without attachment to economic returns, "activity without attachment." Even those who were merchants and landlords performed their roles in support of their religious requirement (Dumont, 1970: 232–234). In Hindu belief the only way people could improve their social position was in subsequent births as a reward for performing their caste roles faithfully. Sincere performance of these roles was again essential to break away from rebirths and find ultimate salvation. The original four *varnas* and *Panchamas* later developed into hundreds of specific castes, or *jatis*. Birth in a caste determined an individual's caste status and occupation. One could not change this position, as one can in a class system. Furthermore, people were required to marry within their own castes.

In this religion-based caste form of social order, the interests of individuals were deemphasized in favor of the interests of society. The individual became socially dependent, personally passive, and generally fatalistic. A strong desire to excel over others economically, overpower others physically, or indulge in pleasure-giving activities did not surge up much. It is for these historical reasons that economic and personal crimes that often arise out of overwhelming desires are, therefore, found much less in India, even today. It is in the context of this general and historical explanation of culture and society in India that crime—economic, violent, and sexual—must be understood.

For example, historically, as material goals were subordinate to religious goals, there was less motivation for property crimes. From the nature of traditional Indian culture and society it is obvious that material goals, such as economic goals, were less important than the religious goal of salvation. As social behavior was based on religious beliefs, material goals were less pressing, and crimes that arose out of economic ambitions were also less. Additionally, since the caste occupational goals stressed were actually roles, and since performance of them should be done with commitment and without anticipation of material gains, the role-perfection expected placed greater control on individual behavior. Finally, whatever economic return they received out of their caste roles seemed sufficient to them. This is because under the caste structure people knew what they would receive as economic compensation for their work. As achievement beyond this was not usually possible, whatever they earned in reality was viewed as acceptable and natural.

By providing general social contentment as a result of channeling people's behavior toward religious goals, the caste system contributed to the general economic underdevelopment of the nation. This system was also discriminatory, especially in relation to certain lower castes, such as the *Panchamas* and *Shudras*. It arrested their economic, social, and educational development. In spite of these and many other exploitative flaws associated with the caste structure, the caste system facilitated a low crime rate.

From the 1980s onward, however, Indian society has begun to change rapidly. The traditional social order is in a state of flux, and the caste form of social order is gradually yielding to a class form of social order. This transformation is not as radical as some might think, since throughout most of India's history higher caste statuses and higher class statuses have corresponded, as did lower caste statuses and lower class statuses. Today, economic motivations are ascendant, and these are helping to advance the economic growth rates. So far, the surge in economic desires has not yet contributed to significant increases in the crime rate since the influences of the traditional society still persist (Vincentnathan, 1985).

The criminal justice system of India is composed of federally coordinated and regulated state level administrative units, which carry out major portions of the administration of justice. The system functions under the general principles of the Indian Constitution and the judicial control of the Indian Supreme Court—the highest court of the land. The president of India is the official head of the country, and state governors are at the state level. However, the regular administration of justice comes under the jurisdiction of the prime minister at the national level, mainly through the Ministry of Home Affairs, and under the chief ministers at the state level. During periods of national law and order crisis the president can assume direct control over the country. Similarly, when a particular state is under political turmoil the president can exert direct control over it, with the assistance of the state governor. At the national level are many police forces, such as the Central Bureau of Investigation, which is similar to the Federal Bureau of Investigation in the United States.

At the state level, the state criminal justice system operates under the authority of the state's chief minister and the state's Ministry of Home Affairs. The director-general of Police is the state's chief enforcement officer. This person is assisted by commissioners of Police in large cities, superintendents of Police in districts, and inspectors and subinspectors of Police in local communities. The High Court is the highest court at the state level, and District Courts are at the district level and its subdivisions. Sessions Courts are for processing serious criminal cases, and Magistrate Courts are for processing less serious criminal cases. Judges are given greater powers to intervene and ask questions at all aspects of court proceedings in the interest of establishing justice and fairness—especially for the accused.

As the legal system is based on Common Law traditions and democratic principles, the rights of the accused are recognized, and they are increasingly provided, especially in the higher courts (Ganguly, 1996b: 612–21; see also Raghavan and Natarajan, 1996). The prisons and jails in every state are under the supervision of the inspector-general in charge, who reports to the director-general of Police. Prisons and jails are often located in the district headquarters. Offenders from rich and privileged groups are often granted better facilities and services than the underprivileged.

As India develops economically, urbanizes, and modernizes, the need for formal criminal justice agencies grows. Village *panchayats* (administrative and justice councils) on which people relied for dispute settlement over the centuries are losing control as people's support for them is declining. This is due to the growth of egalitarian and individualistic values, which often go against *panchayat* decisions based on caste and class inequalities and the need for social harmony. In this context crimes and disputes are increasing, also exacerbated by population growth. For instance, the population increased between 1986 and 1996 by 21.6 percent; crimes by 21.6 percent; and number of police by 21.1 percent (Government of India, 1998: 7). The total number of cases received by courts for trial was 5,297,662 in 1996, but only 843,588 cases were tried and 318,965 convictions were made (Government of India, 1998: 9). The recidivism rate among arrested persons during 1996 was 8.6 percent (Government of India, 1998: 332), which is significantly lower than recidivism rates of many countries. Perhaps the main reason why the crime rates and recidivism rates are still lower in India is because of the continuing hold of the traditional and informal controls. The criminal justice system, however, will have a tougher time in controlling crimes and conflicts and in maintaining order as these controls decline under the impact of modern forces.

PUBLIC PERCEPTION OF CRIME AND CRIME CONTROL

India is a large nation of almost a billion people with relatively little crime. Crime and crime control, at least with respect to ordinary crimes against the person or property, are not of much concern and emphasis. On the other hand, there is some public preoccupation with governmental and political corruption and the associated violence that surrounds the intense political activities of some election campaigns. In 1991 alone, more than 350 people were killed in election-related violence, including public officials, political candidates, and their active supporters (Echeverri-Gent, 1996).

In general, the criminal justice system of India is viewed as a backup to the informal means of social control, heavily dependent on caste, religious, and family considerations. When activated, the criminal justice system is

Table 5.1
Rates of Selected Crimes in India, 1991–1996 (per 100,000 population)

Offenses	1991	1992	1993	1994	1995	1996
Murder	4.6	4.6	4.3	4.3	4.1	4.0
Rape	1.2	1.3	1.4	1.5	1.5	1.6
Dacoity*	1.3	1.3	1.1	1.0	0.9	0.9
Robbery	3.1	3.0	2.8	2.7	2.5	2.4
Burglary	15.5	14.7	13.9	13.5	12.7	12.4
Theft	42.7	40.4	36.3	33.7	32.1	30.6
Riots	12.4	12.1	10.6	10.5	10.5	10.0
Criminal Breach of Trust	2.1	2.1	1.9	1.8	1.7	1.6
Cheating	3.2	3.4	3.4	3.5	3.3	3.6
Counterfeiting	0.5	0.6	0.4	0.3	0.2	0.3

*Dacoity, or gang robbery, often noted in rural areas, is also on the decline.
Source: Government of India, 1998: 156–57.

considered by most Indians to be fair and just, subject to the rules of law. As India modernizes, there is a sense that its law enforcement is becoming increasingly more effective in combatting crime, especially in the rural areas where crimes of violence have historically been more of a problem as compared with urban areas.

CONTEMPORARY CRIME

Currently, crime numbers in India are much lower than in the United States and most European and Asian countries. Even after making allowances for the fact that crime may not be adequately reported, available statistics indicate the rates of many crimes in India are inordinately lower by severalfold in comparison to crime rates in many other countries. For example, in the year 1995, India had a property (e.g., robbery, burglary, and theft) crime rate (N = number per 100,000 population) of 47.3 (see Table 5.1). By comparison, the rate was 4,814 for the United States; 4,883 for Canada; 4,137 for France; 4,824 for Germany; 1,253 for Japan; 1,019 for Singapore; and 853 for Hong Kong (International Criminal Police Organization, 1997).

In general, criminological research and findings indicate that cultural goals and values that encourage crime are often associated with extreme individualism, as these relate to the self-enhancement of oneself above all others, especially in terms of economic motivation (Merton, 1938; Vincentnathan, 1973; Messner and Rosenfeld, 1997); masculinity identification (Miller, 1958; Whiting, 1965; Messerschmidt, 1993); and sexuality, hedonism, and violence (Sanday, 1981; Simpson, 1991).

On the other hand, values and goals that discourage crime are those that

Table 5.2
Crime under the Indian Penal Code, 1951–1996

Year	Estimated Population In millions	Index	IPC Offenses In millions	Index	Rate per 100,000 population
1951	361.1	100.0	650	100.0	179.9
1961	437.7	121.2	626	96.3	142.9
1971	551.2	152.6	953	146.6	172.8
1981	690.1	191.1	1,386	213.2	200.8
1986	766.1	212.2	1,406	216.3	183.5
1991	849.6	235.3	1,678	258.2	197.5
1996	931.9	258.1	1,710	263.1	183.4

Note: Percent Changes in Crime Rates: 1951–1996 = 1.9%; 1951–1991 = 9.8%; 1991–1996 = −7.1%.
Source: Government of India, 1998: 7, 155.

are nonindividualistic, altruistic, noneconomical, nonmasculine, and non–pleasure oriented. These goals and values provide constraints to the "un-controlled" and criminal expression of human motivations. At the same time, they enable the normative standards to remain powerful. Such goals and values, although declining in India, seem to account so far for its more effective control of crime compared with many other nations in the world.

Despite the tremendous increase in population, the crime rate in India has not increased very much and has even decreased in recent years (see Table 5.2). An overview of the raw crime data reveals that the Indian penal code offenses increased by 163.1 percent between 1951 and 1996, whereas the population increased by 158.1 percent, resulting in an increase in the rate of penal code offenses of only 1.9 percent. Between 1951 and 1991 the crime rate increased by 9.8 percent, whereas the population increased by 135.3 percent. Between 1991 and 1996 the population increased by 9.7 percent and the crime rate actually declined by 7.1 percent. The compounded growth rate of population per annum between 1986 and 1996 was 2 percent, and the Indian penal code offenses 2.1 percent (Government of India, 1998: 7, 155).

In a country with a population of nearly 1 billion and extreme levels of poverty, one would expect more crimes than what the statistics indicate. Even considering that crimes are not accurately reported, as in all countries, and that crimes in India have to be more than what statistics reveal, there are reasons to believe that overall crimes in India are lower.

Again, in comparison with many Western countries, violent crime rates in India are lower. However, the difference in homicide rates between India and Western countries is not as marked as the difference in property crime rates, including robbery. Within India, like most nations, there are also striking regional differences in violent crime rates due to differences in the historical circumstances, place of human settlements, urbanization trends, and so forth.

Violence and violent crimes, especially in the past, could be partly explained by the sense of masculinity and the martial image that some caste groups maintain. For example, the warrior castes (*Ksatriya varna*) have traditionally placed strong emphasis on men displaying violence and physical prowess to gain respect and power over other men, their adversaries, and those who belong to lower social and economic statuses—the poor, women, and lower-caste persons. Apart from warrior castes and some tribes that have developed violence as a part of their subcultures, the needs for masculine expression by violence are not widely noted (Vincentnathan, 1996).

In gender relationships, generally, men relate to women with superiority and dominance, and this often results in men using violence against women. These incidents of violence are not usually reported to the police, and many times family, caste, and community elders intervene and try to reconcile the couple involved in domestic violence. These interventions help reduce extreme abuses against women that could otherwise result in an escalation of the number of homicides. Nevertheless, the official rates of battery and torture of women have been increasing in India: 25,946 cases in 1994; 31,127 in 1995; and 35,246 in 1996 (Government of India, 1998: 88).

Another type of violent crime that relates to the subservient position of women and their "commodification" is dowry death; this category includes suicide due to harassment for more dowry and homicides over dowry issues. The practice of dowry originated largely from wealthy business and land-owning castes as a means of distributing the woman's portion of the family wealth at marriage, when she left the family, so that the couple would have a comfortable life. As time passed, such a system became very exploitative for the women and their families and detrimental to the lives of many women. Now, even though the dowry system is illegal and women are entitled to inherit family wealth when their parents die, the bridegroom and his family still demand exorbitant amounts of money and luxury items, both at the time of the marriage and subsequently.

Failure to keep bringing dowry gifts after marriage may lead to ill treatment and abuse of wives. Some wives, unable to bear the ill treatment, commit suicide. In certain cases the husband or husband's family might put suicidal thoughts into the mind of an ill-treated and agonized wife. Sometimes the husband or a relative of the husband kills the wife and tries to make it look like a suicide, accident, or natural death. This practice gives husbands opportunities to remarry and gain more dowry.

For the year 1996, there were 2,747 cases of violations registered under the Dowry Prohibition Act (1961) (Government of India, 1998: 91). Severe penalties were attached to serious forms of cruelty emerging from the dowry practice. However, the dowry system continues to be on the rise without strong social sentiments developing against it and without diligent enforcement activities devoted to preventing it. In fact, for the whole of India in 1996 there were 5,513 dowry deaths reported, an increase of 8.3 percent over the previous year (Government of India, 1998: 88). Of these deaths, dowry homicides amounted to 1,387 during the same year (Government of India, 1998: 113).

Due to the widespread practice of dowry and a consciousness that at every stage of development of the female, from birth to puberty to marriage, females "cause" expenses to their families, female children in general are less preferred than male children. They are less preferred at birth, less pampered, and less nourished. Girls tend to die at a higher rate than boys because of receiving less care and medical attention. Apart from these less obvious ways of hastening the death of female children, the crime of female infanticide also occurs, especially in poorer families. For example, throughout 1997, there were "on an average 105 female infants . . . killed every month in Dharmapuri District" (*The Hindu*, 1998d).

In addition to interpersonal violence, there are also group-based forms of violence. As India modernizes, the conflict that begins to surface between traditional hierarchical notions and emerging democratic values is causing increasing rupture in the social order. Castes, which were once in a rigid hierarchical structure, are now competing with each other for power and privileges, and this sometimes erupts into caste-based violence. Indian communities are also divided by religious, political, and other group identities, which lead to serious ideological differences and disputes and sometimes to communal violence.

The recent surge in Hindu nationalism and fundamentalism encourages violence against lower castes, Muslims, and Christians, and some of these groups in response and in retaliation have organized to defend themselves and their interests (Basu, 1997). Elections as well contribute to the overall violence in India today. Not only are elections times of intense political activity and increased public participation, but they are also times when candidates and their active supporters promote greater caste, class, religious, and other differences, which often stir up violence. Political candidates, elected officials, and their active supporters are often targets of violence. In one of the most intensive episodes in 1991, "some 350 people, including former Prime Minister Rajiv Gandhi, four other parliamentary candidates, and twenty-one candidates running in state legislative assembly elections, were killed in election-related violence" (Echeverri-Gent, 1996: 463).

Moreover, violence continues to be used against the untouchables when they make advancements in their lives or when affirmative action benefits granted to them become an issue (Vincentnathan, 1996). In 1992, for example, there were 24,922 crimes committed against India's deprived castes (Government of India, 1996: 248), which increased to 31,440 by 1996

(Government of India, 1998: 103). Values relating to nonviolence—emphasized within some sections of Hinduism, Buddhism, Jainism, and the Indian Independence Movement, headed by Gandhi—are weakening. Nevertheless, these interpersonal, collective, and political acts of violence have not contributed to overall high levels of violent crime rates in India.

Like the rates of most property and violent crimes, rates of sex crimes, such as rape, are also lower comparatively speaking. For the year 1995 the Indian rape rate was 1.5 (Government of India, 1998: 161), whereas other countries had much higher rates: the United States, 37.09; France, 12.67; Malaysia, 4.87; Sri Lanka, 2.99; and Singapore, 2.76 (International Criminal Police Organization, 1997: 22). However, there are reasons to believe that more of these crimes occur than what the statistics indicate.

In general, rapes are underreported in India, especially because of the embarrassment it can cause the women and the shame it can bring to the family, apart from jeopardizing marriage possibilities. In rural areas, where labor organizations are not well developed and bonded labor may prevail, raping of untouchable women by landowning, higher-caste men is often noted (Sanghatana, 1983) but rarely reported. In 1996, there were 949 reported cases of rape committed against women of untouchable castes (Government of India, 1998: 103). Sometimes rape of women occurs to harass and subdue dissident male laborers who are husbands or kin of those women and to teach other similarly situated men to become subservient and compliant. Overall, however, rape rates are still lower than most other countries because Indian men are less preoccupied with individualism, masculinity, and power.

Nevertheless, sometimes young men tease or harass young women in public and in less guarded places. Behavior such as young men touching young women in anonymous contexts, in crowded areas, in buses, and on trains is also common (*The Hindu*, 1998a). Such behavior often arises out of sexually repressed urges that cannot be fulfilled in relation to strong social controls placed on sexual expression in India. For example, a strict gender segregation is maintained. In classrooms, boys and girls sit in separate areas and do not interact closely. Most marriages are arranged. Kissing and dating are unknown or uncommon. Virginity before marriage is idealized for both men and women.

This behavior also reflects fears about sex and women, which have led men to become overbearing and to assert their physical male superiority against girls/women. Such harassment, referred to as "eve-teasing" in India, is common in high schools and college settings, which may also indicate boys' and young men's fears in relation to girls/women achieving parity with them and the former's desire to intimidate the latter. In 1996 there were 5,671 reported cases of eve-teasing, an increase of 17.7 percent over the previous year (Government of India, 1998: 88–91).

In sum, as late as 1996, the rate of homicide was down compared to the average rate of homicide for the period 1991–1995. "Property" crimes such as robbery, burglary, and theft for 1996 were also on the decline. On the other hand, "violent" crimes such as rape and the kidnapping and abduction of girls had increased during this time. And from the period 1986–1996, such "economic" crimes as cheating, criminal breach of trust, and counterfeiting were up by 20 percent (Government of India, 1998: 31, 39).

CONTEMPORARY CRIME CONTROL

As India modernizes, it is turning from informal means of social control to more formal means of social control. In short, laws are being passed and enforced to control behavior that in the past had been subject to the controls of religion and caste culture. Traditionally, parents usually guarded their daughters very closely to prevent sexual assaults and relationships, which made girls ineligible for marriage and also ruined the family name. Today, by contrast, formal laws exist to protect girls and women from this kind of behavior. For example, in 1961 the Dowry Prohibition Act was passed to encourage equal and respectful treatment of women, to facilitate their marriages without severe economic burdens on their families, and particularly to stop their ill treatment and murder. Apart from this and other national acts, states have also introduced their own laws to protect women. These laws hold that the husband or his family members are culpable of homicide when the wife has committed suicide over dowry harassment and abuse.

More recently, to protect women from eve-teasing, laws have also been introduced. On July 18, 1998, a small group of young men in an autorickshaw (a motorized three-wheeler) severely teased and harassed a college woman on a public road in Madras City, causing her to stumble and fall. Later, she died. The event led to serious political and public discussion of the abuse of girls and women by boys and men, which resulted in the young men of this particular case being charged with murder. In the wake of this event, the creation of a comprehensive ordinance to protect women from such treatment was passed (*The Hindu*, 1998b). The punishment for eve-teasing, according to this new Tamil Nadu ordinance, is imprisonment up to one year or a fine of 10,000 rupees, or both (*The Hindu*, 1998c).

Changes that were consciously introduced during British administration and since Indian independence to motivate the people toward economic development began slowly. Hinduism, by stipulating religious salvation as the goal that people should seek and discouraging attachment to material goals, had provided a general blueprint for life that made the people of India not easily succumb to worldly attractions. The religious and social orders, which were largely complementary to each other for centuries, have now begun to erode. By around the 1970s the economy was starting to develop more quickly, and during recent years, economic growth has been astounding. Nevertheless, even at a contemporary time when growing economic desires are clearly perceivable, and religious beliefs and values less forceful, expression of economic desires in illegal directions is limited by traditional beliefs and values.

Further, by encouraging nonviolence, Hinduism and particularly its branches, Jainism and Buddhism, also contributed toward less violence in society. In a broader sense, violence was thought of as actions that create an imbalance between one's selfish needs and one's environment (Murthi, 1967). Consequently, not only overtly violent behavior but any type of selfish behavior, including theft, was considered violence. The nonviolent orientation was greatly strengthened by various nonviolent movements, such as the Indian Independence Movement led by Gandhi. According to this thinking, all living things, large and small, animal and human, should be loved and given opportunities to flourish. *Himsa* (violence) was denounced and *ahimsa* (nonviolence) glorified (Bondurant, 1958). Even killing animals and killing them for their meat were frowned upon. Support for vegetarianism flourished.

Moreover, during the British rule the lower and despised castes began to adopt the "clean" habits of the higher castes, a trend that intensified after independence. They hoped to shed their undesirable caste identities and gain somewhat acceptable and satisfying caste statuses. For example, there are some "criminal castes" whose ancestors were criminals, and their descendants were also regarded as criminals. Some persons of these castes have continued criminal activities to the present (Yang, 1985). However, in recent times, these castes have begun to give up crime to gain respectability.

Castes that often used violence and also engaged in thievery and extortion, practiced prostitution, or were involved in other behavior considered morally reprehensible by the larger society consciously put forth effort to change their behavior. Caste elders created caste associations for the advancement of their castes. In order to gain desirable images, some castes have changed their caste names, engaged in new occupations, and introduced new myths about a loftier origin of their caste. All these efforts have helped to moralize the various castes, including "criminal castes," who otherwise might have contributed significantly to crime in society. These informal methods of social and crime control also served as a means for "reintegrating" the offender and society.

Apart from the whole cultural development based on religion acting as a general social control, the institutions of family, caste, and community also exert direct control. For Indians, family life is very important, and family matters are well guarded. A clear line is drawn between the inside family life and the outside community life. Parents and children often subject themselves to hardships for the betterment of the family. Children are reared with the importance of maintaining family integrity and name. It is, therefore, hard for anyone to commit a crime and bring shame to one's family. Additionally, the shame to one's family is also a shame to one's kin group and caste. Similarly, if offenses are committed frequently in a community, the community would develop a bad name. Then persons from that community may not be able to find jobs, or families in other communities may not seek marriage alliances with members of that community. Because of such potential problems, parents, caste elders, and community elders give importance to rearing children appropriately and disciplining them properly. When a child acts in an antisocial manner or violates a rule of law, whoever sees it often intervenes to chastise the child, then informs the parents.

When individuals do commit a crime, they often experience shame, identity crisis, deep depression, and suicidal tendencies (Vincentnathan, 1992: 86–87). Family members also undergo similar experiences. Those who are convicted and incarcerated maintain a low profile when they return to the community and tend to alienate themselves from neighbors, friends, and community members. One consequence of these relations is that recidivism rates in India are only 8.6 percent compared to 80 percent in the United States and 40 percent in Japan (Vincentnathan, 1995; Government of India, 1998: 332).

Indian culture and social structure, however, are changing with economic development and Western influence. A Western sense is not only liberating people from the traditional and oppressive hierarchy but is also promoting self-serving actions, a decline in self-control, and friction in relationships with others. In the last few decades the religious, nonviolent, and cleansing orientations, along with institutional controls, have significantly declined. There is increasing violence in TV programs and movies. The patterns of violence and sex in American films are entering Indian films, apart from American films and programs that are directly reaching the Indian public through movie theaters and TV satellite dishes. Some of these violent influences are the result of greater social interactions between India and Western nations. Western cultural influences are dominating India as they are globally, and from a criminological perspective, they are disturbing Indian society (Silbey, 1997).

Indian culture and society are undergoing significant transformations under the impact of science, technology, and economic development. The Indian economy has moved from localized, fairly self-sufficient and community-based operations, as Ghandi wished it to be, to a national economy. More recently, India's highly regulated and closed economy has become more open, with increasing participation at the global level. As India moves more deeply into market exchange relations, attitudes of market consumption, for example, are engendering economic competition, making people see each other as a hindrance to their own achievement, or as an object for profit, which lessens the general value placed on human beings. In turn, committing crime and victimizing others for personal advantage are becoming easier. When crimes and victimizations increase, people will begin to develop an even more cynical and negative picture of human nature, which can further contribute to the devaluation of others and subsequently to increased crime against them.

FUTURE OF CRIME AND CRIME CONTROL

Certain conclusions can be drawn about the future of crime and crime control in India, based on emerging social patterns and crime trends. Despite the fact that India has the second largest population in the world, the crime problem continues to be strikingly lower than in many countries, East and West. The rates of crime for the decade 1986 to 1996 remained fairly stable. The compounded growth rate for all criminal offenses under the Indian Penal Code was only 0.1 percent during this period (Government of India, 1998: 155). This low growth rate in crime is surprising at a time when there has been increasing pressure on land and economic resources, due to population increases, unemployment, widespread poverty, economic inequalities, and growing individualism and economic desires.

A closer look at the patterns and trends in criminal statistics indicates that certain crimes associated with economic development, urbanization, and modernization will increase, and those that are linked to the traditional rural society might show a gradual and slow decline. Violent crime rates, such as the homicide rate, for instance, could decline overall, except in certain states and cultural areas of the north and east that provide greater cultural support for violent behavior and have rates of homicide higher than the national average.

Property and economic crimes will increase in India as the growing economic ambitions in society will be increasingly expressed in criminal ways. These crimes are "functional" to the economy because the motives behind them are also the motives promoting economic development (Vincentnathan, 1973). This will happen as it did in the economic development history of most Western societies. Additionally, the attitudes of consumerism and a general orientation to seek pleasure and enjoyment, which economic development engenders, should increase pleasure-related, such as sex-related and drug-related, although there is no indication of this so far.

As urbanization trends increase, property crimes in cities will increase, and violent crimes may slowly decline. Property crimes will increase because cities usually contain more economically ambitious people. Violent crimes in cities may decline as gaining status through the use of violence becomes obsolete and gaining status through economic gains comes to predominate in the evolving culture.

The rural forms of violent crime and the crimes committed by rural gangs will decline. Already "dacoity," or robbery committed by gangs, which happens mainly in rural areas, is declining as India urbanizes and people become

Table 5.3
Cities and Their Associated State Crime Rates, 1996 (per 100,000 population)

Cities and their States		Violent Crimes		Property Crimes		
		Homicide	Rape	Robbery	Burglary	Theft
City:	Calcutta	0.7	0.2	1.4	1.3	44.5
State:	W. Bengal	2.6	1.1	1.2	1.0	31.7
City:	Bombay	2.1	1.0	4.0	16.2	89.2
State:	Maharashtra	3.2	1.6	1.0	19.1	54.6
City:	Madras	1.0	0.2	1.3	9.2	44.5
State:	Tamil Nadu	3.2	0.6	1.0	10.8	31.7
City:	Delhi	4.1	4.1	5.0	21.3	185.7
	Delhi Area	4.6	4.3	5.4	20.5	180.8
State:	Uttar Pradesh*	5.6	1.2	3.5	7.7	22.0

*Delhi is located on the border of Uttar Pradesh and has a more diverse population, being the
nation's capital.
Source: Government of India, 1998: 161–63.

individuated and groups become weaker. More effective law enforcement
services have also helped to reduce dacoity. Between 1986 and 1996, such
gang robberies declined by 23.1 percent, and these declines were especially
steep in India's urban areas. For example, the share of the cities' dacoity to
the national figure is only 5.3 percent (Government of India, 1998: 39, 53).
Additionally, overall Indian cities have lower violent crime rates than the
particular states in which they are located, whereas their property crime rates
are higher (see Table 5.3).

In order to reduce violent crime and prevent it from increasing, there
should be significant changes in the lifestyles of the people. Unless Indians
move away from hierarchical thinking connected with caste, class, religion,
and gender, and unless they give up violence as a means of establishing their
superiority over others, violent crimes will continue and may even increase.
Indians have to develop democratic attitudes, separate themselves from di-
visive "group-think," and learn to respect others as individuals, with due
regard for their rights. Only then can the hierarchical thinking that promotes
intolerance and violence be replaced by egalitarian views that promote tolerance and peaceful resolution of differences.

REFERENCES

Basu, Amrita. 1997. "Caste and Class: The Rise of Hindu Nationalism in India." In
    James H. K. Norton (ed.), *Global Studies: India and South Asia*. 3rd ed.
    Guilford, CT: Dushkin/McGraw-Hill, 117–22.
Bondurant, Joan V. 1958. *Conquest of Violence*. Princeton, NJ: Princeton University
    Press.

Dumont, Louis. 1970. *Homo Hierarchicus: An Essay on the Caste System.* Mark Sainbury (trans). Chicago: University of Chicago Press.

Echeverri-Gent, John. 1996. "Government and Politics." In James Heitzman and Robert L. Worden (eds.), *India: A Country Study, Area Handbook.* 5th ed. Washington, DC: U.S. Government Printing Office, 429–506.

Europa Publications Limited. 1997. *The Europa World Year Book, 1997.* Vol. 1. London: Gresham Press.

Ganguly, Sumit. 1996a. "India: Between Turmoil and Hope." In James H. K. Norton (ed.), *Global Studies: India and South Asia.* 3rd ed. Guilford, CT: Dushkin/McGraw-Hill, 92–97.

————. 1996b. "National Security." In James Heitzman and Robert L. Worden, (eds.), *India: A Country Study, Area Handbook.* 5th ed. Washington, DC: U.S. Government Printing Office, 561–621.

Government of India. 1996. *Crime in India, 1994.* New Delhi: National Crime Records Bureau, Ministry of Home Affairs.

————. 1998. *Crime in India, 1996.* New Delhi: National Crime Records Bureau, Ministry of Home Affairs.

The Hindu. 1998a. "Crime against Women Increasing in Assam." June 29, 11.

————. 1998b. "Ordinance against Eve-Teasing Likely." July 29, 4.

————. 1998c. "Ordinance against Eve-Teashing Issued." July 31, 1.

————. 1998d. "Female Infanticide Alarming in Dharmapuri Dt." August 2, 1.

International Criminal Police Organization. 1997. *International Crime Statistics, 1995.* Paris: International Criminal Police Organization (Interpol).

Merton, Robert K. 1938. "Social Structure and Anomie." *American Sociological Review* 14, 3: 672–82.

Messerschmidt, James W. 1993. *Masculinities and Crime: Critique and Reconceptualization of Theory.* Lanham, MD: Rowman and Littlefield.

Messner, Steven F., and Richard Rosenfeld. 1997. *Crime and the American Dream.* Belmont, CA: Wadsworth.

Miller, Walter B. 1958. "Lower Class Culture as a Generating Milieu of Gang Delinquency." *Journal of Social Issues* 14: 4–19.

Murthi, T.R.V. 1967. "The World and the Individual in Indian Religious Thought." In Charles A. Moore (ed.), *The Indian Mind.* Honolulu: University of Hawaii Press, 320–340.

Raghavan, R. K., and Mangai Natarajan. 1996. "India." In Graeme Newman, Debra Cohen, and Adam C. Bouloukos (eds.), *International Factbook of Criminal Justice Systems.* Bureau of Justice Statistics: http://www.ojp.usdoj.gov/pub/bjs/ascii/wfbcjsin.txt.

Sanday, Peggy. 1981. "The Socio-Cultural Context of Rape: A Cross-Cultural Study." *Journal of Social Issues* 37, 1: 5–27.

Sanghatana, Stree Shakti. 1983. "War against Rape: A Report from Karimnagar." In Miranda Davies (ed.), *Third World, Second Sex.* London: Zed Press, 197–201.

Silbey, Susan. 1997. "Let Them Eat Cake: Globalization, Postmodern Colonialism and the Possibilities of Justice." *Law and Society Review* 31, 2: 207–35.

Simpson, Sally S. 1991. "Caste, Class, and Violent Crime: Explaining Difference in Female Offending." *Criminology* 29, 1: 115–35.

Srinivas, M. N. 1966. *Social Change in Modern India.* Berkeley: University of California Press.

Vincentnathan, S. George. 1973. "Patterns of 'Serious' Crimes and Suicide in San Francisco, Tokyo, and Madras." Ph.D. dissertation, University of California, Berkeley.

———. 1985. "Caste, Class, and Crime: India and the United States." In Richard F. Tomasson (ed.), *Deviance: Comparative Social Research*. Greenwich, CT: JAI Press, 8: 97–122.

———. 1992. "Social Construction of Order and Disorder and Their Outcomes in Two South Indian Communities." *Journal of Legal Pluralism* 32: 65–102.

———. 1995. "Social Reaction and Secondary Deviance in Culture and Society: The United States and Japan." *Advances in Criminological Theory* 6: 329–47.

———. 1996. "Caste Politics, Violence, and the *Panchayat* in a South Indian Community." *Comparative Studies in Society and History* 38, 3: 484–509.

Ward, Geoffrey. 1997. "India." *National Geographic* 191, 5: 2–57.

Whiting, Beatrice B. 1965. "Sex Identity Conflict and Physical Violence: A Comparative Study." In Laura Nader (ed.), "The Ethnography of Law." *American Anthropologist* 67, 8 (pt. 2): 123–40.

Yang, Anand. 1985. "Bhils and the Idea of Criminal Tribe in Nineteenth-Century India." In Anand Yang (ed.), *Crime and Criminality in British India*. Tucson: University of Arizona Press, 128–39.

6

IRAN

(Developing Nation-State)

Hamid R. Kusha

PROFILE OF IRAN

Iran, formerly known as Persia, is a Middle Eastern country located between the Caspian Sea on the north and the Persian Gulf and the Sea of Oman on the south. On the west, its neighbors are Iraq and Turkey; on the northwest, the ex-Soviet Republics of Azerbaijan and Armenia; and on the northeast, the ex-Soviet Republic of Turkestan. Afghanistan and Pakistan are two other neighbors of Iran on the east and southeast. With a total land mass of 631,660 square miles (1,648,000 square kilometers), Iran is slightly larger than the state of Alaska.

In 1995, Iran's population was estimated at 64,625,455 (Iran, 1995). Iran's ethnic composition is varied, composed of 51 percent Persian, 24 percent Azerbaijani, 8 percent Gilaki and Mazandarani, 7 percent Kurd, 3 percent Arab, 2 percent Balouch, and 2 percent Turkmen (Iran, 1995). Compared to its 1986 census of 48,181,463 (Metz, 1988), Iran has one of the fastest-growing population rates among the developing nations, estimated at 2.29 percent in 1995. Its young population constitutes one of the most difficult problems facing Iran's Islamic government in its attempts to control and regulate people's behavior.

Iran's written history begins with a migratory movement around the beginning of the second millennium B.C., spearheaded by Indo-European groups, such as the Scythians, the Medes, and the Persians. Of these groups, the Medes and Persians are the most relevant to Iran's history and culture, for it was these two groups that were later to create the first world empire under Cyrus, the Great Kurosh Kabir of the Achaemenid empire (550–330 B.C.). Within a decade, Cyrus created a world empire that extended from the Indus River in the east to the Aegean shores of Asia Minor in the west. There were more than 50 different nationalities and ethnic groups who gave homage and tribute to Cyrus's court.

The Achaemenid (Hakhamaneshi) empire reached its zenith of might and power under Darius (d. 486 B.C.). He brought Asia Minor and a number of Greek city-states under Persian headship, although he was unsuccessful in subjugating Athens and Sparta. It was Alexander of Macedonia (d. 323 B.C.) who defeated the Achaemenids and built another world empire. In doing so, Alexander brought the world of the Hellenes to Iran, including some of the Hellenistic notions of law, justice, and punishment that merged with the general legal principles codified under Cyrus. The cultural admixture gave to Iran another source of historical vitality that was expressed in the rise of the Seleucid (312–247 B.C.) and later the Arsacid (247 B.C.–226 A.D.) empires whose Perso-Hellenistic cultural heritages passed to Sasanid Iran (226–651).

This long history, known as the pre-Islamic period of Iran, came to its end with the demise of the Sasanids at the hands of Muslim Arabs in A.D. 642, an event that made Iran an integral part of the world of Islam. From the mid-seventh century to the present, Iran has played a central role in the rise of the Islamic civilization. In the process, it has received and passed on to the world of Islam various social and cultural traditions, including a tradition of law, justice, crime, and penology.

HISTORICAL PERSPECTIVE ON CRIME AND CRIME CONTROL

Until quite recently, Iran has been one of those societies not obsessed with crime (Adler, 1983). This state of affairs has had much to do with the historical anticrime impacts of Iran's religious culture, family, and education system whose combined heritage has inculcated not only a high degree of respect for authority from the general populace but an aversion to crime. It also has been the by-product of a complex system of law, justice, and crime control mechanisms that have evolved from both pre-Islamic and Islamic Iran.

Iranian Religious Culture

Iran likes to take pride for having developed over a long period of history a brilliant, humanitarian, and anticriminogenic (i.e., non-crime-producing) culture. As a heterogeneous society, Iran has seen many invaders ranging from Indo-Aryan tribes to Greeks to Arabs to Turk-Mongols, to name but

a few. In the assimilated Iranian culture, religion has always played a significant role. Moreover, Iran has also given birth to a number of Indo-
European religions, all of which have had wide influence on peoples and
cultures in the Middle East and southern Europe. Zoroastrianism was perhaps the most influential of these religions, impacting on notions of both
sin and crime.

The Zoroastrian religion conceived an everlasting battle between the
Good (Ahura-Mazda) and the Evil (Ahriman). Human beings were,
therefore, perceived as duty bound to be on the side of the Good and to
refrain from committing sin and crime, both of which were conceived of as
part of the realms of Evil. Criminals were looked upon as the agents of Evil
assisted by demons in their sin/crime commission. By contrast, righteous
persons were believed to be protected by Twelve Celestial Angels (Amshas-
pandan), each of which represented a specific month of the year. Righteous
persons refrained from lies, rage, greed, and deception without which one
was believed to be incapable of committing crime.

In Zoroastrianism, sin/crime has both individual and communal bases.
Of special significance was the cause of justice, peace, and tranquility believed to stop crime. Accordingly, the person of the monarch was responsible
to serve the cause of justice. Otherwise, the realm would fall into the
clutches of deception, crime, drought, and darkness. Crime was controlled
through informal means (i.e., family, education, temple and community relations, Zoroastrian belief system) as well as formals means (i.e., government, police, codified laws, King's Court).

With the coming of Islam to Iran, Muslim Arabs brought the genesis of
a new concept of justice, law, and crime control to the Middle East and
North Africa, where the bulk of Islamic conversion conquest activities took
place. Islam, unlike Zoroastrianism, which is a dualistic religion, is a mono-
theistic and universal religion that has a view of sin/crime that is very close
to the Judeo-Christian view expressed in the Ten Commandments.

In the Islamic notion of criminology, there is no place for ghouls, goblins,
and demons. However, there is Satan (Sheytan), who is portrayed as a Fallen
Angel from God's grace because Satan did not submit to God's wish that
all celestial beings pay homage to God's creations, Adam and Eve. Unlike
celestial beings, Adam and Eve were created in the image of God, and
therefore they possessed the innate ability to reason. Human beings, as
Adam and Eve's offspring, are portrayed as rational beings (*'aqil*) in Islam
and therefore are free to choose (*mukhayyir*) between sin/crime and non-
crime. This means that human beings are responsible (*mas'ul*) for their
choices. This, of course, has impacted Islamic penology in that punishment
became a rational means to crime aversion. In other words, crime commission is not under the influence of naturalistic but humanistic forces. This
said, there is also the paramount notion that God is the primal source of

criminal causality. However, God does not make human beings rational. Rather, it is a combination of individual, communal, and social factors that play a criminogenic role.

For example, among Muslim Arabs there are various sayings attributed to the Prophet Muhammad and Shi'i Imams that poverty is the source of all evils in the same manner that greed, injustice, and oppression are criminogenic elements. For bedouin Arabs, tribal honor played a significant role in crime control in that the tribe was the main protector of the individual, matched in importance with the family. Any type of crime that blemished the tribal and/or family honor was frowned upon universally and punished in the harshest manner. Blood feuds were common among bedouin Arabs, often lasting for generations and shedding much blood. Islam put a decisive end to these blood wars by stressing that in the sight of Allah it was sincerity (*ikhlas*) in belief (*iman*) that was of prime significance, and therefore the worth of a Muslim was not in his or her genealogy, family, clan, and tribe but in his or her purity of the faith. Islam also stressed the importance of the community of believers (*umma*) as well as a loving and caring family. In short, crime in any form and shape was derogatory to both one's faith and honor.

Muslim Arabs, as they settled in various parts of the Old World, had to adapt their partially bedouin and partially Islamic tribal/communal form of crime control and punishment system to the social, economic, political, and cultural requisites of a world empire that they had created under the 'Umayyad and Abbasid caliphs. One adoption was to Byzantine-Sasanid styles of governance, public administration, and tax collection strategies in devising their effective forms of central government and crime control. Muslim governors, in short, had to follow a model of justice, law, and punishment that Islam's sacred text, the Koran (Qur'an), had advised for. This adaptation gradually led to the rise of the Islamic Sacred Law (the Shari'ah) and its crime control mechanisms.

The Sacred Law of Islam

The Islamic Shari'ah has produced a sophisticated view of law, justice, crime, and punishment by utilizing the Koran as well as the sayings (*hadith*) and deeds (*sunna*) attributed to Prophet Muhammad and Shi'i Imams. In addition, the use of human rationality (*'aql*), analogy (*qiyas*), and juristic opinion (*ra'y*) are allowed. Like all other natural systems, the Islamic Shari'ah equates crime with sin and advises believers to refrain from sin/crime commission.

Besides temporal crime control mechanisms that included both informal and formal means, the Shari'ah gives a prominent place to God as the final divine arbiter in human affairs. The gist of this is that Allah is the Ultimate Judge (Qazi al-Quzat) who is Compassionate (Al-Rahman) and Merciful

(Al-Rahim) at the same time that He is the Mightiest of all the Mightiest (Jabbar al-Qasimin). He is also knowledgeable of every thing on the earth and in the heavens. Therefore, not an iota of sin/crime (*ma'asi*) and/or injustice (*zulum*) goes unnoticed in the eyes of God. The Shari'ah finds the Muslim judge (or *qazi*, anglicized as the *kadi*), the caliph, and the governor not only duty bound to fight crime but to see to it that the reasons for crime commission are uprooted. The most important reasons have been theorized as injustice, oppression (*ikhtinaq*), corruption (*fisad*), and individual inclinations (*naifs-e'ammareh*). Hence, it was implied that those in any position of authority had to be honest (*amind*), righteous (*muttaqi*), God fearing (*mu'min*), and just (*'adil*).

Islam advises that criminals be dealt with in a swift and yet proportional manner. However, Islam is against cruel and humiliating punishments (Souryal, 1988; Kusha, 1998). This has been a controversial issue, of course, in that the Islamic Shari'ah has provided for a number of punishments that seem cruel and unusual such as the amputation (*qat'*) of fingers of thieves (*sariq*) for theft (*sirqat*); flogging (*jild*) or stoning to death those convicted of adultery (*zina*); flogging of those convicted of consumption of alcoholic beverages (*khamr*) and drugs (*miysar*). At the same time, however, the Koran reminds believers that they should refrain from committing crimes in any form, shape, or context. It also advises believers to be respectful of one another, to be civil, and to be honest, alluding to the Koran's codification abilities in the areas of personal, family, contract, and tort laws as it simultaneously respects the boundaries of homes and private property.

Finally, the Koran implores those in charge of crime control (e.g., the state as well as the judges) to be righteous (*muhiq*) and to follow God's righteous commands (*ahkam, hudud*) both in judgment and in meting out punishment. This divine and righteous path (*sirat*), reminds the Koran, ought to be adhered to by judges and those in the position of high authority if they desire to emulate the Prophet Muhammad's model of applying Islamic law (Fazlur Rahman, 1979). If not, those judges, governors, and military authorities who stray from Muhammad's model will experience horrendous punishment in the next world to come.

Family, Community, and State

Like most societies, the family, the community, and the state have played important interdependent roles in social control and crime prevention. Together, these Iranian institutions have helped to inculcate a respect for law and conformity to social mores, norms, values, and folkways that have generally reproduced a high degree of inequality and subordination over time. Iranian social etiquette, for example, is caught up in respect, honor, and pride in one's family background and class status, serving as a backdrop for an individual's position of respectability in society. Behaviors that blemish these are universally frowned at. They are considered products of lowly up-bringing. On the other hand, power and prestige are due to age, education, and socioeconomic status. Respecting parents, grandparents, elder siblings, and teachers and showing deference to those in positions of authority are, thus, highly valued if not rewarded.

The Iranian body politic, whether at the family, community, or state level, has always been dominated by powerful, patriarchal, and charismatic figures. The Iranian class structure based on the historical (traditional) system of stratification has functioned, until very recently, to perpetuate the unequal distribution of wealth, prestige, and power. In turn, these relations have established the rise of an autocratic/despotic style of government, at home and at the communal level. As a result, individuals at every level of Iranian society have been subject to a high degree of informal control, which, in turn, has helped prevent the spread of predatory crimes, although not those crimes of a nepotistic nature.

Historically, in the despotic/autocratic/patriarchal system of social con-trol, women and children have been treated as second-class citizens. Women, accordingly, need men's supervision and control because women have been considered "irrational," "emotional," and a constant source of "temptation." Although this sexist and derogatory view of women has al-lowed for "honor"-related crimes committed primarily against women, for example, engaging in premarital or extramarital affairs (or even being raped), which may result in death to women, it is also argued that this sexist ide-ology, until recently, has protected women in Islamic societies, including Iran, from such stranger-perpetrated predatory crimes as assault and rape. In any event, there is no Koranic basis for this type of punishment-honor killings. Rather, these honor crimes date back to pre-Islamic practices that have been justified by a certain medievalist and sexist reading of some Ko-ranic injunctions that stress chastity (*iffat*) in an ironically sex-neutral man-ner.

PUBLIC PERCEPTION OF CRIME AND CRIME CONTROL

As far back as most Iranians can remember, common crimes such as mur-der, burglary, and rape have not been considered as issues or social prob-lems. Traditionally, Iran has been a country with little crime, and the people of Iran have not been obsessed with crime and crime control. At the same time, however, as far back as the 1960s, most people can recall that during the periods of both the monarchical rule of the Shah and the Islamic rule of the subsequent postrevolutionary Iranian Republic that the primary crime problem has been that of state repression and political crime committed by governmental agents against dissidents of either of the prevailing regimes. The other publicly perceived crime problem has involved the corruption and lack of appropriate punishments for high-level governmental officials of either regime.

On the other hand, when divorced from political crimes and crimes of corruption, contemporary perceptions of the criminal justice system, especially of law enforcement, are that of fairly efficient, effective, and professional personnel. People report crimes against their property and to a lesser degree against the person to law enforcement and prosecutorial agents, and they expect reasonable results. At the same time, families are protective of their own children's involvement in crime and delinquency, preferring to handle the matters informally, still a bit queasy and uneasy about handing their loved ones over to the criminal justice system for processing.

CONTEMPORARY CRIME

Perhaps nothing reveals the contemporary crime scene in Iran more than the changing forms of women's criminality there. Prior to the rise of the Islamic regime in Iran, women's criminality related, by and large, to vice crime and petty types of larceny and misdemeanors. Under the present Islamic Republic's repressive and misogynous rules and laws, women have now entered into the realm of serious crimes, involving murder (usually of their abusive husbands), aggravated assault in the context of corrupt and totalitarian-style municipal government, and organized crime, especially those that revolve around prostitution rings.

There have also been reports of young married women committing self-inflicted immolation and other forms of suicide. Agance Farance Press reported in its February 1994 report that "a young-14-year-old girl" in Tehran, "pressured by her family to marry a 42-year-old man, set herself ablaze and died," according to the weekly *Zan-e-rooz* [newspaper]. In the same month and year, Reuter (1994) also reported that in another local newspaper account "a married Iranian woman was stoned to death in Tehran's Evin prison for adultery and planning her husband's murder." Finally, in the same year, Amnesty International (AI) reported that a large number of women were arrested in a nationwide crackdown on "vice and moral corruption" and that many of them were sentenced to the punishment of public flogging. According to AI (1994: 164), "[T]hey were among hundreds of women who were reported to have been arrested in Tehran for allegedly failing to conform to the strict dress laws of the Islamic Republic."

At least one thing that has not changed from the regime of the Shah to the regime of the Ayatollah, and that is consistent in both the pre- and postrevolutionary systems of criminal justice in Iran, is the fact that no systematic official crime data pertaining to actual crime (and control strategies) has ever been disclosed. For example, the 1997 United Nations' profile on Iran's criminal justice statistics provides no data on the number of crimes reported to the police, on the number of persons arrested, convicted, and sentenced, or on the number of criminal justice personnel, prisons, and so forth. The lack of "official" data forces a researcher to rely on such alternative sources as Iranian newspapers published both inside and in exile, opposition political groups, and human rights organizations like Amnesty International.

Contemporary crime appears to have entered the Iranian scene around the mid-1960s during a period of rapid development and modernization. Under the rule of the Muhammad Reza Pahlavi (r. 1941–1979), Iran had become strategically aligned with the West, especially the United States, as the Shah was attempting to bring his nation into the modern age. Armed with U.S. moral and financial help, the Shah undertook a reform that he called the White Revolution of the Shah and People, designed to reform Iran's land tenure, education, public administration, judiciary, military, and economy.

The White Revolution gradually bore fruit in incorporating Iran into a Western style of modernization and development, on the one hand. It also opened up a new social era in Iran, on the other hand. The latter proved to be quite disruptive to Iran's Islamic traditions. Along with Westernization came a more brazen consumption of alcoholic beverages, a more widespread use of illicit drugs, and a more permissible entertainment industry that included night clubs, movie theaters, and television shows. By the early 1970s, juvenile offenses, previously unheard of in Iran, began to be of consequence. At the same time, there emerged a view of modern women as competent and capable of engaging in civil, political, and public life. For example, under the White Revolution programs, middle- and upper-class women were allowed to enter a number of professions, including the judiciary, banking and finance, arts, sports, and even policing.

In reaction to these modernizing and Westernizing reforms, an Islamic alternative movement began in earnest, under the auspices of the Ayatollah Ruholla Musavi Khomeini. His battle cry was a return to an Islam that he equated with morality, a respect for law and human rights, and a "crime-free" Iran—an Iranian society free of the wanton waste, bribery, corruption, and misuse of oil revenues associated with the Shah and the ineffectiveness of the modern judiciary in fighting against nepotism and other abuses connected with Western development and modernization.

The 1970s also witnessed the rise of political and antistate subversive activities by revolutionary organizations (e.g., various Marxist-Leninist and Maoist groups or other islamic fundamentalist groups). These types of political activities were inevitable in Iran because under Shah Pahlavi law enforcement had become subject to a dreaded police state whereby no type of political dissent was tolerated. Their political offenses were harshly dealt with by military tribunals. In the prosecution and defense of these cases, only military judges, prosecutors, and defense counsels trained in law participated. Civil defense was not allowed, and the death penalty could be imposed unless the Shah commuted the death sentence to life in prison.

The boom in oil prices, beginning in 1974, also led to the proliferation of both white-collar and financial crimes. These crimes had a demoralizing and delegitimizing effect on the general populace, who saw the Imperial system as corrupt and discriminatory in all its facets. For example, there was the Criminal Court of Governmental Officials that supposedly presided over offenses committed by governmental administrators. Few high-ranking government officials, however, were ever punished for their corruptions and mismanagement of public funds. Instead, corrupt officials were usually removed from office and sent to provincial towns with a new government post or sometimes sent as one of the Shah's ambassadors to some foreign diplomatic post.

In postrevolutionary Iran, under the prevailing Islamic regime, the same practices of governmental abuse against political dissent continue unabated. In fact, with the rise of the Ayatollah Khomeini, Iranian society witnessed a new and harsher phase of the criminalization of dissent. Only this time, it has been in the name of religion rather than modernization. Women have clearly been the biggest losers under the Islamic regime.

Women have been victimized, for example, by the present Islamization of the judiciary in Iran. In spite of the constitutional checks and balances that operate on paper, women have been treated as second-class citizens in all aspects of law and social organization, be it in the family, inheritance, child custody, witness, education, and employment opportunities. Citing the Ayatollah Khomeini's dictum that "women's first job is to be a wife and a mother," the authors of the Parliamentary Human Rights Group maintained in 1994: "For 15 years there has been a deliberate reversal of precious gains by a century-old Iranian women's movement for equal rights" (Reuter, 1994: 1).

The oppressive measures that the Islamic Republic has imposed on females have included the imposition of Vail (*chador*) for women and girls as young as seven years of age, sexual segregation in public, and sexual division of labor in employment practices. From 1980 to the present, because Iranian women have resisted these enforced measures and fought against them, they have become the main target of a forced Islamization that has led to women's brutalization, marginalization, and victimization. In fact, several thousands of women have been arrested, tortured, flogged in public, and executed for their dissident ways, not the least of which includes their active participation in the People's Mojahedin Organization of Iran (PMOI).

After three years of semilegal and semiunderground political activities (1979–1981), the PMOI, a group originally formed to fight the Pahlavi regime and subsequently an enemy of the Khomeini regime as well, moved from merely critiquing Khomeini's policies to leading full-scale armed uprisings against the central government in 1988 and 1989. In 1987 the

PMOI relocated its headquarters to Iraq, where they still maintain their base of operations today. Having established a modern Liberation Army there, composed of PMOI members and ex-political prisoners, they have been lobbying Western European parliaments (and the United States) to be recognized as the only democratic alternative to the Islamic regime. Engaged in armed skirmishes with the central government of Iran, these men and women guerrilla combatants of the PMOI have lost tens of thousands of their allies to death and imprisonment.

In 1986, the PMOI published a book under the title of *List of Names and Particulars of 12,028 Victims of the Khomeini Regime's Executions.* By utilizing these data (see Table 6.1) and other data set documents published by the PMOI (see Tables 6.2 and 6.3), one can ascertain a sense of the extent of the criminalization of political dissent under Khomeini's tenure (1979–1989) as well as under his successors (1989–1996).

In reading Table 6.1, it is instructive to point out that this data set has been gathered under extraordinary circumstances whereby the socioeconomic status (SES) characteristics apply to the actual number of persons who have been executed in this period. This number does not reflect the actual number of executions that the PMOI has estimated at a grand total of 120,000 for the last two decades. At the same time, the PMOI has argued that this data set is being continuously updated, as the spate of political killings and disappearances continues into the present day. Even under the "moderate" president Muhammed Khatami, the state of summary executions and disappearances has not stopped. Since Khatami took office in June 1997, for example, the PMOI has documented another 266 political killings.

In spite of the fact that the Islamic Republic's Constitution recognizes the principles of due process, the Islamic Republic of Iran has been condemned an unprecedented 42 times since 1984 by the United Nations General Assembly and its Subcommittee on Human Rights. The primary reasons for these condemnations have been on the grounds that Iran's Islamic system of justice (1) does not differentiate between political and nonpolitical crimes; and (2) its adjudication standards are highly arbitrary and do not conform to internationally recognized standards of fair treatment and due process.

The PMOI has also documented what it terms state-sponsored terrorist acts outside of Iran. These acts can be considered illegal extrajudicial and extralegal killings of Iranian dissidents in Europe, Asia, and other Middle Eastern countries. They also involve executions and felonious assaults carried out by state secret services/agents against foreign nationals sympathetic with anti-Islamic Iranian dissidents (see Tables 6.2 and 6.3).

The PMOI has also gathered a list of many unofficial prisons, jails, and houses of detention that operate in spite of the official correctional institutions. According to a number of ex-political prisoners, these extralegal

Table 6.1
The Socioeconomic Status of Those Political Dissidents Executed between
1981 and 1986

Age Category	Education Category	Political Affiliation Category	Occupation Category	Marital Status Category	Punishment Category
23.5 years known number executed 6,471	HS known number executed 2,860	PMOI known number executed 11,128	Teaching known number executed 647	Married known number executed 1,644	Executed known number 7,666
>18 known number executed 599	UG known number executed 596	Others known number executed 900	Workers known number executed 630	Single known number executed 5,750	Other forms of execution 4,362
<40 known number executed 91	Unknown number executed 4,975		Professionals known number executed 541		
Total known number executed 7,448 Unspecified 4,580	Total known number executed 7,407 Unspecified 4,621	Total known number executed 12,028 Unspecified 0	Total known number executed 2,433 Unspecified 9,595	Total known number executed 7,394 Unspecified 4,634	Total known number of executions
Grand Total 12,028	Grand Total 12,028	Grand Total 12,028	Grand Total 12,028	Grand Total 12,028	12,028

HS = High School
UG = University/College Graduates
GS = Graduate School
U = Unknown
Note: Base: recorded number of executions between 1981 and 1986: 12,028; estimated number of executions between 1981 and 1986: 50,000.
Source: PMOI, 1986.

centers operate clandestinely by various Secret Service organizations whose exact number is unknown. However, the number is rumored to be around 20, ranging from paramilitary groups called the Hizbullah, the Ansar-e Hizbullah, and the Basij-e Mustazafan to highly organized units of the Revolutionary Guards.

Table 6.2
Summary of Extrajudicial/Extralegal Killings of Iranian Dissidents,
1980–1995

Year	Total	Foreign Targets	Dissidents	PMOI	Kurdish Groups	Other Groups
1980	3	0	0	0	0	3
1981	6	0	3	2	0	1
1982	13	0	5	7	0	1
1983	6	5	1	0	0	0
1984	4	2	0	1	0	1
1985	11	5	0	2	0	4
1986	10	3	1	3	0	3
1987	17	5	4	3	0	5
1988	9	2	3	4	0	0
1989	10	3	0	2	2	3
1990	8	1	1	3	2	1
1991	19	9	1	1	5	3
1992	32	5	7	13	4	3
1993	19	3	3	9	4	0
1994–1995	25	4	1	13	7	0
Grand Total	192	47	30	63	24	28

Source: Adapted from PMOI's Web site: http://www.iran-e-azad.org

The number of political prisoners is almost a state secret. The opposition sources have claimed that around 120,000 political dissidents have been executed in the past two decades. In the *1989 Report on Human Rights around the World*, Amnesty International documented waves of political executions: "Over 1,200 political prisoners were executed. . . . Thousands of others remained in prison, among them an unknown number of prisoners of conscience" (AI, 1989: 254). In its 1994 report, AI (1994: 163) maintained: "In August *Resalat* newspaper reported a senior prison official as stating that the total of 99,900 prisoners were held during the Iranian calendar year ending March 1993. However, no figures were made public regarding the number of political prisoners nor the number of prisoners executed." In the same document, AI also reported: "Torture and ill-treatment of prisoners continued to be reported to extract confessions or statements to be used as evidence at trial" (163). Insofar as the "cruel and unusual" punishments were concerned, the report gave a grim picture: "Amputation and flogging as judicial punishments remained in force" (164). As far back as 1989, AI has consistently reported on the maltreatment of both women and men in prison who have been subjected to sexual abuse and mock executions.

Table 6.3
Extrajudicial/Extralegal Killing or Maiming of Iranian Dissidents Abroad, 1979–1996

Number of Dissidents	Country	Dates	City	Description
4	Austria	1987 through 1989	Vienna	Assassination
3	Dubai	1986 through 1992 and intermittently	Unspecified	Assassination
11	France	1979 through 1996 and intermittently	Paris and unspecified	Assassination/ Aggravated Assault
40	Germany	1982 through 1993 and intermittently	Unspecified	Assassination/ Aggravated Assault
30	India	1982	Unspecified	Assassination/ Aggravated Assault
22	Iraq	1986 through 1996 and intermittently	Solyemaniyeh, or Baghdad, or Kurdish regions of Iraq	Assassination/ Attack with Bombs and Grenade Launchers
3	Italy	1989–1993 and intermittently	Rome	Assassination/ Aggravated Assault
1	Netherlands	1992	Unspecified	Assassination Attempt
16	Pakistan	1982 through 1996 and intermittently	Karachi and unspecified	Assassination/ Aggravated Assault
5	Philippines	1982–1983	Manila	Assassination/ Aggravated Assault
6	Sweden	1981 through 1993 and intermittently	Stockholm and unspecified	Aggravated Assault
14	Turkey	1984 through 1996 and intermittently	Istanbul, Ankara, and unspecified	Assassination/ Aggravated Assault and Kidnapping
4	United Kingdom	1986–1987	London and unspecified	Assassination/ Bomb Injury
3	United States	1981 through 1992 and intermittently	New Jersey, Oklahoma, and Dallas	Assassination/ Aggravated Assault

Source: Adapted from PMOI's Web site: http://www.iran-e-azad.org

CONTEMPORARY CRIME CONTROL

To appreciate the complexity of contemporary crime control in Iran, one must discuss it in relationship to the ongoing legal developments that occurred both before and after the Islamic Revolution of 1979. One must also locate the various crime control strategies within the processes of modernization. Serious modernization began under the rule of Reza Shah Pahlavi (r. 1925–1941) and was fine-tuned under the rule of his son, Muhammad Reza Shah Pahlavi (r. 1941–1979).

Shah Reforms in Courts, Police, and Corrections

In the late 1920s and early 1930s, Reza Shah initiated a number of reforms in Iran's criminal justice system. These reforms required changes in the Iranian Constitution of 1906, which was modified in 1925, 1949, 1957, and 1967. Under the two Pahlavi Shahs, three types of modern laws and courts were recognized in the judiciary. These were civil, criminal, and administrative laws/courts.

The inspiration for the type of modern civil law and courts came from the French system. The civil cases were put under the jurisdiction of District Courts presided by magistrates. Unless the competence of the court was questioned, the judgments of the civil courts could be appealed to the Civil Chamber of the Courts of Appeal, sitting in each principal town of a department. Appeals from these two courts were heard before a Civil Chamber of the Court of Cassation. This was but a single court for the whole country sitting in the capital at the Law Courts in Tehran. After 1965, a kind of small claims courts was institutionalized. Called the Houses of Equities (khanehay-e Insaf), these tribunals were scattered all over the rural areas of the country in order to ameliorate the plight of small claims.

The modernization of the criminal laws and courts were also inspired by the French model whereby criminal cases were referred to "ordinary" and "special" bodies (e.g., courts, tribunals, councils), depending on the nature of the offense under consideration. The ordinary courts were composed of the Police Courts, Houses of Equity, Arbitration Councils, Criminal Courts, and Assize Courts. The special courts were composed of the Military Tribunals, Juvenile Courts, the Criminal Court of Governmental Officials, and Financial Court. As their titles indicate, these courts followed specified substantive and procedural functions, necessitating, at the same time, new and modern ways of categorizing crime and criminal court procedure.

Before modernization, Iranian cities and villages had a combined system of night watches and hue and cries that watched the realm for fire and rogue elements. This system was enhanced by the enforcement of the King's Peace in the realm, which consisted of a network of military garrisons, security-conscious governors, and a system of regional law enforcement that dealt almost exclusively with emergencies, riots, and rebellions, rather than with crime control.

In the early 1930s, a national police force (Plois wa Sharban-ye Kull-e Keshvar) was introduced in Iran. Next to a professional and standing modern army, the police became the beneficiaries of Reza Shah's modernization efforts, as these were extended toward the establishment of municipal police units (Shahrebani) and a precinct- (*kalantari*) style system of enforcing law within each municipality (*shahrdari*). The officers had military ranks, were uniformed, and armed with baton, pistol, and identifying badge numbers.

Modernization efforts also extended to building modern correctional facilities, beginning with Reza Shah and continuing with his son, Muhammad. Modern prisons and detention centers were built throughout the country. Under Muhammad, such modern prisons as Qasr, Evin, and Gohardasht were added to the old ones. The newer prisons were known as Nedamatgah, which is equivalent to a penitentiary reflecting a more humane approach to penology.

In addition to the Municipal Police (Sharebani), Iran's internal as well as provincial security was maintained through the Gendarmerie, regular army, and secret police. The secret police, known as the State Organization of Security and Intelligence (Sazman-e Amniyat wa Ettela'at-e Keshvar [SAVAK]), was to gradually gain tremendous power to detain, arrest, imprison, torture, and execute almost any person deemed to constitute a threat to the state or to the dictatorial powers of the Shah. In effect, by the 1970s SAVAK was almost like a secret state within the official state. It was organized into Eight Departments (Edareh-e Kul), with its branches in provincial towns, and consisted of about 9,000 personnel. On paper, SAVAK was to answer to the Office of the Prime Minister, but the head of SAVAK, usually a military general, reported directly to the Shah and carried out his wishes and commands as orders.

Islamization of Crime Control

The Islamic Revolution of 1979 overturned the Iranian Constitution of 1906 and replaced it with the Constitution of the Islamic Republic of Iran. The battle cry of the Ayatollah Khomeini and his partisans was that Iran, under the constitutional monarchy, had become a corrupt Western entity alien to Islam. By returning to Islam's core values, Iran was to be reshaped into a moral and crime-free society. The main crime control strategy was to "re-Islamize" Iran's informal and formal mechanisms of control, from the institutions of the family, education, and culture to the institutions of law, adjudication, and punishment.

The new constitution calls for an independent judiciary whose Islamic duty is to disseminate justice and to safeguard individual rights and freedoms. The Islamic court system (Mahakem-e Shar'i) of today is based upon a return to the traditional Islamic Shari'ah system. It came into being following two important acts. In August 1982, the Supreme Judicial Council (Iran's Supreme Court) abolished the laws (and therefore the courts) passed under the Shah. All the previous secular laws were declared null and void because they were not based on Islamic norms, concepts, and traditions. In October of the same year, the modern courts were abolished altogether. This has created much confusion and chaos in the judiciary for the past 18 years as the monopolization of judicial power remains in the hands of the Shi'i cleric in Iran. These courts operate according to different conceptualizations of crime, causation, prevention, investigation, and punishment.

In effect, the new Islamic regime reinstitutionalized the categories of crime and punishment according to the Islamic model of medieval Iran. Under the monarchy, law-violating behavior was categorized as (1) crime (*jenayat*), (2) misdemeanor (*jonheh*), or (3) wrong/tort (*khalaf*). This was thought to be modern as it categorized lawbreaking behavior against a set of secular rules and standards rather than according to categories of sin (Sane'i, 1992).

By contrast, under the new Islamic criminal justice system, law-violating behavior is categorized by behaviors that (1) violate God's rights (*haq-e elahi*), (2) violate the general populace's rights (*haq al-nass*), and (3) violate the public's rights. There is also a distinction made between those crimes that are "pardonable" (*qabel-e gozasht*) and those crimes that are "unpardonable" (*qeyr-e qabele gozasht*). Such a distinction is virtually nonexistent in other criminal justice systems. Crimes against God, for example, are not pardonable. And under the interpretation of the current regime, these include any type of antistate, anti-Islamic, or revolutionary leadership activities. The perpetrators of these types of "crimes" are branded as Muharib (one who wages war against God). These types of crimes receive the harshest capital punishments such as public hanging, beheading, and stoning to death.

Not only are there special and clandestine institutions for incarcerating these offenders, but after the Islamic Revolution SAVAK was purged of some of its more notorious elements and refurbished as the ministry of VEVAK (Vezarat-e Ettela' wa Amniyat-e Keshvar). VEVAK has been implicated in secret detention, imprisonment, and torture, as well as in the executions of tens of thousands of Iranian dissidents, inside and outside of Iran, as already discussed.

Under the monarchy, punishment categories were also based on Western and secular rationales. At the same time, Iran adhered both then and now to a number of United Nations' protocols and conventions against cruel and unusual punishments. Under the Islamic regime, it is argued that Islam has the highest regard for human dignity in punishment. Under the present criminal justice system, however, four types of medieval punishments have been institutionalized. These are (1) the *hudud* (boundaries), (2) the *qisad* (*lex talionis*), (3) the *diyyat* (blood money), and (4) the *t'a zirat* (corporal) punishments.

Hudud (s. *hadd*) emanate from the Koran and pertain to those crimes for which *hadd* is prescribed in the Koran. These include adultery (*zina*), male homosexuality (*lavat*), female homosexuality (*musahiqah*), providing means and ways for adultery and sodomy (*qavvadi*), foul language against one's female relatives (*qazaf*), drinking alcoholic beverages (*maskar*), waging war against God (*muharbeh*), spreading corruption on earth (*afasd fi al-arz*), and thievery (*sirqat*). The punishment for these crimes differs in severity, ranging from public flogging (*jild*) for drinking alcoholic beverages to stoning to death for adultery to beheading for male homosexuality to public flogging for female homosexuality.

Qisas is, again, a Koranic term and pertains to those capital crimes for which capital or retributory-compensatory punishments apply. *Qisas* is divided into two categories: murder-related retribution (*qisas-e nafs*) and organ-related retribution (*qisad-e 'uzv*). The punishment for these types of crimes follows a definite biblical perspective of "a tooth for a tooth, an eye for an eye, and a life for a life." However, one's religious affiliation and one's sex are taken into consideration. For example, a Shi'i Muslim male's punishment is less severe than the punishment of non-Muslim males for the same crime. In fact, based on a distinct medieval practice in various Islamic societies, a Muslim male cannot be executed if he murders a non-Muslim male. Sexist distinctions are also made. Whether Muslim or non-Muslim, a female's blood money is valued as half of a male's blood money. Moreover, a female murderer can be executed without any compensation for her blood, but a male murderer's blood has to be compensated by the victim's survivors before he can be executed. Fathers, according to a medievalist interpretation of the Shari'ah, are legally allowed to commit acts of infanticide without any repercussion.

The *diyyats* are crimes for which monetary-compensatory punishments apply. They pertain to any injury that one may inflict (intentionally or otherwise) to different organs of a plaintiff. There are 30 such categories in the Islamic Republic's criminal justice system (i.e., hair, eye, nose, ear, lips, tongue, tooth, neck, jaws, arms and legs, nails, spinal cord, and so on). When assessing the blood money for these body parts, again, discriminatory practices based on gender and religious categories apply. Men's organs are valued more than women's organs.

The *t'azirats* are composed of a wide range of crimes from street crimes to political crimes, including counterfeiting, theft of government documents, slandering the revolutionary Islamic political figures and state leadership, antisocial activities, flight from prisons, and government personnel's law-violating behaviors. The punishments range from public flogging to imprisonment and fines or a combination of the two. As a general rule, petty crimes are dealt with quite harshly and usually in the most degrading manner such as public rituals of defaming the convict, putting a rope on the neck of the convict and walking him or her in public, public lashings, and so on. Crimes by high public officials, which have reached an unprecedented dimension in recent years, however, are dealt with primarily in the form of fines.

FUTURE OF CRIME AND CRIME CONTROL

Under the present Islamic criminal justice system in Iran, offenses are conceived primarily as sin, with punishment as retribution-in-kind. In practice, the present Islamic system of law, justice, and punishment has proven its corruptive and overcriminalization impacts because the system not only utilizes archaic and contradictory notions of crime, but it follows an arbitrary system of law enforcement in which any form of dissent can be considered a crime, subject to the most severe punishments imaginable. The fact that the Islamic regime has actively pursued Iranian dissidents abroad to eliminate them provides some indication of its treatment of dissent at home. Iranian authorities are on record that it is their Islamically prescribed duty to eradicate the opponents of the regime wherever possible.

In addition, in spite of the fact that the ideal of an Islamic justice system is equity in the application of law and punishment, its judiciary (and legal code) deals quite harshly with petty crimes, whereas white-collar crimes are dealt with in the most lame manner (not unlike most Western systems of criminal justice that idealize due process and equal protection while the "rich get richer and the poor get prison," as Jeffrey Reiman has so elegantly put it). As a result, the Islamic regime of the Ayatollah Ruholla Khomeini has witnessed a lot of social and political resistance to its notions of crime and justice, a struggle that has, in turn, led to the Islamic regime's consistent violations of human rights. As Amnesty International (1990) pointed out a decade ago, in relation to the execution of thousands of alleged drug traffickers and other criminals, the procedures before the Islamic Revolutionary Courts in Iran fall short of international standards for a fair trial. Hopefully, the worst of these abuses and political crimes are in Iran's recent past and not the immediate and distant futures.

After the Islamic Revolution, attempts to re-Islamize the criminal justice procedures and the philosophy and punishment of crime and crime control have proven themselves to be grossly criminogenic, because these arcane norms and concepts of law, crime, and justice have not been employed in light of the contemporary social, political, economic, and cultural realities of Iran. Under an Islamic form of government, Iran has not become a crime-free society as the Constitution of the Islamic Republic had wished and envisaged. On the contrary, Iran has become a society with a young, oppressed, and frustrated population who sees its social and economic deprivation in a society that is rich in history, culture, and economic resources as an excuse for becoming a crime-infested country. Unless these Islamic trends are reversed, Iran will suffer more in this century from an already rising cycle of crime, poverty, and social injustice.

REFERENCES

Adler, Freda. 1983. *Nations Not Obsessed with Crime.* Littleton, CO: Fred B. Roth-
man and Company.

Agance Farance Press Report. 1994. February 26. Cited from Internet: http://
www.Iran-e-Azad.org.

Amnesty International (AI). 1989. "Iran." In *Amnesty International: The 1989 Report on Human Rights around the World.* London: Amnesty International
Publications.

———. 1990. "Iran." In *Amnesty International: The 1990 Report on Human Rights
Around the World.* London: Amnesty International Publications.

———. 1994. "Iran." In *Amnesty International: 1994 Report on Human Rights
Around the World.* London: Amnesty International Publications.

Fazlur Rahman. 1979. *Islam.* Chicago: University of Chicago Press.

Iran. 1995. Cited from Internet: http://www.teachersoft.com/Library/ref/atlas/
mideast/ir.htm

Kusha, Hamid R. 1998. "Revisiting the Islamic Shariah Law in Deterring Criminality:
Is There a Lesson for Western Criminology?" *Crime and Justice International*
14, 10: 9, 10, 24–26.

Metz, Helen Chapin I. 1988. *Iran: A Country Study.* Washington, DC: Federal
Research Division of the Library of Congress.

People's Mojahedin Organization of Iran (PMOI). 1986. *List of Names and Particulars of 12,028 Victims of the Khomeini Regime's Executions.* N.p.: PMOI
Publications.

Reuter. 1994. February 1. Cited from Internet: http://www.Iran-e Azad.org

Sane'i, Parviz. 1992. *Hoquq-e Jaza-ye 'Umumi* (Criminal law). Tehran: Ganjeh Da-
nesh.

Souryal, Sam. 1988. "The Role of Shariah Law in Deterring Criminality in Saudi
Arabia." *International Journal of Comparative and Applied Criminal Justice*
12, 1: 1–25.

7

NAVAJO NATION
(Posttraditional Nation-State)

Jon'a F. Meyer and James Zion

PROFILE OF NAVAJO NATION

With 250,000 citizens within 25,000 square miles in three states (Arizona, New Mexico, and Utah), the Navajo Nation is the largest Native American tribe in terms of both population and land base. Although a large number of Navajos live in off-reservation communities bordering their tribal lands, the 143,405 Navajo reservation residents figure is still much higher than the 11,812 Sioux who live on the second largest reservation (Bureau of the Census, 1993: 7). The current economic situation is bleak, as the U.S. Census reports that even among Native American tribes the Navajo Nation is economically substandard. A high percentage of people living in poverty (57.8 percent), a high unemployment rate (30 percent), and a low per capita income ($3,735) characterize the reservation (Bureau of the Census, 1993: 9–10). When compared to figures for the United States as a whole (living in poverty: 15.1 percent, unemployment: 6 percent, per capita income: $15,777), it is clear that the average Navajo is not participating in the American dream.

Sources of income on the reservation still include tourism and traditional arts and crafts: rug weaving, jewelry making, carving, and other folk arts. A number of traditional Navajos continue to tend sheep herds, providing mutton and wool, although herding now has more "symbolic importance" than practical value as a national industry (Lieder, 1993: 29). About one fourth of Navajos are supported by general assistance and welfare payments (Bailey and Bailey, 1986: 261).

Employment, when it can be found, tends to be inadequate. Those who live in the rural areas have little or no access to work. Even in the larger reservation communities, part-time and seasonal work are common. By far, the largest source of full-time careers is the government, including occupations tied to the Navajo Nation's profitable leases to private companies for rights to mine the reservation's vast natural resources (e.g., oil, gas, uranium, and coal). The *Dine'* preference law states that Navajos must be hired over similarly qualified non-Navajos, but there are still many *Bilagaanaa* (non-Indian outsiders) working on the reservation because they bring skills or certifications that are hard to find on tribal lands.

The Navajo political system has evolved into a hybrid of the traditional as well as quasi-traditional and the imposed elements of the U.S. federal government. Navajo culture is strongly based in accommodation, both internal and external. Early Navajo governance focused on consensus and an absence of intimidation. Their peace leaders were elected and had no coercive power over others (Wilkins, 1987). These leaders, *naat'aanii*, were selected for their wisdom, ability to keep the peace, and planning ability. Navajo ancient history (twelfth to sixteenth centuries) also demonstrates their overall flexibility as well as their ability to accommodate other cultural institutions, such as the way the Navajos adapted and incorporated the rich social and political heritages of their neighbors in the Southwest, namely, the Pueblos and the Spanish.

Harmony (*hozho'*) and *k'e* (a difficult word to translate into English, but it connotes the cement that is supposed to hold Navajo society together) were both important institutions to Navajos, referring to peace within oneself, among and between families, and with other tribes and nations. Navajos consider harmonious reciprocal relations to be the pinnacle to which all people should aspire and equate it with a metaphysical beauty that cannot exist otherwise. As an illustration of the significance of *hozho'* and *k'e*, a common Navajo salutation is: "Walk in beauty."

HISTORICAL PERSPECTIVE ON CRIME AND CRIME CONTROL

Crime certainly existed among the tribe before the Navajo Wars and their confinement at Bosque Redondo (i.e., Fort Sumner) in 1864, but anthropological and historical data show that offenders were able to regain status within the community through sincere apologies and making reparations to their victims. Beginning in 1864, the Navajo justice system was transformed into one that they resisted. Incarceration was introduced as a correctional approach by the U.S. federal government. Like many Native American nations, Navajos have great contempt for the promise of incarceration as a solution to their crime problems (Feinman, 1986; Ross, 1996).

Following their victory in the Navajo Wars, the U.S. Army set about designing the Navajo Nation's first federally recognized government in 1865. The system was simple and reflected the military's interests in controlling Navajo citizens. Navajos were divided into 12 villages, each with a "chief" appointed by the U.S. Army and with a "sub-chief" appointed for every hundred citizens. A jurylike process was established in which the 12 appointed "chiefs" served as quasi-jurors for serious crimes, and the U.S. Army post commander served as the judge.

Who controlled crime on the reservation was a major concern when the federal government drew up the Treaty of Bosque Redondo, which was signed by the Navajo Nation in 1868. Rather than allow the tribe to implement its own justice policies, the treaty obligated Navajos to "deliver up" to federal authorities tribal members who committed crimes (Navajo Tribe, 1868/1968, Article 1). This early strategy was but a harbinger of things to come.

At first, Native American tribes were granted some discretion in their political governance. Specifically, until 1922, when the Navajo Tribal Council form of political structure was introduced as a means of facilitating leasing agreements with private oil and gas companies (Wilkins, 1987), Navajos continued to cling to their traditional system of leadership, even during those years in which they were under the control of a U.S. Department of Interior agent assigned to supervise the tribe. The early Tribal Councils consisted of delegates from each of the five Navajo agencies. While the Council form of government has failed to fit Navajo expectations, it has survived nevertheless to the present, subject to political and legal debate as to the meanings of various tribal resolutions, for example.

Following the 1868 Treaty, Navajos were relatively free and able to control their fates with only a modicum of oversight and interference from the federal government. This control included the criminal justice system. However, in 1885, the Major Crimes Act (18 U.S.C., Section 1153) transferred prosecutorial power from the tribes to the federal government for 7 felonies (murder, manslaughter, rape, assault with the intent to kill, arson, burglary, and larceny). Currently, that number has been expanded to 13 crimes.

PUBLIC PERCEPTION OF CRIME AND CRIME CONTROL

Public perceptions of crime and crime control have had less to do with what the Navajos or other Native American tribal persons have thought and more to do with what U.S. government policy has been about in relation to questions of assimilation and integration. Early assimilationist policy makers sought to "Americanize" Native Americans and to transform them into socially accepted (and acceptable) citizens, often through an educational system of boarding schools. At their best, boarding schools deprived children of contact with their families in the name of creating "honorable, useful, happy citizens" who would leave their "paltry reservations" and integrate fully into mainstream American society (Morgan, 1889: 94–96). At their worst, boarding schools separated entire cultures from their language, traditions, and belief systems, substituting English and Christianity as ways of "civilizing" Native Americans. These assimilationist policies also sent Native American children to live with white families.

The enforcement of these unpopular policies by the Navajo police contributed to the Navajo's belief or perception that the police worked only or primarily for white concerns (Phillips, 1954). On the other hand, more "progressive" folk sought an integration based on the incorporation of traditional and European practices. Earlier, for example, several federally sponsored research teams had lauded the unintended survival of Navajo traditional justice elements within the European model. The well-known Meriam (1928) report presented an overall look at Native American tribal life, including the depressing effects of forced assimilation, and concluded that Native Americans would assimilate in due time and should not be rushed into doing so. Subsequent reports of the presence of Navajo traditional practices of justice on the reservations were also favorably reviewed by the Phelps-Stokes Fund in 1939 and by Boyden and Miller in 1942.

However, the spirit of integration gave way to assimilation during the "termination era," 1945–1961, when the federal government attempted to eliminate Native American tribes or transfer responsibility for them to the states in which they were located (Deloria and Lytle, 1983). One of the realities of the termination era was the passage of Public Law 280, which gave 5 states control of the reservation justice systems within their borders. Although Arizona, New Mexico, and Utah were not included on the list of 5, Arizona was included on a list of 10 "optional" states that in terms of tribal versus state control had the Navajo running scared.

To further fuel the Navajos' fear of "losing control" of their justice system and as a means of catalyzing their resistance, an Arizona politician mistakenly argued that Public Law 280 gave his state the authority to assume control of the Navajo courts simply by passing a statute. In 1959, in an attempt to stave off a potential takeover, the Navajo created the Courts of the Navajo Nation, essentially mirroring the neighborhood state courts so that it would be difficult for any state to condemn their policies. By the 1980s, perceptions had come full circle to the effect that the Navajo Supreme Court Chief Justice Nelson McCabe decided it was time to integrate traditional Navajo law back into the Navajo court system. Over time, a nonunified approach to crime and justice on the Navajo reservation has evolved from these "mixed" policies of social control.

CONTEMPORARY CRIME

Despite the Major Crimes Act, statistics maintained by the Navajo Nation courts reveal that they are handling contemporary felonies in a misdemeanor system. This means that they are unable to protect the public from those who pose a serious risk to others or who need intensive therapeutic interventions (e.g., sex offender counseling). The majority of offenses processed through the courts are assaults, in particular those that occur within families. For example, the domestic violence rate for the first nine months of 1998 was 3,100 per 100,000 population. Moreover, even though possession and consumption of alcohol are illegal on the reservation, the second most prevalent offense is driving under the influence. Third are crimes against families, including sex crimes against children. Finally come offenses against the public order, including public intoxication and disorderly conduct (e.g., fighting at *N'daa* [traditional Squaw Dances] and high school dances).

Court caseloads provide a vivid picture not only of the strong role that alcohol plays in the criminality on the reservation but of related trends noted by court personnel. For example, family violence is at an all-time high, and there has been a large increase in violence generally, including random violence where victims are beaten to death for apparently little reason. This trend has been attributed to a growing disillusionment by Navajos and to the recent increases in gang membership.

The lack of opportunities, coupled with a general marginalization of Native American youth, has contributed to a literal explosion in gang membership. Since 1994, tribal gangs have more than doubled in membership, and this growth has been accompanied by a parallel increase in violent crimes on Indian reservations (Brasher, 1997). These increases differ notably from nationwide decreases in violence over the past five years. The gang problem is particularly significant on the Navajo reservation, which has 75 active gangs (Navajo Nation, 1997). Navajo gang members make repeated appearances on the tribal court docket; more than half of the cases processed through the Navajo Nation Family Courts in 1993 were gang-related (Navajo Nation, 1997). In the fiscal year 1997, assaults became the most prevalent type of offense, accounting for one fourth of the criminal docket (Navajo Nation, 1997). Gangs have brought the visual indicators of graffiti and vandalism as well as the violence that typically accompanies them (e.g., knife and gunfights and drive-by shootings).

Research conducted by the Navajo Judicial Branch has found that most tribal gang members are in their teens and are from single-parent families or those with a history of domestic violence. The gangs appear to have begun in the off-reservation cities such as Albuquerque, New Mexico, and Phoenix, Arizona, then crept into the urban tribal county seats (e.g., Window Rock, Fort Defiance, and Chine). Navajos have been members of Hispanic gangs in off-reservation communities for some time now, and gang activity has finally spread to the reservation. Gangs are now one of the most serious crime problems faced by the Navajo Nation.

Tribal suicide and crime rates are high when compared to off-reservation areas, and the causes are the subject of much discussion on and off the reservation. Three factors have been linked to Navajo crime: (1) the negative effects of Indian education policies; (2) the "Long Walk" (the marching, at gunpoint, of Navajos to their internment at Bosque Redondo, during which one fourth of Navajos died or were killed) and their overall experiences at Bosque Redondo, which has been compared to a reeducation camp; and (3) the explosion of gang membership among communities that have been unprepared to deal with it.

CONTEMPORARY CRIME CONTROL

Because of its size, the Navajo Nation has been able to operate its own criminal justice system, including police force, court system, and corrections programs. While it depends on the U.S. federal government for funding to operate its justice system, the day-to-day concerns belong to the tribe. Among other things, they are able to enact laws covering their reservation, allocate resources to support those laws, develop and implement programming, and hire and fire personnel.

At the same time, Navajos (by no means unique among tribal justice systems) have only limited jurisdiction over a number of misdemeanors and civil cases (Indian Civil Rights Act, 25 U.S.C., Section 1302). All other crimes fall under the purview of the federal government. However, U.S. attorneys decline to prosecute in more than 75 percent of reported felonies, including a substantial portion of the tribe's homicides (Feinman, 1986: 196). This situation compels the tribe uniquely to levy assorted misdemeanor charges for alleged felonies, if any kind of prosecution is to occur. Moreover, in some instances, the state in which the reservation is located has jurisdiction over the offense.

Recently, the states have become more aggressive in their prosecution of cases, and given the 1997 ruling in *Strate v. A-1 Contractors*, the states are expected to attempt to exercise criminal jurisdiction over non-Indians for crimes committed on highway rights-of-way areas and, following the 1998 ruling in *Alaska v. Native Village of Venetie Tribal Government* decision, on fee simple lands on and near reservations. Altogether, this creates a confusing tangle of jurisdictional realities in which cases are pursued based on (1) where the offense took place (tribal lands fall generally under the jurisdiction of the Navajo courts, off-reservation land do not); (2) tribal identity (non-Indians and Native Americans from other tribes cannot be tried by the Navajo tribal court system even for offenses occurring on Navajo lands); and (3) the type of offense (Navajos cannot try cases that have been reserved by federal authorities). This justice puzzle also leads to creative charging, in which the tribal courts may prosecute someone for a lesser offense in order to retain jurisdiction (e.g., an offense may be charged as a misdemeanor to keep it in the tribal courts versus the federal courts) or to assert jurisdiction (e.g., an individual may be charged in a tribal court with possession of a firearm used in a shooting in addition to the federal homicide charges he or she might face).

Police

As a tribe, Navajos were without a formal police force until 1872. Before European contact, traditional peacemakers resolved conflicts between tribal members, but there was no police force per se. Instead, everyone policed one another in an informal system of social control, as was typical among traditional peoples (Arthur and Marenin, 1996; T. Austin, 1996; Meyer, 1998).

Following the internment at Bosque Redondo, the U.S. Army assumed the responsibility for policing, a task they found difficult to perform. After many requests by the military for a police force that relied on the use of Navajos (Jones, 1966), Manuelito, 1 of the 12 head chiefs and principal signers of the treaty, became the first chief of police in charge of 130 patrolmen. In addition to their law enforcement duties, they became roving peacemakers.

By all accounts, the first tribal police officers were effective in reducing thefts and returning stolen livestock to its rightful owners (Jones, 1966; Locke, 1992). In addition to these typical law enforcement duties, however, the police became responsible for the enforcement of decidedly unpopular policies, in particular ensuring that Navajo children attended white boarding schools (Hagan, 1966; Vincenti et al., 1972; Locke, 1992). During the Great Depression, in response to a reduced market for meat products, the Navajo police were called in to enforce the greatly detested Livestock Reduction Program, which forced Navajos to give up or significantly decrease their beloved sheep herds (Phelps-Stokes Fund, 1939; White, 1983).

It is likely that these tasks and other extralegal activities such as attempts to acculturate their fellow reservation residents, to adopt white dress and styles, and to eschew polygamy and other native "vices," played a strong role in the public's belief that the police worked for white concerns of assimilation (Phillips, 1954; Hagan, 1961). Tribal police were also used as agents of rumor to spread "propaganda about the happy situation" on their reservations (Debo, 1989). On top of this, Navajo police officers were also performing such extralegal duties as maintaining the government's buildings and grounds, cleaning ditches, and doing other public works and construction.

In 1959, after nearly a century of being policed by the federal government, the Navajo Nation took over the administration of the force and established the contemporary tribal organization of policing, the Navajo Department of Public Safety (NDPS) (Davis, 1959; Vincenti et al., 1972). The NDPS operates in six districts and is headquartered in Window Rock, Arizona, the Navajo capital. Its officers are comparable to other U.S. police except that they lack technical jurisdiction over serious crimes over which only the federal government has authority.

Nevertheless, despite their lack of jurisdiction, the Navajo police are still the first to be called, and they conduct the initial investigations before turning the crime over to the federal government (Feinman, 1986). Moreover, as a part of the "Operation Safe Trails" program, a special task force of Navajo police have been trained by and work with the Federal Bureau of Investigation (FBI) in the investigation of violent crimes. In many ways the Navajo police have long been considered forerunners among tribal police departments. They have been credited with serving as a model for other tribal departments (Jones, 1966). In order to deal with complex jurisdictional issues associated with tribal policing and the powers of arrest, for example, the Navajo police have entered into cross-deputization agreements with neighboring police agencies (Prassel, 1972).

Some have described the Navajo police as a modern force (Hagan, 1966). However, according to annual reports filed by the Indian agents in charge of the reservation, the Navajo police have consistently been underfunded. Today, there is less than one NDPS officer for every 1,000 tribal members, and calls by police for "backup" assistance average about one per hour (Avery, 1997).

Courts

Traditionally, Navajos did not have a formal court system, preferring to rely on the use of peacemakers who lectured offenders about the harm they had caused and their role in society before coordinating reconciliation of the offender and victim. This system was not maintained by the federal government, which established the Courts of Indian Offenses in 1892. Navajos viewed the new courts as foreign tribunals that judged their citizens based on offenses they could not understand and chose not to support (Yazzie and Zion, 1996).

Like a number of other tribes (Mansfield, 1993), Navajos continued to utilize their customary justice practices under the rubric of the European system. The tribe elected as judges those individuals who they felt would make good mediators (Boyden and Miller, 1942), and some cases were deliberately mediated informally at the victims' request. For example, Indian court judges were, in effect, practicing a customary restitution model within a punitive-oriented European model.

In the 1980s, under Navajo Supreme Court Chief Justice McCabe's directive to integrate traditional law into the contemporary tribal court system, the Navajo common law came to be officially recognized and would be the controlling law. This began the arduous task of documenting the tribe's common law principles and discovering ways to implement them into legal practice. In fact, a research team was assigned to interview elders and to closely examine traditional legends and songs for clues of Navajo common law.

One of the most exciting innovations under McCabe's initiative was the design and implementation of the Peacemaker Court in 1982. This program was designed to bring tradition back into the Navajo justice system. In peacemaking, disputants ask a *naat'aanii* (a respected elder or leader who is often related to at least one of the parties) to hear their case and to help them prepare an appropriate resolution to assist both of them in their return to harmony (Tso, 1992; R. D. Austin, 1993; Bluehouse and Zion, 1993; Zion and Zion, 1993).

Some cases are brought directly by citizens who hope that a *naat'aanii*/peacemaker can help them restore their family or neighborly relationships with those who have harmed them. Some of these harms include criminal cases that have been diverted from the courts. If, for example, the parties involved are able to resolve their differences and work out a plan agreeable to both during peacemaking, then the Navajo Nation's prosecutor's office will dismiss charges, as it has done in a number of cases, especially domestic violence situations. This diversion policy provides a regular source of cases to the peacemaker program and demonstrates the endorsement provided by criminal justice decision makers to the peacemaking program. Through the peacemaking process, the victim and offender are reconciled, the offender is provided with ways to prevent further harm, and the community is returned to balance by knowing that the injury has been repaired.

Although it was formally instituted in 1982, the Peacemaker Court did not serve many clients, due in part to the slow speed at which word of new programs travels on the reservation, especially to the more rural districts. To further complicate matters, many Navajos were reluctant to try the new program owing to distrust of the criminal justice system in general. To counteract the low rate of use, the Navajo judiciary branch secured the funds to hire a full-time coordinator in 1991, who educates the public by attending chapter meetings and briefing justice system personnel about the program and its goals, and who retains and certifies the peacemakers in court processes. The coordinator's efforts appear to have made a difference. In 1991, just 46 cases were handled through peacemaking. By 1997, nearly 3,000 peacemaking cases were handled in the seven tribal court districts.

Under the direction of Chief Justice Robert Yazzie, the courts are presently a hotbed of change. Several new programs are in progress, including a merger between peacemaking and probation that has begun to incorporate peacemaking elements into the corrections branch of the criminal justice system. This merger has been funded by a Justice Department drug court grant. The courts are also completing a bench book on domestic violence. Finally, the Navajo Nation Council recently passed the Local Governance

Act to give the individual tribal chapters control over peacemaking. This move is expected to return to the chapters the ability to resolve their own conflicts.

FUTURE OF CRIME AND CRIME CONTROL

Historically, due to their colonization experiences, Native Americans can be considered somewhat culturally schizophrenic. They have adapted to and sometimes thrive in the white world while still wholeheartedly embracing their cultural roots, which are sometimes at complete odds with white culture. The focus on material acquisition, for example, has not been valued among traditional Navajos but is a stronghold Euro-American value. Likewise, the value assigned by European Americans to the physical ownership of songs and ceremonies tends to be nonexistent, whereas Navajos consider them to be true properties that are owned and can be passed down from generation to generation. With modernization, many of the traditional values have been forgotten by the more assimilated younger people, who no longer feel the continued need to live in *k'e*. Still, it appears that these values can be reawakened through peacemaking and follow-up, as has been the case.

At present, Navajo crime control policy cannot be considered a unified approach, and it only sporadically embraces their common law ideals. Individual programs have been instituted, but they are not yet linked into a comprehensible whole. It is hoped that this will come with time, as the Nation completes its reworking of its justice system and after the U.S. Department of Justice adopts a funding program that is less piecemeal in orientation (presently, the government funds only "demonstration" projects rather than providing for infrastructure-based needs). As a result, the present type of funding has sponsored a large number of Navajo Nation projects. However, even the successful programs have not been able to sustain themselves after the federal monies have been exhausted.

In the near future, these kinds of serious budgetary issues serve to prevent any major overhauls from taking place. Change will be slow to come, and the dreams of some kind of integrated crime control policy seem like years away. At the most rudimentary levels, the NDPS still suffers from a poor public image and will need to address this before it can successfully deal with crime and disorder on the reservation. Even the Peacemaking Court programs have experienced intense budget cuts and are in the process of setting up nonprofit, tax-exempt corporations that may signal the future of other tribal initiatives as well.

In conclusion, the Navajo Nation has come a long way in their journey to become what they used to be. Based on their successful implementation of traditional peacemaking programs, they are actively seeking new ways to incorporate their common law into other parts of their legal system. This is

no easy task due to the immense changes to the Navajo economic and political systems during the past century. The Nation has found that the way
to deal with their new "monsters" (e.g., violent crime and alcoholism) is
through relying on their traditional methods that have survived more than
a century of concealment.

The next step in crime and crime control is to firmly incorporate peacemaking into all three branches of the criminal justice system. It has been in
place in the courts, and it is currently making inroads into corrections. The
time is also ripe for the Navajo police to look toward elements of peacemaking as a way to settle disputes in the field and to address community
fears and concerns. Such a transformation would be complicated but could
be couched within a larger community-oriented policing approach. Rather
than just keeping the peace, the police could serve as agents of change and
begin to make the peace.

REFERENCES

Alaska v. Native Village of Venetie Tribal Government, No. 96–1577 (1998).

Arthur, J. A., and O. Marenin. 1996. "British Colonization and the Political Development of the Police in Ghana, West Africa." In C. B. Fields and R. H. Moore
(eds.), *Comparative Criminal Justice: Traditional and Nontraditional Systems
of Law and Control.* Prospect Heights, IL: Waveland Press.

Atkins, J.D.C. 1887. *Annual Report of the Commissioner of Indian Affairs.* House
Executive Document no. 1. 50th Cong., 1st sess., serial 2542.

Austin, R. D. 1993. "Freedom, Responsibility, and Duty: ADR and the Navajo
Peacemaker Court." *The Judge's Journal* 32 (Spring): 9–11, 47–48.

Austin, T. 1996. "Banana Justice in Moroland: Peacemaking in Mixed Muslim-
Christian Towns in the Southern Philippines." In C. B. Fields and R. H.
Moore (eds.), *Comparative Criminal Justice: Traditional and Nontraditional
Systems of Law and Control.* Prospect Heights, IL: Waveland Press.

Avery, M. 1997. "Testimony before Departments of Commerce, Justice, and State,
the Judiciary, and Related Agencies Appropriations for 1998." April 24. U.S.
Congressional Record.

Bailey, G. A., and R. G. Bailey. 1986. *A History of the Navajos: The Reservation
Years.* Santa Fe, NM: School of American Research Press.

Bluehouse, P., and J. W. Zion. 1993. "Hozhooji naat'aanii: The Navajo Justice and
Harmony Ceremony." *Mediation Quarterly* 10: 327–37.

Boyden, J. S., and W. E. Miller. 1942. "Report of Survey of Law and Order Conditions of the Navajo Indian Reservation." Unpublished material reproduced
at the National Archives and Records Administration, Washington, DC.

Brasher, P. 1997. "Gangs Spread to Indian Reservations." Associated Press Wire.

Bureau of the Census. 1993. *We, the First Americans.* Washington, DC: U.S. Department of Commerce.

Davis, L. 1959. "Court Reform in the Navajo Nation." *Journal of the American
Judicature Society* 43, 2: 52–55.

Debo, A. 1989. *Geronimo: The Man, His Time, His Place.* 5th ed. Norman: University of Oklahoma Press.

Deloria, V., and C. M. Lytle. 1983. *American Indians, American Justice*. Austin: University of Texas Press.

Feinman, C. 1986. "Police Problems on the Navajo Reservation." *Police Studies* 9: 194–98.

Hagan, W. T. 1961. *American Indians*. Chicago: University of Chicago Press.

———. 1966. *Indian Police and Judges: Experiments in Acculturation and Control*. New Haven, CT: Yale University Press.

Indian Civil Rights Act, 25 U.S.C., Section 1302 (1968, amended 1983).

Jones, O. L. 1966. "The Origins of the Navajo Indian Police 1872–1873." *Arizona and the West* 81: 225–38.

Lieder, M. D. 1993. "Navajo Dispute Resolution and Promissory Obligations: Continuity and Change in the Largest Native American Nation." *American Indian Law Review* 18: 1–71.

Locke, R. F. 1992. *The Book of the Navajo*. 5th ed. Los Angeles: Mankind Publishing Company.

Major Crimes Act, 18 U.S.C., Section 1153 (1885).

Mansfield, E. 1993. "Balance and Harmony: Peacemaking in Coast Salish Tribes of the Pacific Northwest." *Mediation Quarterly* 10: 339–53.

Meriam, L. 1928. *The Problem of Indian Administration*. Baltimore, MD: Johns Hopkins University Press.

Meyer, J. F. 1998. "History Repeats Itself: Restorative Justice in Native American Communities." *Journal of Contemporary Criminal Justice* 14: 42–57.

Morgan, T. J. 1889. *Supplemental Report on Indian Education*. House Executive Document no. 1. 51st Cong., 1st sess., serial 2725.

Navajo Nation. 1997. "Statement by the Navajo Nation before the United States Senate Committee on Indian Affairs and the Senate Judiciary Committee on Juvenile Justice Joint Oversight Hearing Concerning Increased Gang Activity in Indian Communities." September 17. U.S. Congressional Record.

Navajo Tribe. 1968. *Treaty between the United States of America and the Navajo Tribe of Indians: With a Record of the Discussions That Led to Its Signing*. Las Vegas, NV: KC Publications. Reprinted from the original 1868 treaty.

Phelps-Stokes Fund. 1939. *The Navajo Indian Problem*. New York: Author.

Phillips, D. 1954. "Our Abuse." In R. W. Young and W. Morgan (eds.), *Navajo Historical Selections*. Phoenix, AZ: Phoenix Indian School Print Shop.

Prassel, F. R. 1972. *The Western Peace Officer: A Legacy of Law and Order*. Norman: University of Oklahoma Press.

Ross, R. 1996. "Leaving Our White Eyes Behind: The Sentencing of Natives Accused." In M. O. Niellsen and R. A. Silverman (eds.), *Native Americans, Crime, and Justice*. Boulder, CO: Westview Press.

Strate v. A-1 Contractors, 520 U.S. 438 (1997).

Tso, T. 1992. "Moral Principles, Traditions, and Fairness in the Navajo Nation Code of Judical Conduct." *Judicature* 76, 1: 15–21.

Vincenti, D., L. B. Jimson, S. Conn, and M.J.L. Kellogg. 1972. *Dine Bibee Haz'aanii: The Law of the People*. Ramah, NM: Ramah Navajo High School Press.

White, R. 1983. *The Roots of Dependency: Subsistence, Environment, and Social Change among Choctaws, Pawness, and Navajos*. Lincoln: University of Nebraska Press.

Wilkins, D. E. 1987. *Dine Bibeehaz'aanii: A Handbook of Navajo Government.* Tsaile, AZ: Navajo Community College Press.

Yazzie, R., and J. W. Zion. 1996. "Navajo Restorative Justice: The Law of Equality and Justice." In B. Galaway and J. Hudson (eds.), *Restorative Justice: International Perspectives.* Monsey, NY: Criminal Justice Press.

Zion, J. W., and E. B. Zion. 1993. "Hozho' Sokee'—Stay Together: Domestic Violence under Navajo Common Law." *Arizona State Law Journal* 25: 407–26.

8

NETHERLANDS

(Developed Nation-State)

Henk van de Bunt and Ineke Haen Marshall

PROFILE OF THE NETHERLANDS

The Netherlands is a small nation in Western Europe, situated between Germany, Belgium, and the North Sea. With a population of 15.5 million, the Netherlands is one of the most densely populated countries in the world. The Netherlands is a constitutional monarchy. Its political system reflects the historical reality of a population divided on the basis of different religious views, as well as on the basis of secularized liberal thinking. The Dutch political system is not a two-party system, but rather it has a multiparty system. Daily political functioning is, therefore, dependent upon a willingness to cooperate and make compromises—even with people and parties that go against one's own principles and ideas.

Up to the 1970s, Dutch society was actually divided into four "pillars" (Catholic, Protestant, liberal, socialist). Since then, a strong process of desecularization has developed, and "pillarization" is no longer the foundation for ordering political and social relationships. The arrival of migrant groups has further accelerated the process of depillarization.

Over the past decades, the Netherlands has increasingly become a multicultural host country to immigrants. Currently, almost 17 percent of the population is, to use a uniquely Dutch term, "allochtonous" (ethnic minority). The Dutch make a distinction between "autochtonous" (indigenous) and "allochtonous" people: If one's own country of birth or that of at least one of one's parents is not the Netherlands, then one is defined as a member of the allochtonous population. The four largest minority groups are Surinamese, Turkish, Moroccans, and Antillians/Arubans (about 870,000 in 1996). The increase in these four minority groups in absolute terms in the 1990–1996 period was about equal to the growth in the total autochtonous population (Tesser and Veenman, 1997: 16–17).

Despite the depillarization, the political system is still based on the need for coalitions and compromises. It is important to have some sense of the political functioning of the Netherlands in order to understand the often seemingly incomprehensible decisions made about controversial issues such as abortion, prostitution, pornography, euthanasia, and drugs. Characteristic of Dutch life, these controversial and complex issues are often depoliticized by the input of experts. In a sense, the expert has replaced the minister. There are, for example, lawyers, medical doctors, and social scientists who, to a large degree, shape the political discussions on topics like drugs, abortion, and euthanasia.

This is also true for the area of crime control. The development and implementation of crime policy remain dominated by experts. Although the area of crime prevention and crime control has become an important item on the political agenda, there is very little political party-based attention-grabbing discussion and little political debate about the determination of the direction of crime policy. In this respect, crime is not a political issue. Employment in law enforcement is purely professional; that is, people are selected on the basis of education and abilities, not on the basis of political preference. Chiefs of police, judges, and prosecutors are appointed for life.

Another important feature of Dutch society is its relative high level of prosperity. This economic reality, combined with the Dutch philosophy that the state (government) has an obligation to take care of its citizens to the best of its ability, has resulted in a nation with one of the strongest social safety nets in the world. Although employment opportunities have increased over the last several years, there is a relatively high number of people who do not participate in the labor force. There are a fairly high proportion of people who have been declared disabled (unable to work), and the number of women without a job is high by international standards (Wetenschappelijke Raad voor het Regeringsbeleid [WRR], 1996). The benefits and compensation received by those who are in need of it is also generous compared to most other countries. Similarly, provisions for the elderly and others in need of assistance, including persons who are staying in the Netherlands illegally, are relatively quite good.

Up until 1999, Dutch citizens were paying high taxes and receiving many benefits in return. Presently, however, it has become apparent that the generous level of social welfare benefits is becoming too expensive. As a result, the regulations concerning benefits and welfare have become more stringent, refusing the provision of governmental services (i.e., education and health care) to undocumented aliens. Some observers are now worrying that Dutch society is becoming a colder and harder society.

HISTORICAL PERSPECTIVE ON CRIME AND
CRIME CONTROL

The Netherlands has traditionally been a country with a low degree of crime and violence. Until the 1970s, crime and crime control policies were of little interest to the public or to politics. For the most part, there was no questioning of the manner in which the police or the judges responded to crime. In the early 1980s, however, when there was a period of strong increases in registered criminality, crime began to become an important issue on the political agenda. Even then the problem did not become politicized in the sense that governing parties made them into hotly contested or controversial political issues.

In fact, for the most part, a political consensus about the desirable approaches to the problems of crime and crime control has remained a historical staple in the Netherlands. The approaches have involved, on the one hand, increased efforts to prevent the commission of petty crimes, including better cooperation between law enforcement and public administration. On the other hand, improved equipment and technology for the police and judicial apparatus to combat serious, organized crime has become the order of the day. In short, the policy mantra has been prevention of petty crimes and repression of serious crimes.

The broad political consensus about crime policy should not obscure the fact that Dutch people hold a variety of opinions on the subject of punishment. Although these opinions have changed somewhat in the 1970–1996 period, much of the thinking about crime and related matters has not changed for the past quarter of a century. For example, fewer people today agree with the statement that one should try to change rather than punish criminals. Yet, at the same time, a large majority of the Dutch population remains in favor of alternative sentences for offenses such as vandalism, burglary, and welfare fraud (Sociaal Cultureel Planbureau [SCP], 1998). In a similar vein, capital punishment was abolished in the Netherlands a long time ago. In a recent study, however, a slight majority (52 percent) of the respondents were in favor of capital punishment under certain conditions (Van Koppen, 1997). Nevertheless, the bulk of survey research done in the 1970–1996 period indicated that there was no support among the majority of the population for the reintroduction of the death penalty (SCP, 1998).

Where attitudes seem they had changed most in the area of crime control is with the functioning of the police and the criminal justice system in terms of effectiveness. In other words, the once laissez-faire attitudes toward the law enforcement and judicial apparatus have been replaced by a more critical and scrutinizing public. It appears that the indignation of the Dutch people is directed not so much at the offenders but, rather, at the shortcomings of those who try to control them, a response no doubt related to public disclosures of clearance rates, speed of case processing, and other productivity measures that have been spiraling downward for years.

PUBLIC PERCEPTION OF CRIME AND CRIME CONTROL

The contemporary Dutch media devotes extensive and critical coverage to various crime and crime control practices. Attention has particularly focused on those criminal cases involving procedural errors resulting in offenders being released, the acquittals of high-profile defendants, and the early release of inmates because of prison overcrowding. Serious public debate today, for example, also centers around the investigative techniques (i.e., wiretapping, infiltration) used by the Dutch police in the fight against organized crime. Most recently, there has been an increasing concern by the media, politicians, and the public alike concerning the nature and prevalence of violent crime in the Netherlands.

In the 1990s the Netherlands experienced several highly publicized violent episodes that contributed to heightened public sensibility. The public accounting of these incidents of violence also contributed to violence becoming one of the more pressing contemporary social issues. Typically, these violent representations have been characterized as "senseless" violence, because there have not appeared to be "real" reasons for the violence. The public response to these incidents was immediate and intense: In different towns there were peaceful demonstrations against "senseless" violence. The concern over violence could also be heard echoing among the media, politicians, and experts.

Is the sudden concern with violence an exaggerated response of the Dutch public? Is it only a matter of decreasing tolerance of violence? Most likely not. Police statistics and surveys seem to bear out that there is more violence in Dutch society today than some 20, or even 10, years ago. In particular, this "new" violence has manifested itself among youth, frequently in a school setting. Self-report research does indicate that carrying a weapon (knife) is a relatively common occurrence among Dutch youth. In a nationally representative self-report survey conducted in 1996, 21.5 percent of the interviewed youth indicated they had carried a weapon within the last 12 months (Van der Laan, Essers, and Spaans, 1998: 28).

Increased use of weapons is also a concern expressed in a 1998 report published by the Dutch Ministry of Justice (*Violence on the Streets*). Another recent study of three youth gangs documented that—although weapons (knives, guns) *are* often present when gangs commit crimes—the actual *use* of violence remains fairly limited (Van Gemert, 1998). At the same time, the proportion of juveniles among those arrested for robbery and assault had increased in the late 1990s: Three out of every 10 suspects for robbery are minors, and 2 out of 10 suspects for assaults are minors (Central Bureau of Statistics and Research and Documentation Centre [CBS/RDC], 1999).

Moreover, while public perception of violent crime may be up in the Netherlands, comparatively speaking the Dutch are relatively "free" from violence and victimization. For example, homicide, the most serious form of violence, remains a relatively rare occurrence in Dutch society. In 1996, a total of 273 cases of homicide were registered in the Netherlands (Van den Berg, 1998: 19). At the time, the Netherlands occupied a middle position among European countries with regard to per capita number of homicides. The Netherlands also occupied a middle position with regard to registered violent crime in general (Home Office, 1997).

The International Crime Victim Survey data for violent victimization (which does not include homicide) place the Netherlands with a rate of 1.9 percent among the lowest ranks of violent victimization (De Waard, Schreuders, and Meijer, 1998). Only Austria and Northern Ireland respondents reported lower levels of violent victimization to the interviewers. Thus, in spite of the Dutch people's recent preoccupation with violent crime, the average increase in registered violent crime in the Netherlands in recent years (1993–1996) was modest compared to other European countries (De Waard, Schreuders, and Meijer, 1998). Finland, Belgium, Norway, France, Ireland, England and Wales, Portugal, Germany, and Switzerland all show higher increases in reported violent crime than the Netherlands. Italy, Sweden, Greece, Austria, and Denmark show—according to police statistics— lower levels of growth or even decreases (Netherlands Bureau of Statistics, 1997).

Although the chances of becoming a victim of violent crime remain relatively low in the Netherlands, a proportion of the Dutch population does feel unsafe, in particular in the larger cities. In 1997, about 7 percent of the interviewed population often felt unsafe (Geveke and van Dijk, 1997: 50). These feelings varied by gender, age, victimization experience, and city size (larger cities, lower sense of safety). Older people especially expressed an increasing sense of fear of crime. The same sorts of feelings were typically expressed throughout Western Europe. That is, the Dutch people were not more fearful of crime than most other Western Europeans, according to data from the International Crime Victim Survey. Questions, for example, measuring vulnerability to street crime showed that about one in five Dutch respondents felt unsafe walking alone in their neighborhood at night, which was roughly similar to the overall European average (Mayhew and van Dijk, 1997).

CONTEMPORARY CRIME

Judging from police statistics, the crime problem in the Netherlands has grown tremendously over the last three decades. In the period between 1970 and 1994, registered criminality increased from 266,000 offenses to 1.3 million offenses. Taking into account the growth of population during this time, the number of offenses multiplied by a factor of four (SCP, 1998: 2). Until 1984, there was an average annual growth of about 10 percent in the volume of crimes; in 1985, for the first time, there was no increase at all, followed by more or less stable figures until 1990, when a new growth spurt followed (SCP, 1998). In 1994, the volume of registered crimes was higher than ever before in the Netherlands—10,350 per 100,000 inhabitants.

It should be noted that information technology improved the registration capacities of a number of police departments across the country, at least partially accounting for the increase in registered crime in the 1990s (Kester and Junger-Task, 1994). There is no doubt, however, that the volume of registered crime (and hence the workload of the police) has grown significantly in the Netherlands since the end of World War II. But it makes a tremendous difference whether the growth in the total volume of crimes is due to an increase in the number of relatively minor offenses (thefts or minor assaults) or because of a rise in more serious offenses (robberies and homicides). Therefore, the *total* volume of registered crimes does not provide the most useful information about the seriousness of the problem of crime (Netherlands Bureau of Statistics, 1997). Rather, it is more important to examine the trends by the *types* of crime.

The bulk of property crimes in the Netherlands consists of different forms of theft (i.e., simple theft and aggravated theft). Other forms of crimes against property (i.e., receiving, embezzlement, swindling) made up less than 5 percent of all property crimes in 1996. The rate of property crimes per 100,000 inhabitants (ages 12–79) doubled in the period of 1960–1970 and again in the period 1970–1980 (CBS/RDC, 1999). Overall, the total number of property crimes registered by the police increased by more than 60 percent between 1980 and 1996 (from 500,774 to 833,669). However, after the peak year of 1994 (977,260 property crimes), the number of crimes against property decreased by 14 percent between 1994 and 1996. The volume of property crime appears to have been stablized in 1997 around 840,000 (CBS/RDC, 1999).

In view of the rapidly growing police workload, it is not surprising to find that the proportion of property crimes solved by the Dutch police has generally decreased between 1980 and 1996 (Netherlands Bureau of Statistics, 1997). For example, embezzlement had a clearance rate of 69 percent in 1980 and fell to 36 percent in 1996. As expected, there is considerable variation in the proportion of crimes solved by the police, depending on type of crime. Again, data for this time reveal that "receiving" consistently had a clearance rate of over 100 percent, whereas the clearance rate for "simple theft" was in the 15 to 18 percent range.

Registered crimes against the person (i.e., rape, assault, robbery, attempted offenses against life) showed a relatively strong and consistent growth (Netherlands Bureau of Statistics, 1997). The number of violent crimes in 1997 (about 75,000) was three times that of 1960 (25,000) according to the CBS/RDC (1999). The two most common types of violent crimes recorded by the police were assault and robbery. The fastest increase took place in the crime of robbery, which more than tripled between 1980 and 1996, followed by assault, which more than doubled. This category includes both homicides and aggravated assaults with a fatally wounded victim. Generally, the proportion of crimes against the person solved by the police is considerably higher than that of property crime. Nevertheless, in 1980, 6 out of every 10 violent crimes were solved by the police, as compared with 4 out of 10 in 1996 (Netherlands Bureau of Statistics, 1997).

The recent decrease (1994–1997) in property crimes has not occurred with respect to violent crimes. To the contrary, the total number of violent offenses registered by the police in this period increased by almost one third: from 50,300 in 1994 to 66,700 in 1997. In 1990, the rate of violent crime was 4 per 1,000 inhabitants aged 12 to 79; in 1996, the rate had increased to 5 per 1,000 persons (CBS/RDC, 1999). In particular, the offense of "threatening behavior" had increased from 2,300 in 1980 to 11,100. In 1997, the number of assaults and threats had increased 7 percent and 9 percent, respectively, compared to 1996 (SCP, 1998: 2). Important to note, however, was the fact that violent criminality still only accounted for a small proportion of all crimes known to the police (5.6 percent).

Since 1973, samples of Dutch inhabitants have been interviewed about their experiences as victims of crime. Because of differences in measuring instruments and sampling methods over the 25-year period, developments in criminal victimization in the Netherlands have to be interpreted with great caution. The total number of reported victimizations in 1980 was slightly higher than the comparable number in 1996, with considerable fluctuations during this period. The total number of thefts, violent offenses, and offenses involving destruction of property was estimated to be around 3.8 million in 1996, broken down, respectively, at about 1.7 million, 1.4 million, and 700,000 offenses (SCP, 1998: 6). One year earlier, in 1995, the estimated number of victimizations was higher: about 4.3 million.

Unlike the police statistics, the victim studies do not show a clear trend. The increase in violent crime noted in the police statistics was *not* reflected in the national victim survey that revealed a decrease from 71 to 58 victimization incidents per 1,000 people between 1994 and 1996. To make matters even more complicated, another population survey (Politiemonitor Bevolking) on victimization and related attitudes found trends more consistent with police statistics: a decrease in property crimes and an increase in violent crimes (SCP, 1998: 7). The Politiemonitor reported an increase from 710,000 violent victimizations in 1993 to 777,000 in 1997. In 1993, 0.5 percent of Dutch citizens over 15 had been the victim of a robbery; in

1995, this number had decreased to 0.3 percent, or from 61,000 to 38,000 incidents. However, two other types of violence ("threatening with violence" and "assault") both increased.

The Role of Ethnic Minorities in Crime

As noted in the nation profile, the Netherlands has become a host country to migrants and short-term visitors from a diversity of nationalities and cultures. Common sense would suggest not only that a large influx of new immigrants brings many positive elements to society (i.e., labor, cultural contributions, different foods) but also that it will create a host of social problems, including criminality. This commonsense idea has found ample support, in Dutch as well as in research sites around the globe.

The exact role that migrants, foreigners, and ethnic minorities play with regard to crime (including the issue of racial/ethnic discrimination) remains a difficult and sensitive question. Some questions about this issue remain unsettled, yet tremendous progress in finding some answers over the last several years, in both the Netherlands and in other countries, has occurred (De Haan, 1997). In addition to information on migrants, minorities, and foreigners routinely collected by criminal justice officials, others (e.g., government task forces and university researchers) have become increasingly involved in collecting such data, too.

A statistical analysis of suspects brought before the courts in a government report from 1997 provides an overview of what is known about criminal involvement of ethnic minorities in the Netherlands. The four minority groups (Moroccans, Antillians, Surinamese, and Turkish) living in Dutch society all are overrepresented as suspects. Criminal representation, however, varied. For example, Moroccans and Antillians were relatively more involved in common street crime; next were the Surinamese and then the Turkish. Moroccans, Antillians, and Surinamese were most involved in robbery, property crimes, and violations of the Opium Act, whereas the pattern of criminality of the Turkish more resembled that of the native Dutch (i.e., economical offenses and threatening and assault). In terms of correctional institutions, minority group representation is even more pronounced, in some cases as high as an overrepresentation factor of 10 (*CRIEM*, 1997).

It is, of course, very well possible that this overrepresentation of ethnic minorities in police statistics, courts, and prison reflects discrimination (i.e., differential treatment based on ethnicity or national origin) or unjust selectivity, rather than more criminal behavior. Without claiming that such ethnically based discrimination does not exist in the Netherlands, there is sufficient evidence to conclude that the official statistics on street crime are grounded in genuine behavioral differences (which should not be surprising, given their marginal positions in Dutch society).

Ethnic minorities are also prominently present in organized crime in the Netherlands. The Fijnaut Report published in 1998 painted an alarming picture of the involvement of different ethnic groups in organized crime. The four criminologists who wrote the report concluded, among other things, that there was extensive involvement of local communities of Turkish, Moroccans, and Surinamese in the organized drug business. These communities, in turn, function as links for large-scale drug trafficking. Many members of these communities have family and other personal ties with the source countries of these drugs. Morocco is a source country for hashish; Turkey, for heroin; and Suriname occupies a strategic position between Columbia and Western Europe (Fijnaut et al., 1998).

CONTEMPORARY CRIME CONTROL

In response to the growing public concern with crime, in 1985, the Ministry of Justice published *Society and Crime: A Policy Plan for the Netherlands*. This policy plan stressed the importance of a policy of "differentiation" (i.e., petty crime requires a different approach than that adopted in respect to more serious forms of crime) and "consistency" (i.e., there needs to be a clear and uniform prosecution policy). Strong involvement of local authorities was proposed as the most appropriate way to prevent petty crime. When it came to serious criminality, for example, organized crime, it was proposed that the police and courts, armed with a consistent prosecution policy, should hold exclusive jurisdiction. As we will see in the rest of this section, the practices and philosophies of crime prevention, detection, and prosecution in the Netherlands today reflect the recommendations of the 1985 governmental report.

For example, since the middle of the 1980s, there has been a growing interest in the relatively new phenomenon of "criminal groups" in the Netherlands. These organized criminals have been able to successfully operate illegal markets in drugs, prostitution, and complex fraudulent schemes. They have also been able to protect their illegal activities by using physical intimidation, violence, corruption, and legal business fronts.

In response to these new developments, special squads were established to fight organized crime. These squads began their work in a very permissive climate (e.g., the fight against organized crime must be won), without clear laws regulating special investigative tactics (i.e., observation, infiltration) and without organizational provisions (i.e., responsibility, supervision). By 1997, it had become common knowledge that the largest organized crime squad in the Netherlands had acted in violation of procedures, and a full-scale parliamentary investigation was launched into the methods used by the police in the fight against organized crime.

Sentencing Practices

Internationally, the Netherlands has the reputation of being a country with a lenient penal policy, especially with regard to the use of prison sentences (Downes, 1988). Analysis of historical incarceration data reveals that the average number of inmates per 100,000 inhabitants (15–64 years) showed a continuing decline in the Netherlands between 1842 and 1975 (Van Ruller and Beijers, 1995: 38). Until recently, the Dutch number of inmates per capita was among the lowest in the industrialized world. Van Ruller and Beijers (1995) argue that after 1975, a genuine historical change took place in the Netherlands. For the first time in 150 years, they argue, there was a "structural expansion" of incarceration. That is to say, there was a growth in the number of inmates accompanied by a prison construction program.

Around 1975 to 1977, the long-term trend of declining incarceration reversed and became one of a growing use of imprisonment (Van Ruller and Beijers, 1995). Today, the Dutch face the reality that they are no longer immune to the mounting pressures of a changing world. The recent increase and expansion in the use of prison reflects two facts: First, the average *length* of (longer) prison sentences has increased; and second, the *number* of unconditional prison sentences has increased significantly (Interdepartmental Policy Research, 1997: 6). In fact, the development in the number of "detention years" by category of sentence between 1985 and 1995 (see Table 8.1) has almost doubled (from 5,822 to 10,941). It should be noted that longer sentences have not been given to all crimes. There has been a selective increase in length of sentence imposed. Analysis of the period between 1978 and 1993 showed that systematic and clear increases in the length of sentence have taken place in five offenses: crimes against life (i.e., homicide and aggravated assault), rape, robbery, aggravated theft (including burglary), and offenses related to the Opium Act (Interdepartmental Policy Research, 1997).

Van Ruller and Beijers (1995) have argued that Dutch penal policy did not become more punitive across the board but underwent a sharpening of the distinction between lenient and nonlenient sanctions. Simultaneously, there has been an increase in longer prison sentences, but there has also been a greater diversity in sanctioning. There are now several sentencing alternatives that do not include the use of incarceration. A large proportion of the cases are actually disposed of by the prosecutor (51.1 percent) rather than by the courts (48.9 percent) (Ministry of Justice, 1996: 32). An increasingly popular method of prosecutorial dismissal is the "composition" or "transaction" sanction, which often involves a fine and which prevents a trial. In 1996, for example, 60 percent of all sanctions imposed involved some type of monetary penalty (CBS/RDC, 1999). Another development

Table 8.1
Developments in Number of Detention Years by Length of Sentence

Length of Unconditional Prison Sentence	Number of Detention Years			
	1985		1995	
	number	percent	number	percent
2 weeks or less	185	3	149	1
2 weeks to 1 month	285	5	352	3
1 to 3 months	881	15	1,362	12
3 to 6 months	1,111	19	1,615	15
6 to 9 months	538	9	357	3
9 months to 1 year	439	8	947	9
1 to 2 years	1,018	17	2,361	22
2 to 4 years	673	12	2,002	18
more than 4 years	692	12	1,796	16
	5,822	100	10,941	100

Source: Interdepartmental Policy Research (1997).

is that of community service: In 1994, 9.6 percent of all sanctions imposed involved community service; in 1996, the proportion of sanctions involving community service had increased to 12.8 percent.

Drug Policy

The Dutch drug policy is first and foremost realistic; that is, the policy is based on the premise that it is unrealistic to expect that drug use can be eliminated from modern society. Policy in the Netherlands pursues a two-pronged approach with regard to drugs: treatment and assistance for the user and punishment for the commercial dealer. The foundation of this approach is the belief that addiction cannot be controlled through criminal justice measures. Instead, addiction is viewed as a public health issue. The main objective of drug policy is "to prevent and neutralize the risk resulting from the use of drugs to the addict himself, people in his immediate environment and society at large" (Engelsman and Wever, 1986: 75).

This does not necessarily mean more treatment. On the contrary, the concept of "normalization," which became the key concept of drug policy in 1985, entails a gradual process of controlled integration of the drug phenomenon into society. Integration does not mean acceptance but the notion that "being a junkie" should be demythologized and deglamorized. Normalization also stresses the importance of assuming reciprocity and mutual responsibility in treatment.

Dutch drug policy makes a "risk" assessment and distinguishes between "soft" and "hard" drugs. Although the risks to society have been taken into account, every possible effort has been made to ensure that drug users are not harmed more by criminal proceedings than by the use of the drug itself. The government's adoption of the harm reduction (or "risk") approach was reflected first in the de facto decriminalization of trading and possessing small quantities of soft drugs (i.e., marijuana and hashish) in 1973. The government's rationale for decriminalization was to remove the sale and consumption of soft drugs from the hard drug scene, thereby avoiding the "social stepping stone" mechanism where soft drug users who come into contact with dealers of hard drugs may, in effect, "graduate" to the use of hard drugs.

In the 1980s, the wholesale suppliers of the "coffeeshops," who were in a sense "sheltered" by the tolerance of the retail trade in soft drugs, were largely left alone by the police and the criminal justice system. The Fijnaut Report (Fijnaut et al., 1998) on organized crime also pointed out that a few large criminal organizations in the 1990s had been able to make profits from the soft drug business in the 1980s, virtually undisturbed by any criminal justice interventions. In the middle 1990s, this situation changed drastically. Whereas soft drug users and small-scale dealers are still pretty much left alone by the law, police activities aimed against wholesalers and traffickers have intensified, and the penalties imposed for soft drug trafficking have become severe.

A tremendous paradox has emerged in Dutch drug policy: There is tolerance at the front door of the coffeeshops, yet strict enforcement and punishment at the back door. It was estimated in 1997 that there were about 1,200 coffeeshops—more than half of them being located in the four largest cities (Bieleman, Biesma, and Smallenbroek, 1997). There is now considerable discussion and debate at the level of local government about what to do with coffeeshops. There are towns that do not want to have any coffeeshops in their municipality, and more and more local governments impose a variety of restrictive requirements on these establishments. Meanwhile, soft drug use in the Netherlands has increased significantly. For example, according to a recent study of risk behavior of young people, soft drug use (lifetime prevalence) of today's youth has increased fourfold compared with the 1980s (Junger et al., 1998: 13).

Possession of hard drugs for personal use is usually ignored by police and other justice officials in the Netherlands. In practice, assistance to addicts is of central concern. However, because of an intensification of enforcement of petty criminality in urban areas, many addicts nevertheless end up in the criminal justice loop. Indeed, many Dutch drug addicts are involved in petty crime. It is estimated that about half of the inmates in Dutch prisons and jails have hard-drug-related problems. Just recently, a new law has been implemented that allows incarceration for the purpose of treatment of addicts who are repeat offenders for a period of two years in special institutions.

In the late 1990s there were several estimates of the number of hard drug addicts in the Netherlands: somewhere between 20,000 and 27,000. It appears that the number of addicts has been stabilizing for years now; the average age of addicts is increasing. Because of excellent social and health services, other problems usually associated with hard drug use (e.g., AIDS, malnutrition, neglect, death) are reasonably under control. About 9,000 addicts receive methadone on a daily basis and are under permanent medical care.

FUTURE OF CRIME AND CRIME CONTROL

In 1994, the Centraal Cultureel Plan Bureau, a Dutch government agency, developed a prognosis model of future developments in criminality in the Netherlands. This model incorporated assumptions about the impact of various factors on the level of criminality. These included the proportion of youth, the percent divorced, level of disposable income, unemployment, disability, income inequality, proportion of non-Dutch inhabitants, drug addicts, percentage of cases solved by the police (clearance rate), probability of prison sentence, and length of prison sentence. Based on this prediction model, the future of crime in the Netherlands is not "too bright."

If no policy changes are implemented, the volume of registered criminality is expected to increase by 10 percent by 2002. By 2006, violent crime is expected to increase by 44 percent and aggravated theft by 23 percent. Only simple theft is predicted to decrease, by 16 percent, between 1996 and 2006 (Directie Preventie Jeugd en Sanctiebeleid, 1997).

Recently, in an update of this prediction model, three additional versions were developed, incorporating the effects of possible changes in policy due to increased prevention efforts; increased resources devoted to the police; and increased resources devoted to sanctions. The version that appeared to be the most effective in reducing the level of crime (i.e., in 2006, there will be about 98 percent of the level of criminality as in 1996) was the "prevention model," which had more long-term effects than either the "police model" or the "sanction model," which had more immediate short-term effects. The prevention model incorporates improved security precautions to ward off burglaries but also parental support in the upbringing of their children, prevention of truancy and dropping out of school, and intensive guidance of criminal youth.

Prevention has been, and will continue to be, the cornerstone of Dutch crime policy. It is not a prevention at all costs by repressive measures that exclude, stigmatize, polarize, and marginalize segments of the population. Rather, prevention Dutch-style is pragmatic, such as using increased security measures to protect buildings and property, and it is inclusive, integrative, and tolerant as well. For many foreign observers of the Dutch model, it appears as a rather naive, all-too-tolerant and "friendly" way of dealing with criminality. Granted, the recalcitrant reality shows that the "friendly" model is not without faults, yet in spite of the growing problems with crime, tolerance continues to be a key concept in Dutch crime policy.

We are confident that crime policy and criminal justice administration will continue to have typical Dutch characteristics. Radically repressive solutions for the problems of crime are still taboo in the Netherlands. For example, notions such as "selective incapacitation" and "capital punishment" are not even discussed. On the contrary, solutions for prison crowding are not found in placing too many people in overcrowded prisons or in building additional ones but in early releases. In fact, there now is discussion about placing limits on prison construction.

Recent policy documents (Ministry of Justice, 1997, 1998) about the most pressing crime problems, such as how to deal with "senseless" violence and the high level of involvement of ethnic minorities, reflect that same mentality. For example, the problem of overinvolvement of ethnic minorities in crime is defined in terms of incomplete integration of the ethnic minorities in Dutch society. Accordingly, preventive integration policy is proposed, anchored in better guidance at school, facilitation of integrating school dropouts into the labor market, the lowering of the mandatory school age to four, the use of health clinics to improve both physical and social development, and "interculturalization." The latter refers to the conscious efforts of adopting Dutch institutions of education, welfare, law enforcement, and criminal justice to the situation of ethnic minorities.

Even policies focusing on organized crime stress preventive components. For example, government agencies have to make sure that they do not grant any contracts to businesses financed with criminal (laundered) money. In short, it appears that in spite of the growing problems with crime, tolerance continues to be a key concept in Dutch crime control. The Netherlands, in other words, seems to have a great ability to absorb crime problems, not by exclusion, stigmatization, and marginalization but by inclusion.

REFERENCES

Bieleman, B., S. Biesma, and A. Smallenbroek. 1997. *Cannabis in Nederland*. Groningen: Intraval.

Central Bureau of Statistics and Research and Documentation Centre (CBS/RDC). 1999. *Criminaliteit en Rechtshandhaving 1999. Ontwikkelingen en Samenhangen op het Terrein van de Criminaliteit en de Rechtshandhaving* (Criminality and law enforcement. Developments in criminality and law enforcement). The Hague, Netherlands: CBS and WODC.

Criminaliteit en Integratie van Etnishche Mindereden [CRIEM]. 1997. The Hague: Miinisterie van Binnenlandse Zaken en Ministerie van Justitie.

De Haan, Willem. 1997. "Minorities, Crime, and Criminal Justice in the Netherlands." In Ineke Haen Marshall (ed.), *Minorities, Migrants, and Crime: Diversity and Similarity across Europe and the United States.* Thousand Oaks, CA: Sage, 198–223.

De Waard, Jaap, Mike Schreuders, and Ronald Meijer. 1998. "Geweldscriminaliteir in 15 European Landen. Nederland Middenmotor." *SEC* (April): 5–8.

Directie Preventie Jeugd en Sanctiebeleid. 1997. *Criminele Bergezichten* (Criminal prospects). The Hague, Netherlands: Ministry of Justice.

Downes, David. 1988. *Contrasts in Tolerances, Post-war Penal Policy in the Netherlands and England and Wales.* Oxford: University Press.

Engelsman, E., and L. Wever. 1986. "Drugsbeleid: Is het middel erger dan de kwaal?" *Tijdschrift voor Alcohol, Drugs and Andere Psychotrope* 12 (April): 74–81.

Fijnaut, Cyrille, Frank Bovenkerk, Gerben Bruinsma, and Henk van de Bunt. 1998. *Organized Crime in the Netherlands.* Dordrecht: Kluwer Law International.

Geveke, Henk and Tom van Dijk. 1997. *De politiemonitor in perspektief.* Amsterdam: Projectbureau Politiemonitor.

Home Office. 1996. "Number of Registered Crimes of Violence per 100,000 Inhabitants." *Excerpt for the Netherlands (CBS) and Germany (BKA).* Amsterdam.

———. 1997. *Increase in Registered Violent Crime.* Amsterdam.

Interdepartmental Policy Research [Interdepartmentaal Beleidsonderzoek], Ministry of Justice. 1997. *Substitutie van Vrijheidsstraffen door Taakstraffen.* The Hague, Netherlands: Ministry of Justice, IBO-ronde 1996, Report No. 8, May.

Junger, M., H. Vinken, A. van de Laan, I. Diepstraten, and P. van den Akker. 1998. *Jongeren en Risicogedrag: Definities, Trends en Factoren.* Rijswijk: Ministerie van VWS, Commissie Jeugdonderzoek.

Kester, J.G.C., and J. Junger-Tas. 1994. *Criminaliteit en strafrechtelijke reactie. Ontwikkelingen en samenhangen.* The Hague, Netherlands: WODC.

Mayhew, Pat, and Jan J. M. van Dijk. 1997. *Criminal Victimisation in Eleven Industrialised Countries: Key Findings from the 1996 International Crime Victims Survey.* The Hague, Netherlands: Research and Documentation Centre (WODC), Report 162.

Ministry of Justice. 1985. *Society and Crime: A Policy Plan for the Netherlands.* The Hague, Netherlands: Author.

———. 1996. *Crime and Law Enforcement: About Victims, Offenders and Criminal Law.* The Hague, Netherlands: Author.

———. 1997. *Prognose Sanctiecapaciteit 1998–2002.* The Hague, Netherlands: Author.

———. 1998. "Community Service Orders in the Netherlands." *Violence on the Streets.* The Hague, Netherlands: Ministry of Justice.

The Netherlands Bureau of Statistics. 1997. "Property Crime Registered by the Dutch Police, 1980–1996." Sourcebook: Amsterdam. "Property Crimes Solved by the Dutch Police 1980–1996." Sourcebook: Amsterdam. "Violent Crime Registered by the Dutch Police, 1980–1996."

Sociaal Cultureel Planbureau (SCP). 1998. "Justitie en strafrechtspleging." In *Sociaal*

Cultureel Rapport 1998. Rijswijk, Netherlands: Sociaal en Cultureel Planbureau, Chapter 15.

Tesser, P., and J. Veenman. 1997. *Rapportage Minderheden.* Rijswijk, Netherlands: Sociaal en Cultureel Planbureau.

Van den Berg, W. M. 1998. "Niet-natuurlijke dood in Nederland, 1996." *Kwartaalbericht rechtsbescherming en veiligheid* (Central Bureau Statistiek) 98(2): 17–25.

Van der Laan, Perter, A. D. Essers, and Erik Spaans. 1998. *Ontwikkelingen in de jeudcriminaliteit.* The Hague, Netherlands: WODC.

Van Gemert, Frank. 1998. *Crips in drievoud. Een dossieronderzoek naar drie jeugdbendes.* Amsterdam, Netherlands: Regioplan.

Van Koppen, Peter. 1997. "De doodstraf." In K. Wittebrood, J. A. Michon, and M. ter Voort (eds.), *Nederlanders over criminaliteit en rechtshandhaving.* Deventer, Netherlands: Gouda Quint.

Van Ruller, S., and W.M.E. Beijers. 1995. "Trends in Detentie. Twee Eeuwen Gevangenisstatistiek." *Justitiele Verkenningen* 21, 6: 35–52.

Wetenschappelijke Raad voor het Regeringsbeleid (WRR). 1996. *Tweedeling in Perspectief.* The Hague, Netherlands: Sdu Uitgevers.

9

NEW ZEALAND

(Developed Nation-State)

George Pavlich

PROFILE OF NEW ZEALAND

The islands now called New Zealand were discovered some 1,000 years ago by Polynesian pioneers, and their Maori descendants inhabited settlements across the land (Biggs, 1998). On December 18, 1642, a Dutch explorer by the name of Abel Tasman anchored off the shores of a place some Maori tribes called Aotearoa ("Land of the Long White Cloud"). Although Tasman did not actually set foot on this land, he bequeathed the name New Zealand to Europeans. James Cook, a British explorer, "rediscovered" New Zealand in 1769 and spent six months charting maps, acquiring knowledge of the area, and claiming parts of the land for George III (Williams, 1997). Such explorations opened the way for expanded European settlement that in the early 1800s centered around missionary work and whaling stations (Orange, 1998).

By the late eighteenth century, the indigenous Maori population is estimated to have been between 120,000 and 150,000 people. It declined markedly over the next few decades due to the ravages of intertribal war and the introduction of European diseases (i.e., tuberculosis, typhoid fever, measles). The declining population, the so-described lawlessness of European settlements, the plight of exploited Maori, and expanding commercial ties were among the reasons advanced for British colonization (Pavlich, 1998). Lieutenant Governor William Hobson oversaw the annexation and on February 6, 1840, secured some 45 signatures (and another 500 over the next six months) from Maori chiefs for the Treaty of Waitangi. Although a treaty of cession, the hastily drafted Maori translation of the document did not convey that the chiefs would yield sovereignty to Queen Victoria (Orange, 1998). Over the next decades, this treaty was contested through war and continues to be an important political document for many continuing debates on "bi-culturalism," sovereignty, treaty obligations, land claims, and so forth (Belich, 1996).

Constitutionally, New Zealand is an independent state that takes the form of a monarchy with a parliamentary government. Queen Elizabeth II (of Britain) is the Queen of New Zealand and is represented by a local governor-general. Recently, however, New Zealand has abandoned a Westminster style of democracy and has instead embraced the concept of mixed member proportional (MMP) representation in Parliament. The court hierarchy is headed by the New Zealand Court of Appeals, although final appeals may still, in certain cases, be made to the Judicial Committee of the Privy Council in Britain.

Geographically, New Zealand is a small country in the southwest Pacific Ocean, 1,600 kilometers long and 450 kilometers wide at its widest point. Its long coastline (5,650 kilometers) embraces a mountainous interior, with the highest point at Mount Cook on the South Island (3,754 meters). Two main islands (the North and South), together with several smaller islands, comprise the bulk of New Zealand. At the time the census taken March 5, 1996, the total population of the country was 3,681,546 people (New Zealand, Statistics, 1997). Ethnically, the population includes 523,374 Maori people (14.5 percent of the total), 202,233 people who identify themselves as coming from one of the neighboring Pacific Islands (e.g., Western Samoa, Fiji, Tonga), 82,320 from China, and 43,821 from India.

Historically, New Zealand's capitalist economy was largely fueled by an agricultural base fortified by enduring trade relations with Britain. Until recently, agriculture continued to be the most important source of export earnings and helped to fund the generous "cradle to the grave" social welfare provisions begun in the 1930s (Roper and Rudd, 1993). When the fourth Labour government was elected in 1984, it oversaw dramatic changes to the country and its economy. The New Zealand government turned away from the highly regulated welfare economy and started embracing policies of tight fiscal regulation (monetarism), deregulation for "free markets," and welfare state cutbacks (Kelsey, 1993; Roper and Rudd, 1993). One impact of these changing relations is that the disparity between the wealthy and poor has widened significantly, amidst escalating poverty (Roper and Rudd, 1993; Kelsey and O'Brien, 1995; Kelsey, 1997) and rising trends in the varieties and seriousness of "crime" (Haverman and Haverman, 1995).

HISTORICAL PERSPECTIVE ON CRIME AND
CRIME CONTROL

In New Zealand the emergence of crime as a social category, requiring official control through a formal justice system, is linked to processes of colonization. Prior to British annexation, Maori *iwi* (tribe), *hapu* (clan) and even *whanau* (extended family) embraced complex systems of social control (Hill, 1986; Ward, 1995). There were, for example, several levels at which *tapu* (the sacred) or *rahui* (a ban or censure) could be inscribed over the social fabric (Mead and Fleras, 1980). The fabric of clan-based settlements scattered across the land produced different regulatory systems and patterns of redress. Nevertheless, particular concepts of governance were common enough to have achieved prominence at that time and beyond. In general, the most significant responses to actions that transgressed customs included those of *utu* (recompense) or the *muru* (raiding party) (Ward, 1995).

European settlers brought specific notions of "crime and punishment" with them to New Zealand. However, Maori discourses and patterns of governance were more consequential in practice well after the Treaty of Waitangi was signed. Indeed, much blood was spilled in the decades after 1840 in the attempt to impose British colonial law as sovereign over all New Zealand (Pavlich, 1998). In the process, the expansion of the colonial government raised the profile of a political logic that (1) criminalized behaviors deemed worthy of sanction; (2) relied on formal court systems to define guilt or innocence; and (3) used the same courts to decide on appropriate sentences for the punishment of offenders. Crime control policies were also set up within this logic.

Since its inception as a British colony with close administrative ties to Australia, governors of New Zealand have sought to deploy a criminal justice system with reference points in these countries. As such, the crime control policies and practices have often mirrored international uses of such disciplines as penology, criminology, psychology, and sociology (Pratt, 1992). For example, early New Zealand crime control practices made use of resident magistrates, justices of the peace, and small bands of police/military officers, who were influenced by classical precepts in criminology (Hill, 1986; Pratt, 1992). Such classical thinking viewed people as rational and free beings who act on the basis of pleasure-pain calculations (Beccaria, 1963). Criminals, by this logic, choose to offend for pleasure and need to be punished accordingly. However, in order to deter them from choosing to reoffend, they only needed to be punished in rationally calculated measures of pain that slightly outweighed the pleasure gained by committing the offense (Lanier and Henry, 1998). In modern New Zealand, like modern Britain and elsewhere, prisons emerged as the mainstay of "rational" punishment practices designed to deter individuals from offending. This thinking guided the expansion of New Zealand's punishment regime well into the next century.

PUBLIC PERCEPTION OF CRIME AND CRIME CONTROL

The public perceptions of crime and crime control are based, in part, on officially kept records and rates and, in part, on representations of crime and crime control found in news media, television dramas, graffiti, and so on (Sparks, 1992; Barak, 1994; Ferrell, 1995). Together, these constructions of crime and crime control have helped to forge or shape public perceptions and policy in New Zealand. Presently, the dominant perceptions are of rising crimes against property, person, and the justice system.

These perceptions of increased criminality have generally supported the expanding efforts of crime control in both the public and private sectors. These developing perceptions of crime and crime control tend to reflect or tell only one story about crime and the possible responses to crime. In the course of this chapter, I will address the dominant discourses or stories of crime and crime control. In addition, however, I will recombine elements of these stories, for example, crime and victimization, to suggest alternative frameworks from within which harmful behaviors can be examined and from without which could flow other responses to crime and crime control.

CONTEMPORARY CRIME

When deferring to officially recorded statistics that rely on legal definitions of crime (as enunciated by legislation like the Crimes Act of 1961 and its amendments), or on victim surveys, it is possible to construct different accounts about the present state of "crime" in New Zealand. These accounts or stories attempt to capture, in static (and statistical) form, given moments of crime.

Echoing the primary place accorded to the analysis of officially recorded data (New Zealand Law Enforcement System database), Spier (1997) and Triggs (1998) depict recent trends in crime and punishment. Spier's analysis of prosecution and conviction trends between 1987 and 1996 presents us with snapshots of nontraffic offenses recorded in the following categories: violent, other against persons, property, drug, against justice, good order, and miscellaneous. In general, he tells a tale in which the total number of prosecutions for nontraffic offenses over this period reflect an upward trend, culminating in the highest number of the decade in 1996. Triggs's (1998: 37) analysis of the 1986 to 1996 period concurs by noting that court cases for nontraffic offenses were up some 11 percent. In terms of sure numbers, the New Zealand Police records that 516,369 offenses were reported in 1996, 200,590 of those were prosecuted, and 129,709 resulted in convictions (New Zealand, Statistics, 1997: 250).

Spier calculates a 17 percent increase in the number of convictions from 1987 to 1996, with much of this increase being accounted for by two trends. By far the largest increase (128 percent) pertains to convictions

"against the administration of justice (e.g., breach of sentence, not comply-
ing with bail conditions, contempt of court, and so forth), which represents
10.7 percent of all convictions" (Spier, 1997: 28–29). This number is followed by an 89 percent increase in violent convictions, accounting for 12.8
percent of the total convictions for 1996. However, in 1996, there was a
slight drop (for the first time since 1990) in the number of violent convictions (i.e., 16,576 in 1996 as compared with 16,778 in 1995) (Spier, 1997:
28), even though the proportion of violent convictions remains considerably
greater than it was in 1987. Some of the latter increase reflects an important
change in the way police now respond to domestic violence, taking a firm
line on arresting where there are signs of violence. Spier points to the large
increase in the "male assaults female" category (where most domestic violence is recorded) from 1990 to 1994 but notes, too, that the trend has
evened out (and even decreased in both 1995 and 1996). In addition, the
number of convictions for violent sexual offenses (e.g., rape, indecent assault, unlawful sexual connection) was almost three times as many in 1996
than in 1987 (Spier, 1997: 17). In 1996, 80 percent of victims of such
convictions, whose age was available, were 16 years old or younger.

Furthermore, this story supports the view that there has been a redistribution of patterns of criminal conviction over the decade. Some conviction
categories have decreased slightly. For instance, drug-related convictions are
down 6 percent, mainly as a result of reduced cannabis-related convictions
(even though other drug-related convictions have increased (Spier, 1997:
18). The "other against persons" (i.e., resisting arrest, obstructing justice,
and threatening, intimidating, or sexual offenses not classed as violent) has
decreased slightly by 2 percent over the decade. By contrast, the category
that comprises the greatest proportion of all convictions—"property" (at
43.8 percent)—increased slightly by 3 percent. The number of "good order" convictions (e.g., trespassing, offensive language, carrying offensive
weapons, disorderly conduct, and unlawful assembly) was the highest for
the decade, moving from 8,297 in 1987 to 9,754 in 1996, even though
these remained proportionately constant at 7.5 percent of all convictions in
both 1987 and 1996 (Spier, 1997: 18; Triggs, 1998).

These descriptions may be supplemented with those of a national victimization survey. This study surveyed the likelihood of people becoming victims of an offense (Young et al., 1997). It canvassed a random sample of
4,500 houses and a "booster" of 500 Maori households for the 1995 calendar year, with a 57 percent response rate. Given a low response rate, the
authors treated the results with some caution. Even so, they estimated that
in 1995 there were about 2,079,041 attempted or actual offenses against
households or people over the age of 15.

Only some 13 percent of these were recorded by the police in that year,
confirming the authors' supposition that police records are limited. The
survey found that in 1995 the incidence of violent behavior (i.e., sexual

violation of women and men, indecent assault, grievous assault, other assault, threats and abduction/kidnapping) was 45 offenses per 100 individuals. The equivalent figures for other offenses were 31.6 for household offenses (i.e., burglary, theft); 14 for individual property offenses (i.e., theft from person, willful damage/arson); and less than 1.0 for robbery. They also noted that in a given year the risk of becoming a victim of the following events in New Zealand, on average, is as follows: 1 house in 14 will be burgled; 1 woman in 16 will be sexually violated; and 1 in 5 people will be the victim of some sort of assault.

On the subject of violence, Young et al. observed that 0.5 percent of the entire sample were victimized by violent offenses more than five times, and this group accounted for 68.4 percent of all the violent offenses (e.g., assaults, sexual offending, threats, and abduction/kidnapping). This leads them to conclude that victims of violence are not evenly distributed across New Zealand. In other words, like most places there are particular contexts where violence abounds. The findings contradict popular media portrayals of violence as brutal, "out of control," and mainly perpetrated by strangers so that all people are allegedly vulnerable. Excluding family violence, which is noted as being a significant problem in New Zealand (Morris, 1997), the report noted that much violence "appears to be minor in terms of injuries and items stolen and much of it is described by victims as not having much impact on them" (Young et al., 1997: 84). Moreover, violence is often accompanied with alcohol and confined to particular areas. Also, most victims (outside of family violence) are young men, and many victims of assaults or threats know the offenders.

More specifically, the pattern of conviction and victimization in New Zealand speaks to the "unequal" distribution of offenses and victims. For example, Spier (1997) profiled convicted nontraffic offenders for 1996 and noted that 82 percent of these involved male offenders. This figure increased to about 91 percent when broken down for serious offenses against a person, suggesting the overwhelming role of men in the perpetration of violence. Where ethnic background of the convicted was known, 47 percent were counted as New Zealand Europeans, 43 percent Maori, 9 percent Pacific People, and 2 percent as other. Teenagers comprise 21 percent of these convictions (mainly 17 to 19 age group), 46 percent were in their twenties, 22 percent in their thirties, and 11 percent involved people over the age of 40. Overall, not unlike other contexts, young men comprise a large proportion of those convicted in New Zealand.

Similarly, Triggs (1998) profiled nontraffic offenders by age, gender, and ethnicity. His analysis indicated that Maori and Pacific People are over-represented (relative to their size in the population) in prosecutions. In particular, the prosecution rate per 1,000 people of the population over 14 years of age is 116.2 for Maori, 67.7 for Pacific People, and 20.1 for other ethnic groups. That the Maori are consistently and disproportionately overrepresented in official agency networks alludes to the previously noted story of the unfinished business of colonization (Jackson, 1988).

Together, the above studies paint a picture of crime in New Zealand, with at least three highlights amenable to diverse causal analyses. First, the studies tell the tale of an increasing number of recorded offenses and nontraffic convictions (e.g., a noted 17 percent increase in crime compared with an approximately 10 percent population increase over the same period of time—New Zealand, Statistics, 1997: 107). In particular, convictions "against justice," such as those for breaches of periodic detention and bail, comprised the largest proportionate increase over the 1987–1996 period.

Second, these data (stories) suggest that the number and proportion of convictions for violence have increased, and the acts that result in such convictions may be more serious than before (Spier, 1997; Triggs, 1998). Moreover, victim reports indicated that violence is concentrated in pockets (as opposed to evenly distributed across the population), is correlated with alcohol consumption, and is higher among young men who know each other. Violence often involves acts (inclusive of sexual assault) by men against women, as well.

Third, it is important not to lose sight of the most enduring and highest proportion of all convictions—namely, those relating to property offenses (43.8 percent). Briefly, the high percentage of offenses against property coupled with the higher rates of convictions of violence reflect to some degree the dual desires of consumption and masculine culture characteristic of "free market" economic policies. In the last section of the chapter, I will pick up on these themes as they relate to New Zealand's projected crime and crime control problems of the future.

CONTEMPORARY CRIME CONTROL

New Zealand has embraced community-based patterns of crime control and complemented such developments with the ubiquitous threat of coercive sanctions if conditions of community corrections are transgressed (Cohen, 1985). In the process of the state introducing more options into the control system and using these in concert, there are greater points in which people may fall foul of the law and be swept into an increasingly fragmented justice "system" (Pavlich, 1996). At the same time, a number of criminological theories have influenced the policies and practices of crime control.

Most notably, the positivist school developed by Lombroso (and Garafolo) relied on science to propose that some people were born with criminal tendencies (Pfohl, 1994). The shift from classical "free will" to "nature" implies different crime control policies. Two significant adaptations in New Zealand include: first, the emphasis on classifying convicted criminals for different sorts of prison "treatments"; and second, the positivist tenets found in emphasizing the aims of "correcting," "rehabilitating," and "habilitating," rather than simply the aims of punishing. For example, New Zealand's Department of Corrections has several programs that derive from positivist precepts, and indeed its Psychological Services wing provides a good example of positivist formulations put into institutional practice.

While classical and positivist precepts shaped founding crime control policies in New Zealand, sociological precepts became increasingly central to welfare state control policies, such as preventing juvenile delinquency through social programs and reforms (Pavlich, 1999). After the 1970s, however, amid a rising tide of neoconservative politics and neoliberal economics, classical crime control precepts gained renewed currency internationally (e.g., Wilson, 1975). This complex past has yielded a patchwork of official crime controls.

First, the Department of Corrections oversees diverse and even disparate control institutions. On the one hand, one can identify a call for punitive measures to deter criminals, and this has been heeded in abundance. On average, there were 4,735 inmates in prison (remanded and sentenced) at any one time in 1996, a large increase over the 2,983 figure for 1987 (Spier, 1997; Triggs, 1998). Such data should be seen in light of New Zealand's current capacity to hold 5,000 inmates in 17 prisons. Reflected in such figures is a 27 percent increase in the number of cases that resulted in custodial sentences from 1987 to 1996 (Spier, 1997).

Triggs has also noted that the percentage of cases that attract a prison sentence against the total imprisonable cases increased from 7.4 percent in 1986 to 8.4 percent in 1997. In addition, depending on how we calculate this, the average length of a custodial sentence has increased from 9.5 months in 1987 to 11.7 months in 1996 (Spier, 1997) or from 10.3 months in 1986 to 14.9 months in 1996 (Triggs, 1998). Equally, imposing the more lenient sentence of corrective training through short and focused prison programs has declined markedly from 841 in 1987 to 563 in 1996 (Spier, 1997). All such indications suggest that despite a neoliberal rhetoric of turning away from state control, New Zealand has intensified its reliance on longer custodial sentences as a key mechanism for dealing with crime. New prisons are also to be built; that these might entail privatization of some kind detracts little from a crime control policy that defers to custodial punishment.

On the other hand, the Department of Corrections complements its public prisons with a community corrections system. This system provides for various community-based sentences that include unpaid community service work, supervision under a probation officer, periodic detention (where offenders live at home but are periodically detained at centers to complete community service), community programs (e.g., drug and alcohol), parole, and a home detention pilot program (New Zealand, Statistics, 1997). Of these, periodic detention is used most frequently, especially for traffic and property offenses, but the use of sentencing people to unpaid community service has grown massively (303 percent) since 1987 (Spier, 1997). Much of this growth took place between 1987 (n = 2,056) and 1993 (n = 9,953), with a decline in its use in 1996 (n = 8,285). Supervision as a mechanism of control continues to grow and inclines toward the more punitive end of the community sentences spectrum. In 1996 the 5,503 cases for which supervision was the most serious sentence imposed reflected a 54 percent growth over 1987 (Spier, 1997). The use of monetary fines as a censuring practice is down, although Triggs has argued that a growing acceptance of "reparation" measures for victims is likely to reverse this trend.

Second, and related to the last point, there is a growing faith in the value of "restorative" justice that removes certain people from the judicial system in order to be dealt with in "the community" (New Zealand, Ministry of Justice, 1995). The aim is to "empower" communities to take charge of their destinies and lessen their dependence on state control. Such reasoning has seen the implementation of various sorts of "community-based" programs, including diversion, family group conferences, and community sentencing programs. In certain instances, especially for *Marae*-based (Maori Meeting Houses) justice programs, there is an explicit attempt to institutionalize a "parallel" justice system that can better meet the cultural needs of particular people. For example, Jackson's (1988) report on the Maori within the criminal justice system addressed this exact point.

Third, a Crime Prevention Unit (CPU) was established in 1993 in an attempt to solicit the active participation of "communities" in crime control. The CPU's brief is broadly conceived, but it targets areas of community that are deemed to carry high risks of producing crime (e.g., at-risk families, at-risk youths, situations producing domestic violence) (Pavlich, 1999). Operating with a budget of NZ$3,464,000 for 1996, the CPU is involved with various programs but has been fundamentally instrumental in helping to develop so-called Safer Community Councils. Over 54 such councils exist and are sponsored by local authorities (i.e., city council or *iwi*) according to the *New Zealand Official Yearbook* (New Zealand, Statistics, 1997). Their main role is to develop a community crime "profile" and then to set about applying to fund programs aimed at preventing and reducing crime. It is consequential that such "communities" are required to define themselves in ways that are coterminous with "sponsors" (usually geographically) and that guidelines for profiles and applying for funding are closely guided by authorities. At issue here is, of course, who precisely defines the notion of community and who determines appropriate methods of control.

In sum, what seems to be happening in New Zealand as elsewhere is that despite the talk of community control and rolling back the state, existing structures have not only not eroded, but they have become stronger (Cohen, 1985). One could argue, in fact, that despite the rhetoric of "state reduction" and "community empowerment," New Zealand's crime control network is relying more on both custody and community sentences. The

27 percent rise in the use of prison as a sentencing option, the increase in the average inmate muster, and the increase in the average length of custodial sentences all speak to a growing reliance on punishment through incarceration. Coupled with the large growth in community-based sentences as well, the expanding state control network in New Zealand also reveals a sense of governance at the local level, being driven or directed remotely, mainly through the dictates of management and financial accountability. In the process, the discussions about the use of particular control strategies are increasingly tied to cost, efficiency, and other management issues. In this ethos, questions of justice have come to occupy a dangerously marginal place.

Foucault (1991) has articulated these changes as part of the story of the "governmentalization" of state control, which requires an entirely different way of conceptualizing and practicing a nation's regulatory techniques. These transformations also reveal a fracturing of the very institutions of justice, permitting a radical dispersal of governmental networks (Rose, 1996). Finally, these dispersed networks are not often well coordinated and seldom have a clear political center.

FUTURE OF CRIME AND CRIME CONTROL

The stories of crime and crime control told thus far could be used to suggest rising convictions for criminal offenses alongside expanding control responses. Official discourses might use such indications to point to a growing crime problem that implies a need to deploy even more crime control resources. Should this story gain future currency, debates in New Zealand are likely to center around funding and, more specifically, given the prominence of free-marketing thinking, on privatizing particular control functions, from policing to corrections. Such a future would be consistent with the present practices and would help to reinforce or perpetuate existing policies and conditions.

However, this is a deeply flawed story that will do little to eradicate the quantum of harmful behavior in New Zealand society. One might, for example, note the notoriously problematic character of the officially recorded data that underscores such a story, reflective of state definitions of the problem as well as special law enforcement interests. One might also recognize the serious limits or omissions to the vary bases upon which these stories (data) reside—for example, the silence around the impact of control strategies that *selectively* criminalize, exclude, and punish particular groups of people and their behavior.

More than this, the stories replicate a dubious paradox: that "crime" is always defined within the context of changing political processes. For instance, Parliament enacts, and judges decide upon, laws; or police officers decide in context whether to charge someone with an offense. The constitutive role that changing power plays in establishing the "reality of crime" is all but occluded in the figures of statistically based accounts. At the same time, the official paradigm of crime and crime control hides another story seldom told.

This is the story of a rising "crime control industry" or "crime control complex" that has its own needs and interests that feed off the continued existence of crime. Connected to the rising trends in crime and crime control have been the cultural patterns in behavior associated with the shifts away from welfare state policies and toward free market policies. If it has been the case, as many criminologists contend, that these changes in social and economic policies have widened the gap between rich and poor, creating tension and stress at many echelons of New Zealand society, then this has also increased the risks of criminalities (Haverman and Haverman, 1995). In addition to these socioeconomic factors are the cultural factors that reflect strong "masculine" traits associated with harmful behaviors (e.g., an obsession with sports like rugby, high gun ownership rates, high alcohol consumption rates among young men, and high levels of violence by men against their partners). Together, these factors suggest a future social fabric with a high prominence of violence (Leibrich, Paulin, and Ransom, 1995; Alcohol and Public Health Research Unit [APHRU], 1996; Morris, 1997; Alpers and Walters, 1998).

The relationship between the ways in which structural inequalities of wealth, power, and cultural capital find means of rendering free market economies intrinsically "crime producing" is well documented in the literature (Taylor, Walton, and Young, 1973; Reiman, 1990; Lynch, 1997). As Bauman (1997) has usefully noted, the free market pushes in contemporary societies (like New Zealand) depend on people to participate as effective consumers. For reasons largely related to the widening gap between "haves" and "have-nots," there are growing numbers of people unable to participate as "normal" consumers. No doubt that these "strains" (Merton, 1997) of adopting cultural values without the sufficient legitimate social avenues for obtaining valued goods have propelled many to participate in various offenses, particularly property-related ones.

The future of crime and crime control may also develop in alternative ways and differ from the strategies currently employed. Although it is presently difficult to contemplate speaking of social harm without recourse to the language of crime and punishment—indicating the prominence of officially sanctioned stories in our lives—there are some inklings of an alternative story. There are murmurs of change, with talk of parallel justice stories, or movements contemplating prison abolition. While the political implications of these examples have yet to be fully appreciated, these stories do gesture toward alternate tales of crime control. One may even recover from such murmurs alternative strategies to deal with harmful behavior beyond "criminal censure."

In other words, is it possible to consider harmful behavior in ways other than as "criminal" and in need of "punishment"? This question challenges the foundations of existing practices; it alludes to a future that could recount radically different stories and license very different regulatory regimes. However, no story can lay claim to a single, eternal truth. If nothing else, this implies the value of keeping alive radically different stories. In doing so, we might recover stories and practices that explicitly place themselves in the service of a much older, if nobler, promise: justice!

REFERENCES

Alcohol and Public Health Research Unit (APHRU). 1996. "Young People and Alcohol." Auckland, New Zealand: Author.

Alpers, Phillip, and Reece Walters. 1998. "Firearms Theft in New Zealand: Lessons for Crime and Injury Prevention." *Australian and New Zealand Journal of Criminology* 31: 85–95.

Barak, Gregg. 1994. "Between the Waves: Mass-Mediated Themes of Crime and Justice." *Social Justice* 3: 133–47.

Bauman, Zygmunt. 1997. *Postmodernism and Its Discontents.* Cambridge: Polity Press.

Beccaria, Cesare. 1963. *An Essay on Crimes and Punishments.* Indianapolis: Bobbs-Merrill.

Belich, James. 1996. *Making Peoples: A History of the New Zealanders.* Auckland, New Zealand: Penguin.

Biggs, Bruce. 1998. "In the Beginning." In Keith Sinclair (ed.), *The Oxford Illustrated History of New Zealand.* Auckland, New Zealand: Oxford University Press.

Cohen, Stanley. 1985. *Visions of Social Control: Crime, Punishment and Classification.* Cambridge: Polity Press.

Ferrell, Jeff. 1995. "Style Matters: Criminal Identity and Social Control." In Jeff Ferrell and Clinton R. Sanders (eds.), *Cultural Criminology.* Boston: Northeastern University Press.

Foucault, Michel. 1991. "On Governmentality." In Graham Burchell, Colin Gordon, and Peter Miller (eds.), *The Foucault Effect: Studies in Governmentality.* Chicago: University of Chicago Press.

Haverman, Paul, and Joan Haverman. 1995. "Retrieving the 'Decent Society': Law and Order Politics in New Zealand, 1984–1993." In Kayleen Hazlehurst (ed.), *Perceptions of Justice: Issues in Indigenous and Community Empowerment.* Aldershot, England: Avebury.

Hill, Richard. 1986. *Policing the Colonial Frontier: The Theory and Practice of Coercive Social Control in New Zealand, 1767–1867.* Wellington, New Zealand: V. R. Ward.

Jackson, Moana. 1988. "The Maori and the Criminal Justice System: A New Perspective: He Whaipaanga Hou." Wellington, New Zealand: Department of Justice.

Kelsey, Jane. 1993. *Rolling Back the State.* Wellington, New Zealand: Bridget Williams Publishers.

———. 1997. *The New Zealand Experiment: A World Model for Structural Adjustment?* Auckland, New Zealand: Auckland University Press.

Kelsey, Jane, and Mike O'Brien. 1995. "Setting the Record Straight." Wellington, New Zealand: Association of Non Government Organisations of Aotearoa.

Lanier, Mark, and Stuart Henry. 1998. *Essential Criminology.* Boulder, CO: Westview Press.

Leibrich, Julie, Judy Paulin, and Robin Ransom. 1995. "Hitting Home: Men Speak Out on Abuse of Women Partners." Wellington, New Zealand: Department of Justice and AGB McNair.

Lynch, Michael (ed.). 1997. *Radical Criminology.* Aldershot, England: Dartmouth Publishing Company.

Mead, S. M., and J. Fleras. 1980. "Customary Concepts of the Maori." Wellington, New Zealand: Victoria University of Wellington Press.

Merton, Robert K. 1997. "On the Evolving Synthesis of Differential Association and Anomie Theory: A Perspective from the Sociology of Science" (text of speech given upon receipt of the Edwin H. Sutherland Award). *Criminology* 35: 517–25.

Morris, Allison. 1997. "Women's Safety Survey 1996." Wellington, New Zealand: Victimisation Survey Committee.

New Zealand, Ministry of Justice. 1995. "Restorative Justice: A Discussion Paper." Wellington, New Zealand: Ministry of Justice.

New Zealand, Statistics. 1997. *New Zealand Official Yearbook.* Wellington, New Zealand: GP Publications.

Orange, Claudia. 1998. "The Maori People and the British Crown." In Keith Sinclair (ed.), *The Oxford Illustrated History of New Zealand.* Auckland, New Zealand: Oxford University Press.

Pavlich, George. 1996. *Justice Fragmented: Mediating Community Disputes under Postmodern Conditions.* London: Routledge.

———. 1998. "Political Logic, Colonial Law and the 'Land of the Land of the Long White Cloud.' " *Law and Critique* 9, 2: 175–206.

———. 1999. "Preventing Crime: 'Social' versus 'Community' Goverance in Aotearoa/New Zealand." In Russell Smandych (ed.), *Governable Places: Readings on Governmentality and Crime Control.* Aldershot, England: Dartmouth.

Pfohl, Stephen. 1994. *Images of Deviance and Control: A Sociological History.* New York: McGraw-Hill.

Pratt, John. 1992. *Punishment in a Perfect Society: The New Zealand Penal System.* Wellington, New Zealand: Victoria University of Wellington Press.

Reiman, Jeffrey. 1990. *The Rich Get Richer and the Poor Get Prison: Ideology, Class and Criminal Justice.* New York: Macmillan.

Roper, Brian, and Chris Rudd (eds.). 1993. *State and Economy in New Zealand.* Auckland, New Zealand: Oxford University Press.

Rose, Nikolas. 1996. "Governing 'Advanced Liberal' Democracies." In Andrew Barry, Thomas Osborne, and Nikolas Rose (eds.), *Foucault and Political Reason: Liberalism, Neo-liberalism and Rationalities of Government.* Chicago: University of Chicago Press.

Sparks, Richard. 1992. *Television and the Drama of Crime: Moral Tales and the Place of Crime in Public Life.* Buckingham, England: Open University Press.

Spier, Philip. 1997. "Conviction and Sentencing of Offenders in New Zealand: 1987 to 1996." Wellington, New Zealand: Ministry of Justice.

Taylor, Ian, Paul Walton, and Jock Young. 1973. *The New Criminology: For a Social Theory of Deviance*. London: Routledge.

Triggs, Sue. 1998. "From Crime to Sentence: Trends in Criminal Justice, 1986–1996." Wellington, New Zealand: Ministry of Justice.

Ward, Alan. 1995. *A Show of Justice: Racial 'Amalgamation' in Nineteenth Century New Zealand*. Auckland, New Zealand: Auckland University Press.

Williams, Glyndwr (ed.). 1997. *Captain Cook's Voyages, 1768–1779*. London: Folio Society.

Wilson, James Q. 1975. *Thinking about Crime*. New York: Vintage.

Young, Warren, Allison Morris, Neil Camerons, and Stephen Haslett. 1997. "New Zealand National Survey of Crime Victims 1996." Wellington, New Zealand: Victimisation Survey Committee.

10

NIGERIA

(Posttraditional Nation-State)

Obi N. Ignatius Ebbe

PROFILE OF NIGERIA

Nigeria is situated in West Africa. It is the largest country on the continent Africa, with over 250 ethnic groups. The unreliable 1991 census showed Nigeria as having a population of 88,569,226 people. However, since 1997, Nigerian records report a population of 104 million inhabitants.

Because this region of Africa was inhabited by "gemeinschaft" or autonomous communities before they were colonized and amalgamated by the British in the nineteenth century, Nigeria was a tailor-made country. The British colonial administration ruled Nigeria as a unitary system of government from 1914 to 1960, leaving the Nigerian people with a federal system. Prior to 1914, the British ruled Nigeria through councils (1849–1860) and a chartered company, the Royal Niger Company (1861–1900). In 1900, the British took over from the Royal Niger Company and ruled Nigeria with governors in different protectorates until 1914, and each protectorate was independent of the other.

Postcolonial Nigeria was a capitalist democracy from 1960 until the coup d'état of January 16, 1966, brought a military dictatorship into power. Capitalism is still the economic system in Nigeria. However, the people believe in the extended family system with the accompanying ideological norm that everyone should be "his brother's keeper."

HISTORICAL PERSPECTIVE ON CRIME AND CRIME CONTROL

An indelible cultural history of Nigeria has shown that, far beyond the reach of living memory, violations of conduct norms have always been in existence. And mechanisms, however ruthless and inhuman, were developed to deal with the offender. A breach of a conduct norm has always provoked moral outrage in both stateless and state-organized Nigeria.

In precolonial Nigeria, what is called crime today was so abhorred that it created two classes of people—the Nobles (Nwaafor) and the Outcasts (OSU)—among the Igbos (Ibos). The concept of crime was not applied. Instead, offenses were of two types: *abominations* (public offenses), otherwise called *aru*, or something the Earth abhors, and delicts called *mmehie* (private offenses). People who committed an abomination such as the murder of one's parents, brother, sister, or kinsman; incest; or any offense against the gods were dedicated to the god of the strange land, and they became outcasts or untouchables (Achebe, 1959; Ebbe, 1996). *Mmehie* offenses such as burglary, robbery, stealing, and so on, were disposed of not by imprisonment but by restitution, a fine, compensation, or a communion feast.

The coming of the Europeans to Nigeria in the fifteenth century and its subsequent colonization by the British in the nineteenth century changed the prior customary order. Up to the 1800s, Nigeria was tribally or ethnically organized in chiefdoms, kingdoms, emirates, clans, villages, or gemeinschafts. Gerontocracy or rule by elders, in the main, was the system of authority and leadership. Social order was maintained through strong allegiance to immemorial customs and traditions underpinned in African religions and philosophy. Members' adherence to the social norms including avoidance of taboos and abominations was an obligation owed to the ancestors, the Earth God, and the Holy Spirits (created spirits). Coercion to obey the norms was irrelevant because every adult knew that the negative consequences of violating taboos or committing an abomination could be fatal and could affect children unborn among his or her kindred.

There was no legislature in the collectivities of chiefdoms, emirates, villages, and so forth. Rules and regulations evolved through African religious beliefs and philosophies and were handed down from generation to generation through immemorial customs and traditions. There was social order without criminal law. Justice at the time was a family affair. The authority of the father was not questioned by anybody in his family, as patriarchy and patrilineal formed the order of authority and inheritance throughout Nigeria. In fact, the authority of the father was so relevant and revered by all that in some parts of Nigeria (Igbos) there were no chiefdoms, kingdoms, clanheads, or emirates, because each family was regarded as an autonomous entity.

Conglomeration of families under a central control was regarded as an infringement upon the authority of the father—"The Man." To be a man meant to be the head of a family, a mature, responsible figure subject to no one and offering allegiance only to the Deities. Communal matters were resolved by consensus of family members. This structure of individualistic justice was typical of the Igbo society of Nigeria, where there is "the King in every man" (Henderson, 1972). Even today, virtually every Igboman wants to be a chief, especially those whom the title was denied even in colonial days because of an abomination of their ancestors, a crime they did not commit (Ebbe, 1996).

This individual system of justice that was part of the family-oriented system of justice was subject to the head of the family. In other words, "The Man" was a complete "system of criminal justice." He enforced the rules, decided all cases within the family, and punished all deviant acts committed by family members including those of his wife or wives. His authority was limited to his family only. Any deviant act or private offense/wrong (*mme-hie*) committed by a family member outside the family was regarded as a slur to the reputation of the family, for which the head of the family would (must) punish the deviant very severely.

The notion of crime and criminal was not present yet as there was no criminal law. For those deviant acts that rarely occurred, the punishment was either a fine in nonfinancial terms, reconciliation, flogging, or compensation. In cases of persons who committed abominations, some ethnic groups such as the Igbos dedicated the offender to the gods. There was no capital punishment for clan members. Capital punishment was for strangers. There was no death penalty for kinsfolk who committed abominations. That act of capital punishment, in other words, was tantamount to committing another abomination. So these offenders were dedicated to the gods as untouchables. They worshipped at the Holy Shrine, and they were prevented from communicating with the free-born in any manner (Achebe, 1959).

In some ethnic groups of Nigeria, prior to the advent of the Europeans, the justice system was either headed by the chief, *oba* (emir, king, or clan) head sitting alone as the authority or mediator or by a council of elders with the oldest man as the chairman of the customary court. In some areas "trial by ordeal" was employed to determine the innocence or guilt of an accused. In some cases, the court or the parties may have consulted a diviner, a seer, or a prophet to determine the innocence or guilt of the accused. Today, while the customary court may not use "trial by ordeal," or consult a diviner or a seer to decide its cases, two parties involved in a case may decide to settle their differences by consulting a diviner.

The traditional Nigerian system of penology and corrections did not include imprisonment of the offender for any length of time. For Nigerians, as is true of Africans south of the Sahara, the offender was still a member of the collectivity who should be corrected within the community and not outside of it. For precolonial Africans, it was only through "reintegrative" justice that the offender could be corrected and made to be a rule-abiding member of the community. Unique to precolonial Nigeria was the absence of a formalized police system. Heads of households and entire villages had their ways of keeping out habitual offenders.

Private Security

In all parts of precolonial Nigeria, every head of a household provided physical security for all members of the household through environmental designs in the form of architectural styles of residences, wooden fence barriers, and masonry barriers (e.g., walls of mud, brick, or stones). There was usually only one door or gate for exit and entrance to the compound. When adults left for farmwork in the morning, the security wall exit door would be locked. Baby-sitters who were usually inside the complex were warned not to unlock the gate or door for any stranger.

Access control was the common form of environmental design in precolonial Nigeria. Heads of households allowed only one major entrance in their compound security walls or fences. If there was any footpath created by members of a household, outsiders were not allowed to use it to come to the compound. Most of the time, a crossbar was placed across the footpath or a dog on a leash was tied to a small tree adjacent to the footpath to scare outsiders from using it. The employment of individuals as security guards was not yet conceived. Only emirs or *obas* had a staff of servants who protected their kingdoms as vigilante groups.

Security of Private Property

The head of a household could use his presence to warn potential night burglars not to target his household by making a series of high-pitched, head-voice, exclamatory sounds while either standing on the ground or climbing a palm tree at night. The exclamatory sounds could be sounds of joy, great excitement, or a war song. Additionally, as most burglaries in Nigeria were carried out at night, he could shoot his gun in the air at night as an anticipatory burglary preventive mechanism. Also, when the head of a household suspected the possibility of a night burglary in the village, he could beat his ancestral drum, pretending to appease the spirits of his ancestors. By doing so, he gave notice to the burglars in the vicinity that he was around. It was, and still is, a cultural truism in Nigeria that as long as potential burglars in the town or village knew that the head of a household was at home, they avoided his compound.

Furthermore, some of these precolonial efforts to prevent criminal victimization in Nigeria appealed to transcendental reality. In this vein, some property could be saved from a Shrine Grove. Igbos, Yorubas, and others believe that if anyone steals something from a Shrine Grove, that person will die a sudden death or face a mysterious sickness that would lead to the person's death and to being buried in a tabooed forest (an evil forest). The Shrine Grove is a home of the community's god—the god of their ancestors who had existed and was worshipped from generation to generation beginning from the reach of living memory. Any type of property could be saved in a Shrine Grove (the altar of the town or village).

Security of Real Estate, Cash Crops, and Fruits

Real estate, cash crops, fruit trees, and movable possessions outside the home were secured from vandalism and criminal intervention by using the leaves of sacred trees such as *uboldia* (*umune*) or the youngest leaves of a palm frond (*omu nkwu*). Every native of the locality knew the evil consequences of tampering with any property with sacred leaves placed on it. The negative consequences were the same as those for stealing properties from a Shrine Grove. In fact, the sacred leaves protected anything displayed for sale from theft.

In addition, some people used ash from their kitchens to secure a property left on a roadside or displayed for sale by an absent seller. It was believed that stealing anything that had kitchen ash on it would result in the thief's sudden death upon eating anything cooked in a kitchen, sending him or her back to the ashes from which he or she was incarnated.

Village Security

In precolonial Nigeria, the community or village council was the highest court of justice. Also, the emirs and *obas* were the highest courts in their kingdoms. Each village was made up of people united by ties of consanguinity. A town council, as it is known in Nigeria today, was a rare or nonexistent entity. The village or community council was headed by the oldest person in the village or a person who inherited the leadership from his father.

Each village constructed various barriers against outside invasion or invasion by burglars from neighboring villages. The village council constructed physical security barriers at various pedestrian access routes to the village, especially those leading to unfriendly villages, while routes to friendly villages were kept open. Village councils established rotational community watchmen who stood guard at strategic routes to the village, ready to apprehend any strangers entering the village at night. The use of sentries was a frequent practice whenever there were waves of burglaries and robberies taking place.

During the daytime, every adult male was expected to look out for strangers or criminal ex-offenders wandering around the village, especially around the village market square. If they saw an ex-offender shopping around in the village market, they had to watch him until he left the village. Anyone caught offending in the village was killed without trial and buried the same night.

Colonial Crime and Crime Control

Criminal law and crime emerged in Nigeria with the European penetration into the chiefdoms, kingdoms, emirates, clans, and villages of the region in the eighteenth and nineteenth centuries. In the process of colonization, each colonial power introduced its laws, political organization, and system of justice (Elias, 1954, 1972; Nwabueze, 1963; Okonkwo and Naish, 1964; Ebbe, 1985a, 1996). The use of coercion was employed to get the natives to adhere to the alien laws and system of justice. By 1800, the British and other Europeans had built trading posts in many towns along the Atlantic coastlands of Nigeria. Nigerians traveled from remote parts of the hinterland to the coastal towns to trade with the Europeans. Over time, the coastal towns of Lagos, Warri, Bonny, Badagri, Opobo, Calabar, and Port Harcourt became highly urbanized.

In 1849, when Lagos was annexed and subsequently colonized by the British, the formal system of policing began. The Lagos Constabulary was established to control and prevent crime at the colonial trading posts and residences and at the colonially controlled urban centers. When the British government granted a charter to the Royal Niger Company Limited in 1861, a paramilitary police force was established to ensure colonial territorial security, to prevent all crimes, and to keep resistance of various kingdoms, emirates, and towns under control. The paramilitary police force of the Royal Niger Company stationed companies and squads of the force only at urban areas and seaports. Over 95 percent of Nigeria, that which was rural at the time, had no colonial constabulary controlling crime. Consequently, the precolonial systems of crime prevention and control were still in practice there.

When the British took direct administration of Nigeria in 1900, after revoking the charter of the Royal Niger Company, British Colonial Governor Lord Lugard established modern police models in the north and south regions of Nigeria (Niven, 1937). After the amalgamation of the northern and southern Nigeria protectorates in 1914, the modern Nigerian police force was in place. It was at this time that British colonial administrators introduced the provincial and district political divisions. Squads of the Nigerian police force were stationed at all provincial and district headquarters, which were the residential quarters of the chief administrative colonial officers. Although the colonial police were located at the district headquarters from 1920 to 1960, the traditional systems of crime prevention and control were retained in most areas of Nigeria.

The colonial administration focused on their economic interests. In effect, all colonial crime prevention strategies concentrated on the security of life and property of the colonial masters. The rural areas were ignored. Thus, the traditional system of policing and crime prevention predominated there. The village councils and their subjects saw the colonial police as an agency for political repression and economic exploitation rather than for crime control or prevention. During this period, crime was more of an urban phenomenon than a rural problem.

The result of the imposition of the colonial legal system over the precolonial or traditional system of control was the development of a Nigerian criminal code fraught with British normative standards imposed upon Nigerian citizens (Elias, 1954). This criminal code, in many cases, criminalized conduct norms of the Nigerian people, for example, the bigamy statute. Enforcement of such laws was ineffective because there were no complainants. Okonkwo and Naish (1964) have also noted that some behaviors defined as criminal in the Nigerian criminal codes were based on alien values and standards and, as such, were not internalized and obeyed by the people for whom the laws were meant to control. For some citizens, such laws as trespassing, matrimonial causes, and real estate use were nonexistent.

Not a few of these laws were enacted by the colonial administrators to protect or forge their own interests (Ebbe, 1985a). They revoked, for example, those statutes that were opposed to their interests such as real estate law and bigamy law and retained those laws that served their interests. Crime was certainly, then, a product of "culture conflict," among other factors, because colonial laws in Nigeria criminalized conduct norms of the people, and many of the citizens had no reason to internalize the alien British values imposed on them.

In this context, the Nigerian police force was created by the colonial regime as a repressive force for securing conformity. The masses saw the colonial police forces as repressive mechanisms not to be cooperated with in any way. In the absence of community cooperation, offender apprehension became very difficult (Okonkwo, 1966). Accordingly, between 1861 and 1965, strategies were developed by the Nigerian police to control crime among various cults, involving murder, witch-hunters, political involvement, and traditional terrorist rulers.

Unmistakably, throughout the period 1950 to 1960, when Nigeria received its independence from Britain, the Nigerian police force engaged in various crime control and prevention activities, such as patrolling the highways, streets, harbors, and shopping centers. The decade of the 1950s was the decade when the Nigerian regional governments were granted self-government. The Nigerian premiers of the regional governments were able to establish regional police units. In the eastern region, the Okpara Mobile Police Force was established to prevent international smuggling from the then–French Cameroon and the Spanish island of Fernando Po (now Equatorial Guinea) and highway robbery.

During this period of semiregional autonomy (1955–1959), up to 90 percent of the Nigerian society was rural, and the traditional system of crime control and prevention there still predominated. The police were located very far away from the rural towns and villages. It was only when a serious crime, such as murder or aggravated assault, was committed that a village head, a warrant chief (created by the colonial masters), a victim, or relatives of a victim would invite the police to the rural village to make an arrest.

PUBLIC PERCEPTION OF CRIME AND CRIME CONTROL

When a head of state is part of a crime problem, and it is known to everyone in the country that their head of state is a mafia boss, it is very hard to implement an effective crime control policy. Many people think, What is the point? In fact, crime control in a country like Nigeria is regarded as a wild goose chase. In a state of rampant political-criminal nexus, to nullify law enforcement, the police were drawn wholesale into the widespread corrupt activities of organized crime.

The problems of crime and the perceptions of crime and corrupt crime control did not emerge until the 1970s, when the oil boom brought enormous wealth to the Nigerian economy. The crime problem in Nigeria is generally explained in terms of the problems of modernization, such as urbanization, industrialization, uncontrolled rural to urban migration of both unskilled and semiskilled youths, illegal immigration from other African nations, culture conflict, unemployment, mismanagement of natural resources, and criminogenic national leadership—the latter emanating from military dictatorships whose wholesale elite criminality have reinforced the crimes of the underprivileged classes, the civil service, and the police.

Military dictatorship in Nigeria is viewed as exacerbating the crime problem. For more than 30 years, the Nigerian Army ruled the country by martial law. Since January 16, 1966, Nigeria has been subjected to seven military dictatorial regimes. With the exception of the present military dictator, General Abdulsalam Abubakar, and General Obasanjo, who came to power because of the death of a previous military leader, all of the other five military leaders came to power via coup d'état. In each of the five coups d'état, the claim for carrying out the coup was that the previous regime was corrupt.

However, what the Nigerian people have learned from over three decades of military regimes was that each military regime became more corrupt than the previous regime that had been overthrown. The degree of corruption, head of state–criminal connection, and cabinet ministers/political–criminal nexus became so widespread that telling the truth in Nigeria, in any situation, became a sin. Consequently, Nigerian youths became entrapped in a culture of wholesale elite organized crime and corruption, thereby making Nigeria a "predatory" state—a state where the head of state uses the National Bank as his personal belonging (Gahia, 1990; Oroh, 1990; "New Law," 1993; Mba-Afolabi, 1995; "Nigeria Recovers," 1995; Okpa, 1995;

Nwankpa, 1998). In such a climate, public perceptions of crime and crime control have also been twisted and rendered inoperative.

CONTEMPORARY CRIME

A major study of Nigerian criminals was conducted in 1980 involving 450 inmates from four major prisons (Kirkiri, Ikoyi, Maidugur, and Enugu). This study of incarcerated criminals found, among other things, that the "typical" male criminal was:

A property offender

Possessed of inadequate education and income

From low-class parents

From a broken home (inadequate family socialization)

In a state of poverty

Undergoing the strangeness and anonymity of the city

Holding a low-paying job

Likely to commit an offense alone

Likely to be married with many dependents

Likely to be below 35 years old (Ebbe, 1982: 167–68)

In another study that examined "correlates of female criminality in Nigeria" in the 1980s, it was found that the types of crime committed by the female inmates had an affinity to the contemporary roles of Nigerian women. Most Nigerian women are petty traders. Hence, most of their crimes were property crimes and crimes without victims. Of all the crimes for which the women were incarcerated, smuggling contraband goods claimed the highest percentage (28 percent), followed by stealing (18 percent) and possession and selling of marijuana or cocaine (11 percent). In addition, most of the women were living in urban areas and had weak attachments to their families prior to the offense that led to their imprisonment (Ebbe, 1985a: 92–93).

In another study, Ebbe found that heterogeneity in the urban areas led to weakened social control, which resulted in higher rates of crime and delinquency but not in the usual places. For example, higher rates of crime and delinquency were found in high- and medium-rent areas rather than low-income areas (Ebbe, 1989). It seems that in the former areas there is a lack of social integration and effective social control. In the latter areas, by contrast, there seems to be a high degree of parental control of juveniles and parental fear of coming in contact with the police if their kids get into trouble with the law (Ebbe, 1989: 763). Also, there seems to be "an incongruity between the residence of most [adult] offenders and the location of their offenses," as the extended family values and ethics of mutual responsibilities express themselves in the notion that "it is folly to rob or steal from a relative to whom one would apply for patronage in times of trouble and need" (Ebbe, 1989: 759).

Today, many offenders carry out their criminal activities in rural towns despite the deadly consequences. Still, crime in Nigeria is an urban phenomenon. Crimes of all types have emerged in Nigeria since the 1970s when the oil boom brought enormous wealth to many homes. At the same time, there are many poor youths who could not find employment in the cities as birthrates surpassed death rates. In effect, the people explosion that followed brought uncontrollable numbers of surplus population to the urban areas.

In general, the crime rate has increased as a result of increased urbanization caused by the creation of new government institutions, by new business enterprises by countries who have recognized Nigeria's political independence, and by the migration from rural to urban areas by people with little or no skills for lucrative jobs (Odekunle, 1978; Ebbe, 1982, 1985b, 1992). Crimes in the rural towns and villages remain domestic and occasional.

Unfortunately, the Nigerian police force (NPF) has not proved equal to the task of controlling the surging high incidence of crime in both rural and urban areas. Also, the NPF has no systematic records of crimes committed in Nigeria. This makes the study of crime rates in Nigeria very difficult. The available records (see Tables 10.1 and 10.2) are unreliable, because among other things, they do not include crimes committed in rural districts and towns. In addition, the NPF has not published "official" crime statistics since 1990.

Finally, with elite, civil service, and police corruption, organized crime has grown by leaps and bounds. Consequently, the political-criminal nexus has become a proven correlate or fact of life in Nigeria (Ebbe, 1997). Under elite corruption, the police have also become an agency for shielding and executing criminal enterprises. Presently, the elite are "beyond incrimination."

CONTEMPORARY CRIME CONTROL

The postcolonial period in Nigeria began on October 2, 1960. After Nigerian independence on October 1, the Nigerian police force came under the control of Nigerians. Within three years, the strength of the Nigerian police increased its number from what it had been in the colonial era. However, the number was still not enough to police the rural areas. The creation of more districts out of all the former colonial districts in 1960 brought the police closer to the rural towns and villages than ever before.

Table 10.1
Rates of Crime Based on Offenses Known to the Police, 1986–1987

Types of Offenses	1986 Number of Crimes Reported	1986 Cases Solved Percent	1986 Crime per 100,000	1987 Number of Crimes Reported	1987 Cases Solved Percent	1987 Crime per 100,000
1. Armed Robbery	1,217	66.7	1.52	1,436	57.2	1.77
2. Assault (Aggravated and Simple Assault)	56,832	85.4	71.18	52,117	61.6	64.31
3. Auto Theft	5,139	41.7	6.43	6,288	36.4	7.75
4. Burglary	11,223	41.6	17.81	15,319	41.2	18.90
5. Counterfeiting	541	48.4	0.67	581	42.9	0.71
6. Drug Offenses	316	42.8	0.39	422	46.9	0.52
7. Forgery	283	39.7	0.35	189	41.3	0.23
8. Fraud	387	29.3	0.48	287	35.2	0.35
9. Manslaughter	738	65.2	0.92	618	54.9	0.76
10. Murder	984	54.7	1.23	849	61.5	1.04
11. Rape	1,238	49.4	1.55	1,116	42.2	1.37
12. Smuggling	449	28.5	0.56	364	39.8	0.44
13. Stealing (Theft)	68,322	48.5	85.57	69,767	45.0	86.09
14. Strong-arm Robbery	826	49.9	1.03	944	49.9	1.16
Total	151,495	—	189.76	150,297	—	185.47
Population	70,835,000			81,035,000		

Notes: The rates of crime are computed based on the police reports, and the country's population was estimated from the 1991 Nigerian census report of 88,569,226.

Sources: Annual Reports of the Nigerian Police Force 1986–1989 and the Nigerian Year Book 1986–1989.

Table 10.2
Rates of Crime Based on Offenses Known to the Police, 1988–1989

Types of Offenses	1988			1989		
	Number of Crimes Reported	Cases Solved Percent	Crime per 100,000	Number of Crimes Reported	Cases Solved Percent	Crime per 100,000
1. Armed Robbery	1,529	46.5	1.83	1,389	44.9	1.61
2. Assault (Aggravated and Simple Assault)	55,334	62.4	66.31	54,116	53.0	62.97
3. Auto Theft	6,291	42.8	7.54	5,282	47.6	6.14
4. Burglary	13,862	41.8	16.61	12,678	49.3	14.75
5. Counterfeiting	488	37.7	0.58	472	41.7	0.54
6. Drug Offenses	593	45.9	0.71	588	45.2	0.68
7. Forgery	326	51.8	0.39	336	46.1	0.39
8. Fraud	457	13.3	0.54	492	37.8	0.57
9. Manslaughter	629	65.3	0.75	543	49.4	0.63
10. Murder	838	61.6	1.00	928	54.7	1.07
11. Rape	963	44.2	1.15	1,032	47.7	1.20
12. Smuggling	291	35.4	0.34	287	42.5	0.33
13. Stealing (Theft)	72,368	50.3	86.73	69,454	49.9	80.82
14. Strong-arm Robbery	851	50.8	1.01	865	46.6	1.00
Total	154,820	—	185.55	148,462	—	172.76
Population	83,435,000			85,935,000		

Notes: The rates of crime are computed based on the police reports, and the country's population was estimated from the 1991 Nigerian census report of 88,569,226.

Sources: Annual Reports of the Nigerian Police Force 1986–1989 and the Nigerian Year Book 1986–1989.

Nevertheless, crime control in the rural areas remained barbaric. For example, burglars caught in rural towns and villages had little chance of having their day in court. The men who caught them inflicted great bodily harm, then let the burglars go. The burglars usually died shortly thereafter, often before reaching their homes. Such cases were never reported to the police. This system of crude criminal justice began in the colonial period as a reaction to the English colonial system, which citizens viewed as having too many loopholes that set criminals free.

The crude, vigilante criminal justice that evolved in postcolonial Nigeria is still applied in some rural towns of Nigeria today. In fact, in the 1970s and 1980s, some urban areas such as Lagos, Onitsha, Aba, Port Harcourt, Enugu, Ibadan, Kano, and Benin City recorded incidents of robbers being burned alive with motor tires sprayed with gasoline. Shaming the offender by stripping him stark naked, then making him carry the item he stole on his head while dragging him half dead to the nearest police station as lashes are rained on his body is common practice today in Nigerian cities. Sometimes robbers are stoned to death by angry crowds though they are sometimes rescued by the police from throngs of angry people.

The contemporary crime control and prevention roles of the Nigerian police concentrate on sporadic patrol of the highways and mounting roadblocks to check for stolen vehicles, automobile and driver's licenses, and traffic violations. The frequent patrol of the neighborhoods to establish police presence in the cities and to catch criminal offenders in the act, common in Western urban centers, is not characteristic of Nigerian police law enforcement strategy. Instead, the Nigerian police resort to static law enforcement in which the police do not patrol the neighborhoods looking for legal violators and instead wait for victims or concerned citizens to report crimes (Ebbe, 1989, 1996).

In 1996, the federal government established a new crime prevention unit called "Operation Sweep." Operation Sweep is a paramilitary police force. It was created out of the Nigerian police force, whose members were given military training and charged with the responsibility of patrolling all of the major highways, busy seaports, and large city neighborhoods notorious for harboring dangerous criminals.

Crime Control at the Local Level

A local government area (LGA) in Nigeria today is equivalent to a county in the United States. Each local government area has a police subheadquarters. The LGA Council uses the police to control and prevent crime in its jurisdiction. The towns and villages under an LGA can go to the LGA police depot and report crime or encourage the police to investigate a criminal incident. In each LGA, the police mount roadblocks at major roads leading to the LGA to check the identity of persons driving into or through the LGA in order to know a stranger's mission in the area. Many armed robbers from different local government areas have been apprehended by this roadblock method of policing.

The LGA Council encourages towns and villages under its jurisdiction to continue to use the informal, traditional methods of crime prevention to help the police. Also, the LGA Council encourages cooperation between the police, rural town councils, and village councils to coordinate successful crime prevention strategies and offender apprehension endeavors.

Crime Control at the Village/Town Level

At the village or town council level, the traditional methods of crime control and prevention are still in vogue. Wooden and bamboo fences are still found at poor people's (heads of households) compounds. Also, the construction of mud and clay walls as antiburglary barriers at lower-class compounds is still very common throughout all the regions of Nigeria. As of May 1998, over 65 percent of all Nigerians still lived in the rural areas.

Town or village councils still maintain vigilante groups to prevent crime and apprehend offenders. Today, when a village vigilante group apprehends an offender, they take the offender to the village chief. The chief determines whether the offender should be taken to the police at the LGA headquarters or be disposed of by a fine and compensation to the victim, depending on the gravity of the offense.

Crime Control at the State/National Level

Nigeria has state and federal courts. At the state level, the Magistrate's Court is a court of original jurisdiction in criminal matters. An appeal can be made to a State High Court, which is the highest court of each state. The Magistrate's Court can dispose of an offender with a penalty as high as seven years of imprisonment without parole. And the State High Court can sentence an offender to a life of imprisonment. Nigeria also has a death penalty. If an offense involves the death penalty, the State High Court may transfer the case to a Special Tribunal, a Federal High Court, or the Nigerian Supreme Court.

Federal courts in Nigeria consist of the Supreme Court, the Federal High Court, and the Special Tribunals. The latter were established to handle armed robbery cases, drug trafficking, and counterfeit and currency offenses. Parole does not operate at any of the levels of the courts in Nigeria.

Nigerian prisons are classified in terms of maximum, medium, and minimum security, as is the case in most countries today. The Nigerian minimum security prisons are like the open prisons in Germany. There are no walls or barbed wires. The inmates there have committed petty offenses and have perpetrated such trivial offenses repeatedly. The Nigerian prison can be an offender's final home. Nigerian prisons today, as in 1980, are still predominantly filled with poverty-stricken men under the age of 35, with little or no education.

FUTURE OF CRIME AND CRIME CONTROL

The crime rate in Nigeria will continue to rise for as long as the social, political, and economic conditions continue to deteriorate and the gap between the haves and the have-nots continues to widen. Police corruption is a serious obstacle to effective crime control endeavors. The Nigerian police need to be reorganized to provide for internal control. In this view of "policing the police," Nigeria needs a strategic law enforcement agency stronger and more effective than the regular police. Such a strategic agency should be assigned to monitor transnational crimes and crimes involving domestic espionage, counterfeiting, bank fraud, embezzlement, political crime, civil service corruption, and police corruption. Such an agency would also be monitored by the police.

Men and women alike, at least in the near future of Nigeria, will continue to engage in roughly the same criminality. However, as women's crimes have been shaped by their presence or absence from the paid labor force, it is anticipated that their criminality will spread beyond smuggling contraband to include activities in the areas of embezzlement, forgery, and fraud. More important, organized crime, civil service corruption, and police corruption will continue unabated as part and parcel of the military dictatorship(s). Finally, under ineffective police operations, traditional methods of crime control and prevention and crude vigilante justice will continue to be employed as a source of redress for the masses.

REFERENCES

Achebe, Chinua. 1959. *Things Fall Apart*. New York: McDowell Obolenski.
Annual Reports of the Nigerian Police Force. 1990, 1989, 1988, 1987. *Offenses Known to the Police*. Lagos, Nigeria.
Ebbi, Obi N. I. 1982. *Crime in Nigeria: An Analysis of the Characteristics of Offenders Incarcerated in Nigerian Prisons*. Ann Arbor, MI: University Microfilms International.
———. 1985a. "The Correlates of Female Criminality in Nigeria." *International Journal of Comparative and Applied Criminal Justice* 9: 83–95.
———. 1985b. "Power and Criminal Law: Criminalization of Conduct Norms in a Colonial Regime." *International Journal of Comparative and Applied Criminal Justice* 9: 113–22.
———. 1989. "Crime and Delinquency in Metropolitan Lagos: Study of Crime and Delinquency Area Theory." *Social Forces* 67: 751–765.
———. 1992. "Juvenile Delinquency in Nigeria: The Problem of Application of

Western Theories." *International Journal of Comparative and Applied Criminal Justice* 16: 353–70.

———. 1996. *Comparative and International Criminal Justice Systems: Policing, Judiciary, and Corrections.* Boston: Butterworth/Heinemann.

———. 1997. "Political-Criminal Nexus in Nigeria: An Excerpt." *Trends in Organized Crime* 3 (Fall): 73–77.

Elias, Taslim O. 1954. *The Groundwork of Nigerian Law.* London: Routledge and Kegan Paul.

———. 1972. *Law and Social Change in Nigeria.* Lagos, Nigeria: Evans Brothers.

Gahia, Chukwuemeka. 1990. "Why They Struck: Coup Plotters Flaunt Their Reasons to Unseat Ibrahim Babangida." *African Guardian* 7 (May): 21–22.

Henderson, R. 1972. *The King in Every Man: Evolutionary Trends in Onitsha-Ibo Society and Culture.* New Haven, CT: Yale University Press.

Mba-Afolabi, Janet. 1995. "Haven for Fraudsters." *Newswatch* 4 (December): 17–18.

"New Law against Money Laundering Underway." 1993. *Nigerian News Update* 15 (January): 8.

"Nigeria Recovers Assets from Detained Bank Chiefs." 1995. *Nigerian Times* 1–14 (September): 29.

Niven, C. R. 1937. *A Short History of Nigeria.* London: Longmans, Green and Company.

Nwabueze, Boniface B. 1963. *The Machinery of Justice.* London: Butterworth.

Nwankpa, Emeka. 1998. "Two Abacha Ministers, Kin Share $2 Billion." *Guardian News* 3 (December): 1–2.

Odekunle, Femi. 1978. "Capitalist Economy and the Crime Problem in Nigeria." *Contemporary Crises* 2: 83–96.

Okonkwo, Cyprain O. 1966. *The Police and the Public in Nigeria.* London: Sweet and Maxwell.

Okonkwo, Cyprain O., and Michael E. Naish. 1964. *Criminal Law in Nigeria (Excluding the North).* London: Sweet and Maxwell.

Okpa, Ejike. 1995. "I Am Not One of the Corrupt Nigerian Military Officers." *Nigerian Times* 1–14 (September): 9.

Oroh, Abdul. 1990. "One Coup, Many Issues." *African Guardian* 7 (May): 23–24.

11

POLAND

(Developing Nation-State)

Wojciech Cebulak and Emil Plywaczewski

PROFILE OF POLAND

Poland is located in Central Europe on the Baltic Sea coast. In 1998 the population was 38.7 million. From the standpoint of nationality, Poland is a country that is almost uniform. There are relatively few ethnic minorities, about 1.5 million in all, mainly Ukrainians, Byelorussians, Germans, Czechs, Slovakians, Lithuanians, Jews, and Gypsies. There is also little religious diversity, as about 35 million people are Roman Catholic and some 543,000 are Orthodox Christians.

As a result of World War II, there occurred a sharp decrease in the nation's population, from 35 million people in 1939 to 24 million in 1946. The decline in people (over 6 million or 17.2 percent killed), relative to its overall population, represented the biggest population loss of all the countries involved in the war. Between 1945 and 1967 the country experienced a high birthrate, but in the 1980s and 1990s, a major slowdown occurred. The average population density is 123 people per square kilometer, with the highest in the Lodz, Warsaw (the capital), and Katowice Districts (or *voivodships*). Sixty-two percent of the country's population live in cities and towns, and there are 42 cities in the country with over 100,000 residents (*Nowa Encyklopedia Powszechna*, 1996).

Poland is an industrially based economy that until 1989 was dominated by a planned, socialist-style and state-owned political economy, strongly influenced by the economic system of the Soviet Union. At that time, comprehensive and long-term processes of economic restructuring were initiated as a departure from the socialist economy toward a free market, Western-oriented type of system. These consisted of the introduction of new tax rules and many other measures geared toward rendering the economy capitalist. Unfortunately, many other aspects of socioeconomic life have been addressed insufficiently, for instance, the much-needed social insurance reforms.

Since 1989 there have been increasing levels of poverty and unemployment. At the same time, beginning in the 1990s there were increases in the gross national product (2.6 percent in 1992, 3.8 percent in 1993, and about 6 percent in 1995), and in the period 1990–1995, foreign investment increased substantially from $2.6 billion in 1993 to over $5 billion at the beginning of 1995. Nevertheless, since 1991 Poland has found it difficult to retain a positive balance in foreign trade. In 1992 the balance was negative by $269 million, and by 1994 the negative balance had increased to $4.3 billion, 32 percent of which was trade with countries from the European Community (EC).

In short, these are strenuous economic times in Poland—in part, because the state's budget has a composition of revenue and expenditure that is different from the budgets of economically well-developed countries, a legacy of decades of the socialist system; in part, because it is very difficult to maintain a budget balance under conditions of radical economic transformation, especially when the state budget sector of the economy needs reform and the sources of state revenue are changing.

Politically, Poland is a unitary republic, and its most recent constitution is from 1997. The nation's political system is based on the division into the legislative, executive, and judicial branches of government. The legislative branch is made up of the Sejm and the Senate. The 460 Sejm deputies and the 100 senators are elected in popular elections for four-year terms. The main function of the Sejm is to legislate laws that the Senate can confirm, amend, or reject. Another important role of the Sejm is to conduct parliamentary control over activities of the executive branch of the government as well as to participate (sometimes with the Senate's role as well) in designating officials for some of the highest state offices. The Sejm and the Senate working together constitute the National Assembly whose functions include, among other things, the enactment of a new constitution, which is then subjected to popular vote in a national referendum. The executive branch consists of the president, elected popularly for a five-year term, and the Council of Ministers headed by a prime minister, all of whom are appointed by the president with the Sejm participating.

HISTORICAL PERSPECTIVE ON CRIME AND CRIME CONTROL

In the People's Republic of Poland (1944–1989), state criminal policies were initially designed and implemented under the extraordinarily difficult conditions of the situation immediately after World War II. The 1944–1947 period saw both the gradual liberation of Polish territory, the establishment of national and local agencies of the people's socialist government, and other events and legal measures that were designed to make Poland a socialist country. At the same time, a number of legal measures were declared that were of an interventionist nature or that increased the severity of criminal legislation. Strengthening the power of the people's socialist government became an important task of criminal law, thus protecting the political establishment being born. Criminal law also played a role related to "settling accounts," as manifested by various decrees that attempted to deal with cases of responsibility that had arisen during World War II.

It should be stressed, however, that during that period the Penal Code of 1932 remained in force, which was a major achievement—among other reasons because it was based on some progressive assumptions of the Sociological School of criminal law. In socialist Poland, many amendments were made to the Code, but another means of enacting criminal legislation was through various "supplementary laws" whose main task was to protect the new socialist regime and especially the state-owned and centrally managed economy, which was the economic basis of the regime. Another task of criminal law at the time was to create legal means of repressing political and economic opposition to the government.

The Penal Code of April 19, 1969 (the second Polish penal code after independence was regained in 1918) had the philosophy that the criminal law was also one of the main means of establishing the desired model of the state of so-called real socialism, with its central managed economy and totalitarian sociopolitical system. The approach did not differ by much from that of the legislation of the 1945–1969 period. Harsh criminal sanctions, especially for crimes against socialist property, economic crimes, and political acts against the state itself, played a very significant role at the time and had a big impact on criminal policy with regard to other types of crimes.

Research on criminal policy of the 1960s and 1970s revealed a decrease in the absolute number of crimes (from 2,476,147 crimes in 1965–1969 to 1,889,587 in 1971–1975) and in the number of criminal convictions (1,292,587 to 987,854, respectively). There was also a decrease in the number of recidivists and criminals who were reconvicted within the meaning of the Penal Code. However, one should keep in mind that some of the decrease was apparent only because a portion of less serious crimes was transferred into the category of infractions. Thus, the decreases were partially "artificial" because they were merely statistical and not reflective of the real crime situation (Buchala, 1978).

Against the background of other European countries, the situation with regard to the distribution of various penal sanctions, especially the role of imprisonment, was particularly bad. Whereas in most of Europe fines became the main type of punishment (over 80 percent of all sanctions in many countries), in Poland during the 1970s fines not accompanied by other punishments did not exceed 10 percent of sanctions, whereas another 10 percent constituted the punishment of limitation of liberty. The punishment of deprivation of liberty (imprisonment) without conditional suspension constituted about 25 percent of all penal sanctions, whereas deprivation of liberty with conditional suspension of its execution was on the average about 35 percent.

During the 1980s, the dominant role of the punishment of imprisonment in the overall picture of criminal sanctions was also a strong feature of criminal policies. As a result, the number of prison convicts exceeded 100,000 and approached the 130,000 mark at some points, which resulted in very high incarceration rates; for example, in 1973 the rate was 327 people per 100,000 inhabitants. By 1986, the rate was still high but had dropped to 290, even though the crime rate during this period had risen approximately 33 percent (from below 1,000 during the period 1974–1980 to about 1,500 in 1984–1985 per 100,000 inhabitants).

Regarding the ultimate sanction, the death penalty, the average number of executions was 12 in the 1970–1987 period. Beginning in 1988 a de facto moratorium on the death penalty was introduced; none of the ultimate sentences pronounced by the District Courts were confirmed by the Supreme Court. Instead, most of these death penalty cases were converted into 25-year sentences of imprisonment.

PUBLIC PERCEPTION OF CRIME AND CRIME CONTROL

Recent surveys of public prosecutors and judges as well as the general public reveal that the death penalty in Poland is favored by close to three quarters of the population. For example, according to a 1994 survey of 784 public prosecutors and judges, 75 percent of the former and 61 percent of the latter were in favor of retaining the death penalty (*Prawo i Zycie*, 1995). Meanwhile, a 1997 public opinion poll showed that 74 percent of Poles were in favor of retaining it, whereas 21 percent were in favor of abolishing the death penalty (CBOS, 1997).

At the same time, it appears that the current liberalization trends in criminal policy by the independent courts in Poland are supported by the people, a product most probably due to the societal emotional scars from the communist period. In other words, Polish society is very sensitive to the issue of human rights. Therefore, the public perception of all cases of real or alleged violations of those rights result in very aggressive (not to say irrational in some cases) responses by many defenders of civil and human rights.

Unfortunately, the beneficiaries of these interventions have mostly been convicted criminals themselves, rather than crime victims or witnesses. Conversely, it has been rare that human rights activists would intervene on behalf of victims of robbery or assault, for example, who have not been able to get justice because the case has been dragging forever in the justice system.

Increasing crime rates during the 1990s, moreover, have not resulted in altering the liberalization of crime control policies in Poland.

CONTEMPORARY CRIME

Central and Eastern European political and economic transformations that have been occurring in Poland since 1989 have resulted in many social changes. Some of these are unfortunately pathological phenomena, including a rise in criminality. Rapid and often uncontrolled social and economic change has brought about many new criminogenic factors that are mainly of an economic nature. Among the many concurrent factors that have created particularly advantageous conditions for the spread of crime are:

1. The inadequacies of the legal system in not catching up with developments in society that have created loopholes in the law that are taken advantage of by criminals;

2. The international connections of the criminal world under the conditions of liberalization in travel to and from Poland and the easing of restrictions on the flow of merchandise across borders;

3. The increasing unemployment and the rising percentage of the population living in poverty, along with the simultaneous discrepancies between the poor and the new class of rich businesspeople, which create frustration that often results in illegal behaviors;

4. The inadequate allocation of financial resources for the needs of the justice system coupled with a declining workforce in law enforcement.

After 1989, unprecedented rises in the crime rate began to occur in Poland (see Table 11.1). In 1990, for example, the number of recorded crimes rose by over 60 percent, from 547,569 the year before to 883,346. The overall crime rate increases have continued in the 1990s, culminating in over 992,000 in 1997, a 10.5 percent increase from 1996 (Komenda Glowna Policji, 1998).

Victimization surveys, however, have demonstrated that the "dark figure of crime" remains very high in Poland. It is estimated that police are not aware (on the average) of three fourths of the crime really committed. Naturally, the percentage varies with crime type: Some 80 percent of thefts of private property, 70 percent of assault with bodily injury, over 60 percent of robberies, and 45 percent of burglaries are never reported to police. The overall reporting rates have been much lower in Poland than in Western countries, which should also be kept in mind when interpreting the official crime statistics (Siemaszko, 1997).

Throughout the 1990s, crime has been mostly concentrated in the biggest city centers, such as Warsaw, Katowice, Gdansk, Krakow, Szczecin, Wroclaw, Poznan, and Lodz Districts. The rates of crime in these cities have

Table 11.1
Crimes Recorded, 1985–1997

Year	Crimes Recorded	Rate per 100,000 Population
1985	544,361	1,463
1986	507,913	1,356
1987	508,513	1,350
1988	475,273	1,255
1989	547,569	1,442
1990	883,346	2,317
1991	866,094	2,264
1992	881,076	3,296
1993	852,507	2,215
1994	906,157	2,351
1995	974,941	2,526
1996	897,751	2,325
1997	992,373	2,568

Source: Statistical Reports of the Information Bureau, Main Police Headquarters, Warsaw, 1998.

also increased. The regions with the highest crime rates are the Warsaw District (3,736 crimes per 100,000 population), the Szczecin District (3,658), and the Gdansk District (3,656).

Crime committed by foreign nationals has also been rising in Poland. Considering that in 1997 alone 88.3 million foreigners came to visit Poland, it is no wonder that such huge movements across the country's borders could not have gone unnoticed by criminal groups. Among foreigners suspected of having committed criminal acts in 1997, citizens of the countries of the former USSR constituted about 70 percent (the other most frequent nationalities were Germans and Romanians). The most frequent crimes are burglary, larceny of private property, robbery, and dealing in stolen goods. Citizens of the former USSR also increasingly commit murders, robberies with guns, thefts of cars and their transportation abroad, extorting money from other Russian nationals temporarily in Poland, organized prostitution, failing to register with proper authorities upon arrival, and unlawful extensions of stay in Poland.

Crimes against the Person

The main trends of violent crime in Poland are an increase in the number of crimes committed with guns and explosives, an internationalization of violent crime, a gradual increase in the participation of foreign nationals (especially from the former USSR), and an increase in the phenomenon of "settling scores" in the form of murder, aggravated assault, kidnapping, and terrorist acts. In the 1990–1997 period, the number of recorded murders increased 49.7 percent to 1,093 in 1997. The motives for murder have been gradually changing.

Since 1990, for example, murders associated with domestic (family) violence, robberies, rape or sexual assault, and acts of unknown circumstances have all been decreasing. On the other hand, murders committed in the context of hooliganism and "other" categories, including "settling scores," have increased. The socially disturbing category of killings as part of "settling scores" was simply unheard of prior to 1990, when 2 acts were reported for the first time. By 1997 the number of such killings had risen to 59. Similarly, the number of aggravated assaults (with guns or other dangerous weapons) has also been on the rise: from 495 in 1990 to 1,389 in 1997.

The most dangerous aspect of the changes in the picture of violent crime has been the spread of weapons as instruments of committing murder. It is noteworthy that up until the mid-1990s murder by guns was so infrequent that it was statistically insignificant. But by 1996 and 1997, a rapid increase of such cases (278 and 260, respectively) had been reported. The spread of the use of guns also applies to some other crimes, especially robbery and extortion. Not only have the rates of gun use increased since 1990, but perpetrators of these acts have displayed an increasing brutality with their usage. Behind the increasing use of guns by criminals lies the increasing easiness of obtaining weapons, demonstrated by the rising number of weapons confiscated by law enforcement from illegal users.

Armed robberies have been targeting gas stations, foreign currency exchange units, and cargo-carrying vans, including armored trucks carrying cash. Such acts were virtually unknown in the 1980s. The most dangerous form of highway robbery involves the "holdup" of cargo-carrying vans. Perpetrators of these acts have become increasingly ingenious in their methods; disguising themselves as police officers was especially popular in the late 1990s. The goods stolen most often are electronic equipment, coffee, and large volumes of cigarettes.

Crimes against Property

Private property has been increasingly endangered since 1990, unlike state-owned property, whose overall volume has been falling due to transformations of the economy, especially in terms of privatization. The main form of stealing private property is through burglary of privately owned motor vehicles, businesses, and homes. Burglary with theft of private property has been the most frequent crime against property for years. The year 1990 was the peak year, with over 313,000 crimes, which was 35 percent of all recorded crime in Poland. Car theft has increased 10-fold since 1990, reaching the highest level in 1997 (over 53,000 crimes).

The theft of cars has been associated with the presence of international organized criminal groups and their increasing professionalization and specialization. The increasing professionalization of these perpetrators is exemplified by the smuggling of motor vehicles by international, specialized groups who have become very good at forging vehicle identification marks and documents and transporting the vehicles abroad quickly. In recent years, Polish customs officials have been seizing over 3,000 stolen vehicles per year as attempts are made to smuggle them out of the country.

As a result of changes in the country's economic system, the picture of economic crime has also changed. Crimes like speculation, using shortage goods, mismanagement, or creating a deficit in a unit of state-owned property have all been on the decrease and have given way to new forms of economic crime that are associated with the transformation of the economy into a free market. The main new types of economic crime include obtaining large volumes of merchandise under false pretenses by perpetrators who run illegal businesses; obtaining massive bank loans under false pretenses, frequently with the participation of corrupt bank officials; custom fraud and tax fraud committed in an organized manner, frequently resulting in long-term income for the offender and enormous losses to the state treasury; introducing financial means derived from crime into the legal economic system (money laundering); and intellectual piracy in areas of cinematography, photography, and computer software. Most of the above crimes involve some kind of fraud, especially pertaining to obtaining goods, services, loans, credits, and bank guarantees under false pretenses.

Organized crime has also become a major law enforcement and social problem. In 1996 the justice system revealed that there were 377 functioning organized criminal groups in the country, with 4,744 identified members, including 158 groups having 522 foreign nationals coming from 37 countries (e.g., Ukraine, Russia, Germany, Vietnam, Albania, and Bulgaria). These organized criminal groups have been mainly active in the following areas: crime related to production and trade in narcotics, extortions, robberies, kidnappings, tax fraud and other financial fraud, forgery of money, smuggling of goods, money laundering, dealing in guns and explosives, forgery of documents, and bomb attacks (Komenda Glowna Policji, 1998).

CONTEMPORARY CRIME CONTROL

The transition away from a centrally planned economy to a free market economy has had a significant impact overall on crime control in Poland, the consequences of which one could argue have been both positive and negative. In restructuring the economy and the state apparatus to facilitate the transition to the new economic system, there has been a reduction in both the manpower and financial resources of the criminal justice system as the problem of crime has become more serious and challenging. In the first few years of the 1990s, both the number of police officers and budgetary allocations for law enforcement suffered radical decreases. For example, there were 121,707 police jobs in 1990 but only 105,000 in 1992.

The fall of the communist system in Europe and the resulting sociopolitical transformations in Poland have also required changes in the legal system. These have affected both the structure and operation of the courts as well as the policies and practices of punishment. Today, the judicial branch of government consists of the Supreme Court, common courts, and courts of special jurisdiction. The Office of the Public Prosecutor is subordinated to the Minister of Justice, and its task is to prosecute violations of the Criminal Law (*Nowa Encyklopedia Powszechna*, 1996).

The new Constitution of 1997 contains a section entitled "Personal Freedoms and Rights" that includes a statement of the "nullum crimen sine lege" principle—the rule that every person who has been detained or imprisoned should be treated in a humanitarian manner; a declaration of the right to compensation for the illegally imprisoned; the right to defense counsel at all stages of the criminal proceedings; presumption of innocence; and the right to a fair, public, and speedy hearing of one's case by a procedurally correct, independent, and impartial court. Trials may also be made secret due to reasons of decency, security of the state, public order, protection of private lives of the parties, or some other important private interest; but even in those cases, verdicts are always announced publicly (Constitution of the Republic of Poland, Articles 41–45, 1997).

In addition, there are the Constitutional Tribunal and the Tribunal of the State. The former makes declarations on the constitutionality of laws and on the commonly binding interpretation of laws. The latter determines matters of constitutional and sometimes criminal responsibility of the state's highest officials like the president and members of the Council of Ministers. Finally, the Supreme Chamber of Control has been established to control economic, financial, and organizational activities of state administrative agencies, among others, and the Civil Rights Spokesman guards against violations of citizens' rights and freedom that have been declared in the Constitution and other legal documents.

Official state penal policies have also been influenced by the sociopolitical changes. In actuality, however, work on the new set of penal codes (the Penal Code, the Code of Criminal Procedure, and the Code of the Execution of Penalties) began at the end of 1980 (under the old political regime). One of the strong factors behind the movement for a new legislation was that criminal policies conducted on the basis of the 1969 Code had been strongly criticized by academic circles (Plywaczewski, 1991). The first drafts of the new codes were ready in 1981. But the introduction of martial law in December of that year resulted in a suspension of the proceedings of the Codification Commission. Work on the new criminal legislation was resumed in 1987, with drafts of the new codes ready in 1991. The main intention behind the new legislation was to abandon the ideology of total-itarianism, human rights violations, and arbitrary and irrational application of harsh criminal sanctions that led ultimately to a disastrous level of prison overcrowding. Finally, on June 6, 1997 the Sejm enacted the three new codes, which became effective on September 1, 1998.

Beginning with 1988, one can see very clearly a gradual process of soft-ening the harshness of penal sanctions. A continuous decrease of the pop-ulation of inmates is one proof of this trend: Whereas there were over 95,000 people behind bars in 1985, over 108,000 in 1986, and over 96,000 in 1987, the figure for 1988 was slightly over 80,000 and for 1989 about 58,000 (the year of amnesty). The falling trend continued in 1990 (about 45,000 inmates), but there were increases in 1991 and 1992 (about 56,000 and about 61,000, respectively). As of 1998 the number was between 60,000 and 65,000. Nevertheless, as the number of crimes have increased since 1990, the courts have not returned to the trend of applying impris-onment whenever possible (Hirsch et al., 1997).

As early as 1998, a number of very disturbing trends in criminal policies were observed. First, the clearance rate for crimes whose perpetrators were not known at the time of crime detection could be described as disastrous (about 20 percent). Second, even if police succeed in apprehending the offender, most cases are discontinued by prosecutors during the course of pretrial proceedings (only 20 percent of prosecutorial proceedings result in the filing of an indictment in court). At the same time, the number of pretrial detentions has fallen continuously over the past few years. Third, the few cases that manage to get to court result in conditional suspension of the execution of penalty, including cases involving serious crimes. Fourth, even if the offender is really incarcerated without a suspension of the penalty, he or she is very likely (about 90 percent of cases) to be released on fur-loughs, with some convicts spending up to three months in the community. On top of this, close to 50 percent of inmates take advantage of conditional early release from prison.

This is not to suggest that there is some kind of direct or causal link between the less frequent use and reduction in the severity of the penal sanction and crime. Rather, the rise in crime must be seen in the context of the high price that Poland has been paying for the political, social, and economic transformations since 1989. Changes in the economy, market re-forms, and a liberalization of the law, taken together, were bound to result in negative trends in the overall picture of pathological phenomena, includ-ing a rise in crime (Holyst, 1996).

Finally, the contemporary assessment of crime control is that for several years now the Polish justice system has faced a very difficult situation of personnel shortages as well as rising organizational and financial problems. Prosecutors and courts find themselves under the burden of impossible case-loads that are increasingly backlogged as cases keep piling up. The number of prisoners behind bars and in juvenile detention centers is also growing. In sum, the situation demonstrates that the system of crime control is in deep crisis and requires immediate action. However, the current legal framework, personnel shortages, state financial picture, and lack of modern technical equipment all compound the crisis (Siemaszko, 1996).

FUTURE OF CRIME AND CRIME CONTROL

In the near future, there are no indications that crime rates are going to decrease in Poland. The current predictions are that the ongoing political, economic, and social changes will continue to have their impact on the nature of criminal acts—meaning that a lot of contemporary trends in crime will become even more dangerous to the well-being and lives of Polish citizens. The main sources of this increased danger are thought to stem from the following criminal activities:

1. Murder, especially committed with robbery or for reasons of "settling scores" like making somebody pay back a loan, turf battles including terrorist bomb attacks, and criminals exacting their own punishments against one another;
2. Robbery with use of guns, especially against commercial establishments, railway cargo, and armored trucks;
3. Increased flow of foreign nationals resulting in increased levels of crime committed by some of them;
4. Crime related to drugs.

Furthermore, in the future the activities of organized crime will continue to increase the size of the underground economy and economic crime more generally. Specifically, organized crime will be especially influenced by factors like:

1. The economic crisis in the country and the state of law designed to deal with it (e.g., loopholes in the law, the liberalization of criminal law, and the increasingly tight tax laws);
2. The further development of the entertainment industry, which has already become a battleground for organized criminal groups;
3. The increased production and trade in controlled substances;
4. The continuing flow of foreign nationals, some of whom will form organized criminal groups based on criteria of ethnic origin (i.e., Albanian, Turkish, Russian, Byelorussian, Ukrainian, and Vietnamese groups are predicted to be especially active);
5. The continuing brutalization of criminal acts committed with guns and explosives.

And as the underground economy continues to develop, it will exact enormous costs (i.e., tax losses) from the state treasury as well as decrease economic efficiency, for instance, through unfair competition. Moreover, the lack of proper legal regulations to combat money laundering will continue to contribute to its spreading, which will, in turn, boost organized crime and expose bank officials to the dangers of corruption. At the same time, the cooperation between domestic organized criminal groups and their foreign partners will increase, too, as will the penetration of Poland by foreign groups. In sum, it is predicted that organized criminal groups will become increasingly more sophisticated, investing their financial means (e.g., laundered money) in legal enterprises. This will, in turn, result in these criminal groups playing a more dominant role in such enterprises as the entertainment industry, the real estate market, construction businesses, stock exchanges, insurance companies, and banks.

Finally, it is predicted that a completely new class of offenders will appear: people of high social prestige and very good interpersonal connections who regard illegal activity as routine business. Using previously established contacts in the political and economic establishment, they will try to ensure participation of top public officials, offering them business advantages or by making contributions to political parties in return for tax and custom concessions, favorable loans, revealing state secrets, or providing economic information. Some of these symptoms are already present in Poland.

In terms of the future of crime control, it is expected that many of the provisions of the new criminal legislation should effectively improve crime fighting. For example, the problem of witness fear of revenge by criminals will be addressed by introducing a new type of witness—the "incognito witness"—whose identity will be secret and who will not testify at trials. Instead, the only way for defendants and their counsel to ask questions of such witnesses will be to use the court or the prosecutor as intermediaries (Komenda Glowna Policji, 1998).

The situation of crime victims is also expected to improve radically under the recently passed criminal legislation. The new Penal Code makes the severity of punishment dependent on, among others, the perpetrator's attitude toward his or her victim, including the issue of whether the offender repaired the damage. It is argued that these new provisions improving the victim's position will make Polish codes unique in the world in their progressive approach (Waltos, 1998a, 1998b).

The overall outlook for the future remains gloomy. But there is no other choice than to remain hopeful that somehow, at least, the worst symptoms of the crisis will gradually be addressed. There certainly seems to be enough awareness of the problems and enough goodwill to initiate steps toward getting back to "normalcy" where there was once less crime and more effective crime control. Of course, the problem is how to secure enough finances, infrastructure, and organizational changes to transform the goodwill into concrete results.

REFERENCES

Buchala, Kazimierz. 1978. "Polityka karna w latach 1970–1975 na tle ogolnych zasad wymiaru kary" (Criminal policy in 1970–1975 against the background of general principles of sentencing). *Zeszyty Naukowe Instytutu badania Prawa Sadowego*, no. 9: 41–64.
CBOS. 1997. *Komunikat z badan* (Public Opinion Research Center, research report). Warsaw: Author.
Hirsch, Hans Joachim, Piotr Hofmanski, Emil Plywaczewski, and Claus Roxin. 1997. *Prawo karne i proces karny wobec nowych form i technik przestepczosci* (Criminal law and criminal procedure facing new forms and techniques of crime). Rev. ed. Bialystok: Temida 2.
Holyst, Brunnon. 1996. "Economic Crime in Poland during the Period of Changes in the Social and Economic System (Selected Problems)." *Eurocriminology* 10: 185–225.
Komenda Glowna Policji. 1998. *Raport o stanie i prognozach przestepczosci* (Main Police Headquarters: Report on the state of crime and future predictions). Warsaw: Author.
Nowa Encyklopedia Powszechna (New common encyclopedia). 1996. Vol. 5. Warsaw: Wydawnictwa Naukowe PWN.
Plywaczewski, Emil. 1991. "Kriminalpolitik und die neusten Reforbestrebungen in Polen [Ausgewahlte Fragen]" (Criminal policy and the most recent reform plans—selected questions). *Revue Penale Suisse* 1, 108: 1–23.
Prawo i Zycie (Law and Life legal weekly). 1995. 25. Warsaw.
Siemaszko, Andzej (ed.). 1996. *Quo Vadis Iusticia?* [praca zbiorowa] (Where are you going justice?). Warsaw: Instytut Wymiaru Sprawiedliwosci.
———. 1997. *Przestepczosc nieujawniona w Polsce* (Unreported crime in Poland). Warsaw: Instytut Wymiaru Sprawiedliwosci.
Statistical Reports of the Information Bureau. 1998. "Crimes Recorded by Main Police Headquarters." Warsaw.
Waltos, Stanislaw. 1998a. *Kodeks postepowania karnego-wprowadzenie* (Introduction to the Code of Criminal Procedure). Warsaw: Wydawnictwa Prawnicze PWN.
———. 1998b. "Krzywsa i prawo" (Injury and law). *Prawo i Zycie (Law and Life* legal weekly), June 9–16.

12

RUSSIA

(Developing Nation-State)

William Alex Pridemore

PROFILE OF RUSSIA

The geography of contemporary Russia extends more than 5,500 miles east to west and from 1,500 to 2,500 miles north to south. Containing within its borders vast steppes of dark fertile soil, unending forests, sunny southern resorts on the Black Sea, and the frozen tundra of the Arctic Circle, Russia is the largest country in the world and stretches across 10 time zones, with a geographic area 75 percent greater than the United States. This area holds abundant natural resources such as precious diamond and gold deposits, producing 15 to 20 percent of the world's crude oil and iron ore and more than a quarter of its natural gas (Russian Embassy, 1998).

In 1998 the Russian Federation was home to 147 million (U.S. Bureau of the Census, 1998), with another 20 million Russians living outside the country in republics of the Commonwealth of Independent States (Harris, 1993). About 80 percent of the population live in European Russia (Lappo, 1992), with approximately 10 percent residing in Moscow and the surrounding oblast (Heleniak, 1994). The middle decades of this century saw rapid migration from rural areas to cities, and nearly three quarters of the Russian population now live in urban areas (Kingkade, 1997). At the time of the revolution in 1917, more than three fourths of the population lived in rural areas. Today, with 169 urban settlements boasting more than 100,000 residents each (GosKomStat Rossii, 1993), Russia has become a "country of large cities" (Harris, 1970).

Containing more than 120 ethnic groups within its borders, Russia is also a country of diverse peoples (Bakirov, 1993). Although 80 percent of the population are reported to be ethnic Russian, 4 percent Tatar, and 3 percent Ukrainian, the 1989 census revealed 36 ethnic groups with at least 100,000 people (Schwartz, 1991). All of these groups pragmatically assimilated during Soviet rule, but many have managed to maintain distinct cultural identities (Bakirov, 1993). Ethnic groups have had differential access to power and economic opportunities in the past, presenting them with socioeconomic disadvantages then and today (Sacks, 1995).

In the final days of the Union of Soviet Socialist Republics (1991), the union was split into 15 successor states, the largest and most populous of which is the Russian Federation. The Federation consists of a complex system of 49 regions (*oblasti*), 21 republics (*republiki*), 10 autonomous areas (*oruga*), six territories (*kraya*), two federal cities (Moscow and Saint Petersburg), and one autonomous region (Russian Embassy, 1998). The executive and legislative branches of the government are popularly elected. The upper house of Parliament—the Federation Council—consists of 2 representatives from each of the 89 Federation members. The lower house—the State Duma—has 450 deputies representing smaller districts.

The dismantling of the command economy and the transition toward a free market began in earnest in 1992. Since that time, production dropped, inflation skyrocketed, unemployment worsened, and poverty became widespread. Central planning had left local economies poorly integrated. Soviet industrial infrastructure was dated, and parts needed for repair nonexistent or long in arriving. Moreover, Russia's lack of hard currency at the beginning of the transition, in combination with a low level of foreign investment that did not match its industrial and natural potential, has prevented the importation of technology needed to modernize the country (Panel, 1992).

Although inequality existed in the former Soviet Union at a level not in accordance with official ideology, it was not as extreme as it is today. World Bank (1997) calculations show a per capita gross domestic product (GDP) of $2,400 for 1996, but this average is not likely indicative of the true situation, as variation is increasing across business sectors and geographic regions. For example, only a year into the transition the per capita income of the "richest" region (the Far East) was nearly twice that of the "poorest" region (central Chernozem) in Russia (*Izvestiya*, 1993).

Social stratification has increased due to variation in wages among different business sectors. Though this polarization is exacerbated now, it should be noted that there was a clear differentiation in earnings during the Soviet years due to political considerations, such as decisions concerning which sectors were most crucial to the Party's economic plans (Connor, 1997). Today, in some regions workers in the gas industry make nearly twice as much as those in the coal industry and more than twenty-five times those laboring in the glass industry (Shaw, 1993). A year after the breakup of the

Soviet Union, the top 20 percent of Russian wage earners were receiving 41 percent of the income; the bottom 20 percent, only 7 percent.

According to official Russian data, unemployment was 3.3 percent in mid-1997. An International Labor Office report, however, puts this number at 9.6 percent (Labour Market, 1997). This may not present a true picture, as hidden unemployment is growing (Starikov, 1996), and many workers who retain their jobs may go unpaid for months at a time. The increase in unemployment, official and unofficial, and the decline in productivity, along with the Russian government's reduced spending on social needs, have led to all kinds of devastating social problems, including widespread poverty, decreased life expectancy, increased infant mortality and homicide rates, and so forth.

HISTORICAL PERSPECTIVE ON CRIME AND CRIME CONTROL

Russia is an ancient state, dating back more than a thousand years, and its history is rich and complex. For the purposes of contextualizing the development of crime and crime control in twentieth-century Russia, a simple introduction to the history of this century is provided. In 1904–1905, Russia experienced an unexpected defeat in the Russo-Japanese war. "Bloody Sunday" also occurred in January 1905, when the guard began firing into a crowd of 200,000 workers who had marched on the Winter Palace in St. Petersburg to petition the Tsar for better working conditions. Hundreds of men, women, and children were killed that historic day. A decade later, World War I took a heavy toll on Russia as approximately 2 million people were lost in the poorly managed war campaign. In 1917, in what was then Petrograd (St. Petersburg), hunger and discontent led to riots. Only this time, soldiers mutinied instead of firing upon the people.

On March 1, 1917, Tsar Nikolai II abdicated the throne, and power was passed to a provisional government. In October of that same year, Vladimir Il'ich Lenin's Bolsheviks stormed the government strongholds and arrested the leaders of the provisional government. A civil war ensued, and it was not until 1921 that Lenin's party prevailed. The enigmatic leader died less than three years later, and the reins of the Communist Party were eventually wrested by the Georgian Josef Stalin. Stalin soon forced collectivization upon the peasants, believing this would be an inexpensive and dependable means of feeding the growing cities and aiding the massive increase in industrialization mandated by the first Five Year Plan. During Stalin's regime, there were famines and political purges of undesirables that took some 3 million lives in 1932–1933 and political purges of undesirables that accounted for another 700,000 shot to death and more than a million sent to labor camps in 1937–1938 during the Great Terror (Tucker, 1990).

By the time the Germans invaded in June, 1942, the Russians had used the second and third Five Year Plans to build a daunting war machine. Collectivization, mass deportations, and Party purges, however, had left Russia without a trained officer corps. The Russians, accordingly, suffered tremendous civil and military casualties during World War II, including losing the lives of some 25 million people. Stalin, the architect of the Gulag, famines, and purges that resulted in approximately 20 million deaths, died in 1953.

The Ukrainian Nikita Khrushchev became head of the Communist Party and began a process of de-Stalinization. His secret speech in 1956 to the 20th Party Congress condemned Stalin's crimes against the Russian people. Liberalization ensued as the new leader attempted to decentralize economic power and fight corruption within the Party. The Central Committee of the Communist Party became increasingly disenchanted with Khrushchev and relieved him of his duties in 1964. Khrushchev's liberalization was followed by Leonid Brezhnev's conservative reaction. The liberal reforms were disbanded, and Brezhnev reinstated Stalin's place among the heroes of the Soviet Union while tightening internal controls. Repression increased, and officials of the political economy became increasingly corrupt—the General Secretary himself was known to be intimately tied to organized criminal activities.

Brezhnev died in 1982, and the next two Party leaders, Yuri Andropov and Konstantin Chernenko, would die after serving only about a year each. Mikhail Gorbachev then became General Secretary of the Communist Party. Gorbachev recognized the dangers of the slumping economy and of the policies of Brezhnev's regime. He filled important posts with "fresh blood" and began campaigns against corruption and alcoholism. Glasnost (openness) called for a more transparent and accountable bureaucracy and allowed public criticism of the old regime, and perestroika (restructuring) opened the economy to limited private enterprise and ownership. As the old command economy began to crumble, however, the limited private sector was not strong enough to take up the slack. Supplies diminished and prices rose. Although individual freedoms increased dramatically under Gorbachev's leadership, the stumbling economy could not support him. The last gasp of the old guard occurred in August 1991 when it attempted to wrest power from Gorbachev. The coup attempt failed, Boris Yeltsin took control, and within days the Communist Party was banned and Gorbachev resigned as its chief. The leaders of Russia, Ukraine, and Belarus met four months later, agreed that the USSR no longer existed, and announced the formation of the Commonwealth of Independent States. In December of 1991 the hammer and sickle of the Soviet flag disappeared from the Kremlin and was replaced by the banner of the new Russian Federation.

Crime

The confluence in Russia of revolution, World War I, and civil war created highly criminogenic conditions in the country during the mid- to late 1910s (Zeldes, 1981). Police forces were fighting in the world war or engaged in a civil struggle at home, leaving no one to protect citizens from each other or to investigate crimes. Overall crime rates peaked in 1924 and declined throughout the rest of the decade (Shelley, 1979). Closer scrutiny, however, reveals that much of the decline was due to the decriminalization of some minor crimes and recategorizing them into administrative offenses (Solomon, 1981) and that there was actually an increase in the official number of cases of bribery and hooliganism due to campaigns against them. Although political offenders were added to the list of criminals in the 1930s, their offenses were "administrative," so they did not show up in official crime rates.

A situation similar to the years following the revolution occurred during World War II; crime rates, especially juvenile delinquency, rose dramatically. The war's devastation left little order, and thousands of orphaned adolescents resorted to criminal activities to stay alive. Later, as the Russian baby boomers hit adolescence at the close of the 1950s and the early 1960s, crime rates again increased. Butler (1992) reports that, barring a few cases of sizable increases or decreases, the overall crime rate was relatively stable from the mid-1960s until the early 1980s. Along with Gorbachev's restructuring in the mid-1980s, however, came dramatic increases in violence, juvenile delinquency, and organized crime.

In 1961, the Ministry of the Interior was reorganized and became responsible for the collection of crime data. Soviet officials began releasing crime data to researchers and the public in 1985, and now data aggregated to the regional level are released regularly. Even with a more reliable system of data collection and a willingness to share information, any statistics should be approached with caution due to the usual problems associated with measuring instances of crime.

Soviet-Specific Crimes

The ideology of communism applied to crime and crime control in unique kinds of ways. First, communist ideology mixed with the Soviet's perception of widespread threat to society resulted in crimes uncommon to Western societies. Second, the problems associated with a centrally planned economy stimulated the development of a "black market" or hidden economy. Hooliganism, agitation, parasitism, and speculation were examples of crimes against Soviet Russia that are either rare or nonexistent in Western societies with market economies.

Hooliganism was defined as a form of public social misconduct (Zeldes, 1981; Butler, 1992). Its ambiguous definition allowed it to be used at various times against vagrants, drunks, and those who committed assault. In general, however, hooliganism was applied almost universally to intoxicated juveniles and young men who exhibited offensive behavior in a public place. Anti-Soviet agitation and propaganda was another type of behavior more or less restricted in Soviet Russia. As Ralph Slovenko suggests in his foreword to Zeldes's 1981 book, the Soviet Union acted more like a cause than a country. Officials were obsessed with ideology, and speaking out against the communist cause was forbidden, sometimes to the point of repression and even execution. The decriminalization of certain types of hooliganism began in the late 1970s, but it was not until the 1980s that the state ceased to prosecute "anti-Soviet agitation" and related crimes (Foglesong, 1997).

Parasitism and speculation are also closely linked to communist ideology. Parasitism was generally defined as being without a job for a set period of time, which the Soviets believed resulted in living off of society without contributing to its well-being (Zeldes, 1981). Since jobs were supposedly provided for everyone, being unemployed meant that one was a parasite living off the work of others, and this was a crime in Soviet Russia. Speculation is a major component of a free market and anathema to communist ideology. Article 154 of the Criminal Code made it illegal to buy and resell goods at a profit, which was fundamental to a "private-property mentality" (Schwartz, 1991). Petty speculation began to be decriminalized in the late 1970s, and the number of prosecutions for parasitism was halved during the 1980s (Foglesong, 1997).

At the same time, it is important to underscore that laws against speculation, and against such crimes as "padding" (i.e., falsifying economic reports to meet quotas) and "expediting" (i.e., using bribes and mutual influence to procure necessary but scarce services and raw materials), were not strictly enforced. Similarly, managers who committed economic crimes that benefited the factory or firm (i.e., "corporate" crime) often had investigations against them halted by Party officials (Solomon, 1992). It is likely that leaders recognized the utility of this behavior and the hidden (shadow) market, which provided goods and services that the command economy could not, so it was tolerated by officials. Meanwhile, corruption occurred at the highest levels, and embezzlement, bribery, and organized crime were common. These elements were well established by the time perestroika began and provided the foundation for the high level of organized criminal activity that was to flourish in Russia following the breakup of the Soviet Union.

In sum, the centrally planned economy was the keystone to Soviet Russia. Shortages, both for producers in terms of raw materials and for consumers in terms of goods and services, resulted in a shadow economy that competed with the state economy. In the process, criminal behavior was created within and outside the system. Faced with difficulties in procuring needed inputs on one end and the necessity of meeting quotas on the other, factory chiefs used "expediters" to obtain raw materials. They also entertained and provided gifts of scarce goods to suppliers and provided illegal bonuses to workers as incentives to meet quotas (Adler, 1993). Lower down the social hierarchy, pilfering from the workplace became an accepted way to boost low incomes. For example, a worker at a shoe factory could steal shoes to shod his or her family or to trade with a neighbor who worked in a state store and had access to fresh bread and other goods. This was a daily event. Poor security, record keeping, and supervision on the part of factory chiefs facilitated its existence (Schwartz, 1991).

Criminal Justice Policy

The legal keystone of Soviet crime control policy was the assertion in Article 39 of the Constitution that the law shall be based not upon the protection of individual rights but on the individual's obligations to society and the protection of the collective (Allen, 1993). This focus on social protection was enhanced by the centralized control of the Communist Party over all aspects of life and the definition of societal interests. Thus, criminal policy could be dictated according to the Party's interpretations of Marxist-Leninist philosophy. Legislation in the postrevolutionary era was a mixture of preventive and repressive measures influenced by the positivist criminology of the period and the Bolsheviks' need to shore up political control (Solomon, 1978).

The Bolsheviks' "revolutionary legality" and antilaw perspective were discarded by Stalin, who viewed the role of law as a mechanism for the creation and maintenance of a centralized Soviet government (Solomon, 1996). Law was neither a good in and of itself nor a source of social change but was instead an instrument used to stabilize the country and solidify Stalin's power. This was done through increasing the range and intensity of repression, as Stalin employed the criminal law beyond its normal use. Terror was not the chief form of control, however, and Stalin's word was not absolute. Officials and criminal justice practitioners sometimes resisted, for example, and refused to hand out the harsh punishments mandated by strict legislation. Following Stalin's death, repression lessened, and preventive and educational measures gradually regained significance, but the key features of Stalin's system remained until perestroika.

The Party's political power and monopoly over decision making, together with its stress on crime reduction and convictions at the expense of procedural rules, resulted in arbitrary and dictatorial enforcement (Dobek and Laird, 1990). Numerous agencies were invested with legislative authority, and the amount of policy created was overwhelming. Many laws delineating offending behavior and prescribing punishment were not published, and legal definitions of socially dangerous acts were often vague ("hooliganism," "anti-Soviet propaganda," "agitation"), offering inordinately wide discretion to enforcement agents. Keeping track of this deluge of policy was confusing enough for officials; Russian citizens were bewildered and came to live by another unwritten rule: "Everything is prohibited unless allowed by law."

The Police

The paternalistic, ideological, and repressive nature of the Soviet regime led to an intrusive police force with a broad mission and wide-ranging powers (Shelley, 1990). The nationalized police force was controlled from the center and was employed as a tool to implement Party policy. Its authority was nearly absolute at times, and this authority usually prevailed over the written law. Though the *militsia* (police) did not lead political repressions, they were accomplices in controlling the Party's political enemies. Beside policing political and traditional crimes, they were responsible for controlling economic crimes as well, making for a police force with extensive powers.

The police became increasingly professional under the Soviets, though still often corrupt and always closely tied to central Communist command. Under Stalin the *militsia* was a repressive instrument for the autocrat. Khrushchev wrested control of the police back to the Party, narrowed its mission to nonpolitical traditional and economic crimes, and remanded more accountability to the Russian citizens (Shelley, 1990). Under Brezhnev the police became more efficient and updated their technical capabilities, although at the same time becoming increasingly political and corrupt. More than 200,000 employees were released from the Ministry of the Interior following Brezhnev's leadership, but as the most visible and proximate symbol of corrupt power, the *militsia* still faced a legitimacy crisis. The force was further humiliated as Gorbachev's changes led to (1) unending reports of corruption and brutality in a newly free press, (2) increasing protections and freedoms for citizens, which produced more crime and reduced the police's ability to use coercive tactics to combat it, and (3) widespread and sophisticated organized crime at a time when the police lacked money, power, and a mandate to keep up with the criminal element.

The Procuracy

The prosecutor's office—or as it is known in Russia, the procuracy (from the Latin *procuria*, to supervise)—was the "premier institution of the Soviet legal establishment" (Smith, 1992: 1). Stalin and Procurator-General Andrei Vyshinskii ceded special powers to the procuracy: The office supervised the investigation of the accused while at the same time securing the protection of the accused's rights. In other words, the investigator was supposed to be a neutral figure searching for both incriminating and exculpatory evidence. But since the procuracy was ultimately evaluated on its ability to secure a conviction, the office could overlook the use of coercive techniques by the investigators or the *militsia* in order to maintain high conviction rates. There was thus little worry of being confronted with the knowledge of abuse of the accused's procedural rights since the procuracy's remarkable powers meant that the office supervised itself (Dobek and Laird, 1990; Smith, 1992).

During certain periods, especially the late 1950s and throughout the 1960s, the procuracy did provide some protections to citizens. For example, in a system lacking proper judicial review, many people turned to the procurator's office for relief from illegally imposed fines and complaints concerning housing and pensions (Smith, 1997). Overall, however, due to the abuses of power and the public's view of the procuracy as a means of state control, it was yet another agency facing a legitimacy crisis as the Soviet Union began to dissolve.

The Judiciary

Throughout Soviet times an assumption of guilt on the part of the judiciary was common, so much so that as late as the 1980s a survey by *Moskovskaya Pravda* (1987) found that over 40 percent of judges questioned assumed the guilt of the defendant before the trial began. And since the use of jury trials was rescinded following the revolution in 1917 (Allen, 1993), judges made the final decision of guilt or innocence and sentenced the offender.

The ultimate decision in some cases was not the judge's, however, but the Party's. An impartial and independent judiciary did not exist in Russia; judges were expected to follow Party dictates. The Communist Party was the true interpreter of the law in all matters—this came from the notion of *pravo kontrolya* (the right of supervision): Communist officials made all decisions vested with Party or ideological interests. The Party selected candidates to be placed on the ballot for judicial elections and, when necessary, used "telephone law" to make the necessary political or ideological decision in a case and pass it along to the presiding judge. Finally, the role of the judiciary and the basis for its evaluation were the same as for the police and the procuracy—to aid in the reduction of crime—and effectiveness was measured by their conviction rate. Evidentiary rules and legal procedure thus meant little. All of this resulted in an astounding conviction rate in the Soviet judicial proceedings of 99.7 percent (Dobek and Laird, 1990).

The Correctional System

The correctional system of the Communist regime is perhaps the most widely discussed control mechanism of Soviet society. Article 20 of the Criminal Code gave a tripartite mission to the prisons: just deserts, deterrence, and rehabilitation (Terrill, 1997). Except for the years of the Great Purges, rehabilitation was probably the most important function, and ideology played the dominant role in rehabilitating and reeducating prisoners. Political education was mandatory and meant to mold prisoners into model Soviet citizens who followed the socialist way of life, labored diligently, and adhered closely to all laws (Amnesty International, 1980). Weekly classes with propaganda-laden discussions and explications of Soviet law were common. These meetings were universally despised among inmates and often farcical—the political prisoners, especially those inmates in the Gulag, were highly educated and more versed in Marxist-Leninist thought than their instructors (Getty, Rittersporn, and Zemskov, 1993).

Conditions in the Gulag were spartan, and high death rates were common, due in large part to epidemics, poor medical services, and untrained personnel. Malnutrition was widespread and debilitating, given the harsh conditions of the camps and the physically demanding regimen of "socially significant labor" mandated by the government. Over a million inmates died in the camps between 1934 and 1953 (Getty, Rittersporn, and Zemskov, 1993). Abuse against inmates by a guard force that was undertrained, underpaid, and living in conditions scarcely more accommodating than those of the prisoners was common.

A final unique aspect of control under the Soviets was the assignment of political and religious deviants to psychiatric hospitals for "treatment" (Slovenko, 1983). Psychiatric diagnoses were made by state-employed psychiatrists, and after this determination, the accused lost any remaining procedural rights and was not allowed to view his or her file—including the name of the doctor, the diagnosis, and recommendations for treatment (Amnesty International, 1980). By and large, these were normal individuals whose crime (and diagnosis) was to be perceived as politically dangerous by officials. They were given diagnoses such as "nervous exhaustion brought on by her search for justice," "schizophrenia with religious delirium," and "delusional ideas of reformism" (Amnesty International, 1980: 184). The "special psychiatric hospitals" were highly secretive institutions, with no provision in the Criminal Code governing their conditions. Such measures eventually disappeared, and these psychiatric units are now under the auspices of the Ministry of Health.

PUBLIC PERCEPTION OF CRIME AND CRIME CONTROL

The contemporary institutions of crime control continue to face problems of internal corruption and stigma associated with the legacies of the various legitimation crises involved with policing, the procuracy, the judiciary, and corrections during Soviet rule. On top of this, rising crime rates, administrative positions held by the same officials who inhabited such posts under the Soviet regime, and the government's current inability to fund even the most basic programs necessary for these agencies to function efficiently and effectively, have all had obvious negative consequences on the public perception of crime and crime control.

In other words, the distrust held by Soviet citizens for each institution of criminal justice administration and control has not disappeared. Still in the minds of the Russian people are the Soviet criminal policies and system of criminal justice with few procedural protections and a resulting crime control that was not only arbitrary and subject to unpublished decrees and bureaucratic regulations but unable to enforce its laws against privileged members of society. Individuals were unprotected by the state as the Party intervened into the functioning of the courts.

Today, Russian citizens are wary of the police and have lost confidence in the *militsia*'s ability to do its job, which has become a major reason for not reporting crimes. At the same time, increases in both the level and seriousness of crime in the country over the past decade, and decreases in the state's ability to control deviant behavior, have increased Russian fears of crime and victimization. Repeated opinion polls have revealed that the fear of criminal victimization is as important to Russians as the current economic and political troubles (Terrill, 1997). Moreover, these same polls suggest that citizens have become less tolerant in their views toward offenders, calling for tougher policies from lawmakers and more punitive measures for lawbreakers.

CONTEMPORARY CRIME

The rise in crime rates began in the years leading to the collapse of the Soviet Union, and increases since that time have also been dramatic. Although most countries of the former Soviet Union have experienced similar problems with crime, Russia's rates have tended to be higher than in the other Republics. Increases have been common across different types of crime and across the urban/rural demarcation, but they are not uniform; some regions have experienced much higher rates of increase than others (Ministerstvo Vnutrennikh Del [MVD], 1996, 1998).

Although absolute numbers differ substantially, both official and mortality data show an approximate doubling in homicide rates during the 1990s. Using mortality data from the World Health Organization (1995), Russia now has an annual homicide rate (about 32 per 100,000) that is more than three times greater than in the United States (about 10 per 100,000). The percentage of homicides as a share of all violent crimes in Russia has been increasing, and homicide rates among women and juveniles have risen faster than the overall rate. The use of firearms in both homicides and crimes involving serious bodily injury has become more common as well.

Nikiforov (1994) claims that youth and senior citizens have been the most victimized cohorts in Russia. He also states that 81 percent of all victims and 63 percent of those receiving serious bodily injury during a crime were victimized by a family member or friend. Victimization surveys have also shown a high level of unrecorded crime in Russia (Alvazzi del Frate and Goryainov, 1994). For example, more than a third of bodily injuries and sexual crimes have not been reported to the police. Other reasons for not reporting crimes to the police, besides lost confidence in law enforcement, were also common to victimization surveys: trivial nature of crime, fear of reprisal, avoidance of publicity, and the victim's own involvement in criminal activity.

About a third of the victimizations that have been reported have received no response or were concealed by the police because they were perceived to be unsolvable. Citizens' low level of reporting and the *militsia* failure to register and investigate many crimes have severely hampered the ability to control the crime problem, as public confidence in governmental agencies decreases, the true level and costs of crime remain hidden, and policy makers and policing agencies are unable to adequately respond since they do not possess valid information.

Women

Russian women have faced victimization in the transition in terms of both socioeconomic status and crime. Attention to the situation of women was a stated element of glasnost, but the ensuing economic and political crises buried this initiative. Unemployment has been much higher among women, and those who have worked have received wages well below the average for men. Rising divorce rates and the introduction of fees for services in health care and education have left basic expenses well beyond the means of many women and their children as they experience the feminization of poverty in Russia. The country lacks a strong women's movement to bring these conditions to the fore, however, and academic studies of gender and gender relations are still in their infancy (Sillaste, 1994). It is therefore unlikely that these issues—and their intersection with criminality and victimization—will receive the attention they deserve any time soon.

Violence against women, for example, has only recently begun to receive serious attention in Russian society. Domestic violence was rarely acknowledged under the Soviets and data never made public. Today, Russian women are two and one-half times more likely to be killed by their husbands or lovers than women in the United States, who, in turn, are themselves about two times more likely to be victimized in this manner than women in most other developed countries (Gondolf and Shestakov, 1997). Women with low incomes and minority status have been at an even higher risk. Unfortunately, housing shortages and the generally low economic status of women make it nearly impossible for most women to find their way out of abusive relationships.

Juveniles

The amount and intensity of crime committed by juveniles are increasing in Russia. The country has no separate juvenile justice system to cope with the problem, and the mechanisms it does possess to handle delinquents are taxed by a lack of resources. Further, there have been no programs designed to treat the larger percentage of youthful offenders with mental and emotional problems.

Finckenauer (1996) reports that the overall rate of growth in juvenile delinquency is 10 times higher than increases in adult offending. The 1980s experienced an increase in violence and participation in subcultural groups in the country (that did not abate in the 1990s) as drug and alcohol abuse rose at a time when teens were becoming increasingly disenchanted with the communist system and exhibiting heightened consumeristic desires (Finckenauer and Kelly, 1992). Supplies of Western goods were not available from the command economy, and adolescents turned to the black market both to fulfill their demand and to gain the means (via theft and prostitution) to purchase what they wished. For children and adolescents, these structural changes occurring in transitional Russia often mean a weak educational system, few recreational outlets, poverty, divorced parents, and poor supervision. These factors have translated into criminal involvement, violence, and victimization, not unlike the periods in Russia following the civil war and World War II, when similar factors were associated with rising rates of juvenile delinquency.

Organized Crime and Corruption

Organized crime and corruption did not originate with perestroika or the transition but have an animated history in Soviet Russia. Party officials tolerated the black market because it provided supplies of goods and services to consumers that the command economy could not and because they often benefited personally from its existence. Connections between officials and the criminal element were common. The organized criminal clans in Soviet Russia laid the foundation for the illegal structures that exist today, and the former *nomenklatura* were uniquely situated to take advantage of privatization.

As the transition developed, criminal groups, the government bureaucracy, and the business sector have operated together in a "criminal oligarchy." Since there is no civil law tradition in Russia, many transactions are unregulated. Criminal groups, moreover, bribe (and coerce) officials for preferential treatment, and they extort business owners to gain racketeering profits (Center for Strategic and International Studies [CSIS], 1997).

Organized crime groups maintain a strong presence in both legitimate and illegitimate markets. They control narcotics and weapons trading, gam-

bling, prostitution, and racketeering (Kryshtanovskaia, 1996). They take advantage of impoverished military and government agencies to procure
weapons, raw materials, and communications and transportation networks.
They recruit highly skilled military and policing officers for security and to
organize operations. They are also "illegally" involved in "legal" ventures,
blurring one with the other. They either own or control major banking
structures and oil, food, and raw material companies. It is estimated that
the black market's share of Russia's gross domestic product is 40 percent,
and Ministry of Interior officials estimate that through extortion, organized
crime has its hands on 40 percent of private companies, 60 percent of state-
run businesses, and 50 percent of banks in Russia (CSIS, 1997).

The history of ambivalent attitudes toward the law and the custom of
completing extralegal business transactions continue today. Political elites
often carry out their duties in a capricious manner and sometimes go beyond
the bounds of the Constitution. The heavy tax burden imposed on businesses virtually assures that they will maintain two sets of books, thus encouraging them to do business outside the legal framework and dissuading
them from using legal means of dispute resolution (Coulloudon, 1997).
These "anti-rule-of-law constituencies" act in ways that continually under-
mine their effectiveness and ability to combat crime and to support law and
order.

At the local level, most businesses prefer not to be involved with criminal
organizations but are forced to pay tribute. This may often be an attractive
deal for business owners, however, as these groups create a *krysha* ("roof"),
which offers services to the owner such as protection, collection of debts,
and even business and legal advice. As these criminal groups become involved with legal operations and diversify their holdings, they become increasingly complex and professional organizations. They often create legal
security services that allow them to obtain gun permits and for which they
can recruit heavily from the military, KGB, and police structures. Sports
clubs and charitable organizations are also popular legal fronts for organized
crime, from which they embezzle funds or use the status of the organization
to smuggle products tax free into or out of the country (Kryshtanovskaia,
1996; CSIS, 1997). Most Russian criminal organizations have also been
quick to use violence and will target nearly anyone. They have been heavily
armed, and public shootouts and assassinations have not been uncommon
(i.e., the MVD [1997] estimates there to be about 500 contract killings per
year).

In sum, officials can do little to stop organized crime and the corruption
within their ranks. Organized crime groups can buy positions as aides to
members of the Duma. Administrators can be forced or bribed to issue
permits and licenses to build or sell or import. Government officials are paid
to divert state goods and services for private use. Tax agents can be manip-

ulated to reduce tax burdens of organized crime's legal ventures. Informants within policing agencies are bribed to tip off local crime syndicates of an impending raid or arrest. These are only a few examples of the many ways in which the state and criminal element cooperate.

CONTEMPORARY CRIME CONTROL

The structure and mission of contemporary crime control institutions in Russia are experiencing dramatic changes. The transition is no small matter to these institutions: The shift from a totalitarian state and a command economy to democracy and a free market is a new path, and the fundamental philosophies are at odds with each other. Crime control agencies in general are usually reluctant or resistent to change, and this has been the case in Russia. Further, the formation and implementation of new criminal policy have been unable to keep pace with the social, political, and economic changes.

The Police

The structure and mission of the *militsia* are changing at a time when internal and external difficulties threaten to thwart this shift. Internal problems include staff shortages, low salaries, lack of necessary equipment, and corruption (Williams and Serrins, 1993). The small size of the officer corps is exacerbated by its low level of training and experience, creating an absence of skilled investigators and thus a lower rate of crimes solved at a time when serious crimes are increasing.

The unavailability of resources is not new to the *militsia*, which experienced cutbacks under Brezhnev and Gorbachev. However, the general lack of funds in Russia today makes the police situation even worse. Communications systems and transport pools are out of date, and computerization of records is in its protean stage. Meager resources means low salaries for administrators and officers. This makes it difficult to hire and retain qualified recruits, leaving the *militsia* littered with incompetent officers. Low salaries also make officers susceptible to corruption, many of whom find ingenious ways to pad their income.

In addition, the related activities of mafia-related crimes, from extortion to contract killings to plundering Russia's raw materials, contribute further to low morale within the ranks. Nevertheless, progress is occurring within the *militsia*. Both the U.S. Federal Bureau of Investigation (FBI) and German police authorities are currently aiding the MVD in its coordination of the police, and the U.S. National Institute of Justice is providing support for the Ministry in its effort to computerize operations. Military downsizing in Russia has meant that the *militsia* can find new recruits in the form of conscripts, and now more women are being hired as officers, although most are still assigned to office jobs or to work with juvenile delinquents (Terrill, 1997).

The Procuracy and the Judiciary

The procuracy continues to exercise more power than any other agency within the system, but the office is caught up in a legal and political struggle to retain its status. First, its strong supervisory role presents a challenge to the creation of an independent judiciary (Smith, 1997), a key factor in the development of legal order in Russia. Second, widespread crime and corruption in the country are being used by the law and order faction in Parliament as an excuse to maintain a strong procuracy. The fear of crime and the push to exploit this also make already shaky procedural protections even more tenuous.

Formerly, courts in Russia were administered by the Ministry of Justice, but as of 1998, a separate Court Department oversees their functions. The accused's right to counsel has been expanded, as has the court's attention to procedural protections (Terrill, 1997). The jury system was reinstated soon after the breakup of the Soviet Union, but its use is relegated to the most serious crimes and to limited areas of the Russian Federation, owing largely to the inherently expensive nature of this endeavor (Solomon, 1997). The use of jury trials has also been hampered by the maintenance of broad appellate powers for higher judges (Foglesong, 1997). There is little deference to the findings of the trial court, and appellate courts commonly repeal decisions on matters of fact, not legal issues. Juries are employed infrequently—there were less than 1,100 jury trials in Russia between 1993 and 1997.

The judiciary's accusatory bias and lack of independence were recognized as its major faults in the past. Both of these are still major threats today, but the problems may spring from different sources. For example, the conviction rate dropped from 94 percent in 1980 to 84 percent in 1990, largely a function of fewer people being convicted without sufficient evidence (Foglesong, 1997). However, although there is more emphasis placed on procedural protections and the rights of the accused, a Code of Criminal Procedure is yet to be adopted, and there is a lack of qualified advocates and judges across the country. Also, the frequency of criminal cases almost doubled between 1988 and 1995, and the number of civil cases more than doubled from 1993 to 1995 (Solomon, 1997). The shortage of the primary participants of the courtroom and the rising number of cases mean congested dockets and prolonged investigations that result in pretrial detention periods that commonly last 10 months. These issues create lingering suspicions of accusatory bias within the courts.

Corrections

Russian prisons have a checkered history, and the fundamental ambition today is to humanize the system. Throughout the 1980s, communist officials made concerted efforts to reduce the prison population, mostly through alternative punishments and reformational programs, reducing the prison population by about 60 percent in the decade and the rate of incarceration down to 300 inmates per 100,000. However, by 1993, a dramatic increase in the custodial population (in response to the increasing criminality) had moved Russia into the position of having the highest incarceration rate in the world, 558 per 100,000 (Mauer, 1995).

The prison system is operated by the Ministry of the Interior and guarded by male *militsia* troops. The Ministry has recognized, however, that the role of a police officer and the role of a prison guard are not identical; it is in the process of creating special guard detachments trained specifically for work in the prisons (Nikiforov, 1994). In the prison system, men are separated from women and juveniles from adults. The death penalty is available, but the maximum length of incarceration for any one offense, according to the 1996 Criminal Code, is 25 years. The average sentence actually imposed is 5 years 6 months; the average time served is 3 years 1 month (King, 1994). Movement within the system to different types of regimes is possible and can be used to reward or punish inmates based upon their behavior while incarcerated. Furlough is also available to inmates who maintain a good record of behavior in prison and are not deemed to be a social threat. Parole is an option as well, but King (1994) estimates that only about 8 percent of inmates leave prison substantially early for good behavior.

In 1994 there were 764 corrective-labor (*ispravitel'no-trudovich*) colonies and 13 cellular prisons (Nikiforov, 1994), as well as 160 "remand" prisons where the accused await their trial (King, 1994). Most inmates are sent to labor colonies, and between a third and a half are sent to the Siberian Far East or Far North, where colonies are often isolated and the weather is harsh. Though theoretically the regimes become increasingly more exacting in moving from "general" to "reinforced" to "strict" to "special" types of colonies, in fact, the first three vary little, and only the latter shows significant signs of tighter control than the others. The prison infrastructure is left over from the Soviets, who constructed prisons to be used for labor. Thus, inmates live not in cells but in military-style barracks grouped together in a compound—within which they are relatively free to move about—with an industrial plant nearby.

Living conditions are poor within these institutions. The remand prisons hold several times their inmate capacity. Though not as crowded, the colonies are (1) disease ridden (i.e., inmates die from tuberculosis at 17 times the rate of the Russian population), (2) often unable to maintain the basic dietary needs of the inmates, (3) becoming more violent, and (4) without essential medical facilities. Inmates are allowed conjugal visits and food packages, but most prisoners are too far from home to have family members visit, and food parcels are often picked through or pilfered before they reach the inmate. It is a rule that all inmates must work, but prison industries are no longer state subsidized, and only a fraction of the inmates are provided meaningful jobs.

Most prison guards, especially those in more isolated colonies, live in similar conditions to the inmates. Ministry of Interior officials and prison administrators do not deny the existence of these problems and are trying to combat them, but with few resources, poor infrastructure, staff shortages, and high crimes rates, they are incapable of remedying the situation. Again, administrators face these negative elements at a time when they are attempting to reclaim legitimacy for a prison system that has been humiliated by a history of slave labor and terror.

In sum, contemporary crime control mechanisms are reciprocally related to rising rates of crime and corruption in Russia. The history of and conditions within these institutions have created opportunities for corruption, whereas their inability to counter criminal behavior (which has tripled since perestroika began) reduces any deterrence factor they may possess. The future of crime and crime control will have to find critical ways to balance these contradictory relationships.

FUTURE OF CRIME AND CRIME CONTROL

Russia has experienced tremendous changes during the 1990s. The moorings of Soviet life were uprooted and a totalitarian regime fell. The move toward a less intrusive government, protected individual freedoms, and a market economy seems inevitable. The transition period, however, will be protracted, and given Russia's unique cultural and historical experience, the result will not be a mirror image of Western-style democracies. At the same time, along with these developments have come painful costs, including an alarming increase in criminal activity and severe strains on criminal justice institutions.

This overview of crime and crime control has presented a country besieged by bleak conditions that are likely to prevail in the near future. The transition is essentially about the role of the state in the affairs of the country, which must retract itself from capricious controller to a facilitator that applies the law uniformly (Gray and Hendley, 1997). Where past reforms in Russia were meant to unify power in the hands of the state, new reforms must be used to strengthen democratic norms and legal order. The appearance of democratic legal institutions in the country is not new; pre-Bolshevik Russia also had these trappings (Berman, 1963). Then, as now, however, their presence does not guarantee the infusion into the system of the fundamental premises of democracy. Similarly, the supply of law is likely to go unused without the demand for it from rule of law constituencies who will benefit from and lobby for it (Gray and Hendley, 1997; Holmes, 1997).

On the other hand, the legal profession is becoming increasingly popular, which is likely to improve the supply and quality of advocates and judges. Likewise, the judiciary's development of self-governing organizations will allow it to impose standards of training and conduct, as well as providing an outlet for legal debate and creating a claims-making body capable of pressuring other branches of government (Solomon, 1997). Overall, the ability of the procuracy and the judiciary to adapt to their new roles and to carry out their new functions will be one of the vital steps in creating legal order in the Russian Federation.

Another fundamental hurdle is the natural strain faced by Russia in trying to promote economic development via privatization (which itself provides opportunities for corruption) while at the same time attempting to implement democratic reforms. In different words, capitalism does not equal (and sometimes opposes) popularly held views of democracy. Those who have made their fortune may eventually begin to reinvest profits into the Russian economy and thus begin to seek a stronger legal environment to protect and support their gains. But Russia's resources are vast, and there are many who still wish to illegally profit from them, and as long as the rule of law is absent and the state has little coercive power, public theft and insiderism will continue. The contention over the roles of the criminal justice actors in the new Russian legal system has become heavily politicized, and legal reforms, as well as the economic and political reforms to which they are inherently connected, will likely take decades to develop.

Positive changes have occurred, however, and there is reason for guarded optimism in some areas. To be sure, old Soviet structures, laws, and bureaucrats remain, but the legitimacy of totalitarian control has dissolved. The demographic shocks experienced by the population are abating (Heleniak, 1995), and Ministry of Interior [Ministerstvo Vnutrennikh Del] data (1997) show plateaus and even decreases in many crime categories for 1997—though this may be the result of the *militsia*'s practice of not recording insoluble crimes (Alvazzi del Frate and Goryainov, 1994; Solomon, 1997). In time, crime control institutions should become more efficient in combating crime and more protective of Russian citizens as they develop legal cultures and improve their capabilities with increased resources, more highly trained personnel, and modern techniques. However, as King (1994) notes, given the history of abuse within these agencies, it is not enough for them to claim that they have corrected the errors in their ways. Individual actors and the institutions themselves must make a conscious and publicly visible effort to prove their move toward legal order is sincere.

REFERENCES

Adler, Nanci. 1993. "Planned Economy and Unplanned Criminality: The Soviet Experience." *International Journal of Comparative and Applied Criminal Justice* 17: 189–202.

Allen, G. Frederick. 1993. "Restructuring Justice in Russia: A New Era of Challenges." *International Journal of Comparative and Applied Criminal Justice* 17: 173–80.

Alvazzi del Frate, Anna, and Konstantin Goryainov (eds.). 1994. *Latent Crime in Russia.* United Nations Interregional Crime and Justice Research Institute Issues and Reports, No. 1. Rome: United Nations Interregional Crime and Justice Research Institute.

Amnesty International. 1980. *Prisoners of Conscience in the USSR: Their Treatment and Conditions.* London: Quartermaine House Ltd.

Bakirov, Vil Sovbanovich. 1993. "New Ethnic Relations Generated by the Disintegration of a Multi-national State: The Case of the Former USSR." Paper presented at the Italian Sociological Association and the Institute of International Sociology of Gorizia's International Conference on Ethnic Groups, Borders, Europe; Brioni, Croatia.

Berman, Harold J. 1963. *Justice in the U.S.S.R.: An Interpretation of Russian Law.* Cambridge, MA: Harvard University Press.

Butler, W. E. 1992. "Crime in the Soviet Union: Early Glimpses of the True Story." *British Journal of Criminology* 32: 144–159.

Center for Strategic and International Studies (CSIS). 1997. *Russian Organized Crime.* Washington, DC: Author.

Connor, Walter D. 1997. "Observations on the Status of Russia's Workers." *Post-Soviet Geography and Economics* 38: 550–57.

Coulloudon, Virginie. 1997. "The Criminalization of Russia's Political Elite." *East European Constitutional Review* 6, 4: 73–78.

Dobek, Mariusz Mark, and Roy D. Laird. 1990. "Perestroika and a 'Law-Governed' Soviet State: Criminal Law." *Review in Socialist Law* 2: 135–61.

Finckenauer, James O. 1996. "Russia." In Donald J. Shoemaker (ed.), *International Handbook on Juvenile Justice.* Westport, CT: Greenwood Press.

Finckenauer, James O., and Linda Kelly. 1992. "Juvenile Delinquency and Youth Subcultures in the Former Soviet Union." *International Journal of Comparative and Applied Criminal Justice* 16: 247–61.

Foglesong, Todd. 1997. "The Reform of Criminal Justice and Evolution of Judicial Dependence in late Soviet Russia." In Peter H. Solomon, Jr. (ed.), *Reforming Justice in Russia, 1864–1996: Power, Culture, and the Limits of Legal Order.* Armonk, NY: M. E. Sharpe.

Getty, J. Arch, Gabor T. Rittersporn, and Viktor N. Zemskov. 1993. "Victims of the Soviet Penal System in the Pre-War Years: A First Approach on the Basis of Archival Evidence." *American Historical Review* 98: 1017–49.

Gondolf, Edward W., and Dmitri Shestakov. 1997. "Spousal Homicide in Russia versus the United States: Preliminary Findings and Implications." *Journal of Family Violence* 12: 63–74.

GosKomStat Rossii. 1993. *Chislennost' naseleniya Rossiiskoi Federatsii: Po goradam, rabochim poselkam i raionam 1 Yanvarya 1993* (The population of the Russian Federation: By city, workers' settlements, and regions on 1 January 1993). Moscow: Respublikanskii Informatsionno-Izdatel'skii Tsentr.

Gray, Cheryl W., and Kathryn Hendley. 1997. "Developing Commercial Law in Transition Economies: Examples from Hungary and Russia." In Jeffrey D. Sachs and Katharina Pistor (eds.), *The Rule of Law and Economic Reform in Russia*. Boulder, CO: Westview Press.

Harris, Chauncy. 1970. *Cities of the Soviet Union*. Chicago: Association of American Geographers.

———. 1993. "The New Russian Minorities: A Statistical Overview." *Post-Soviet Geography* 34: 1–27.

Heleniak, Timothy. 1994. "The Projected Population of Russia in 2005." *Post-Soviet Geography* 35: 608–14.

———. 1995. "Is Russia's Demographic Situation Improving?" *Post-Soviet Geography* 36: 644–46.

Holmes, Stephen. 1997. "Introduction." *East European Constitutional Review* 6, 4: 69–70.

Izvestiya. 1993. February 13, 4.

King, Roy. 1994. "Russian Prisons after Perestroika: End of the Gulag?" *British Journal of Criminology* 34: 62–82.

Kingkade, W. Ward. 1997. *Population Trends: Russia*. Washington, DC: United States Bureau of the Census.

Kryshtanovskaia, Ol'ga V. 1996. "Illegal Structures in Russia." *Russian Social Science Review* 37, 6: 44–64.

Labour Market. 1997. *Russian Economic Trends*. [Online], October. Available: http://cep.lse.ac.uk/datalib/ret/update/oct97/labour.htm

Lappo, G. M. 1992. "Urban Policy in Russia: A Geographic Perspective." *Post-Soviet Geography* 33: 516–32.

Mauer, Marc. 1995. "The International Use of Incarceration." *The Prison Journal* 75: 113–23.

Ministerstvo Vnutrennikh Del (MVD). 1997. *Sostoyanie prestupnosti v Rossii, za 1997 god* (The condition of crime in Russia in 1997). Moscow: Author.

———. 1998. *Prestupnost's i pravonarusheniya, 1991–1995* (Crime and delinquency, 1991–1995). Moscow: Author.

Moskovskaya Pravda. 1987. May 17, 3.

Nikiforov, Ilya V. 1994. "Russia." In Graeme Newman, Adam C. Bouloukos, and Debra Cohen (eds.), *World Factbook of Criminal Justice Systems*. [Online]. Available: http://www.ojp.usdoj.gov/bjs/pub/ascii/wfbcjrus.txt

Panel on Patterns of Disintegration in the Former Soviet Union. 1992. *Post-Soviet Geography* 33: 347–404.

Russian Embassy. 1998. [Online]. Available: http://www.russianembassy.org

Sachs, Michael Paul. 1995. "Ethnic and Gender Divisions in the Work Force of Russia." *Post-Soviet Geography* 36: 1–12.

Schwartz, Lee. 1991. "USSR Nationality Redistribution by Republic, 1979–1989: From Published Results of the 1989 All-Union Census." *Soviet Geography* 32: 209–48.

Shaw, Denis J. B. 1993. "News Notes: Russia's Division into 'Rich' and 'Poor' Regions." *Post-Soviet Geography* 34: 323–25.

Shelley, Louise. 1979. "Soviet Criminology after the Revolution." *Journal of Criminal Law and Criminology* 70: 391–96.

———. 1990. "Policing Soviet Society: The Evolution of State Control." *Law and Social Inquiry* 15: 479–520.

Sillaste, G. G. 1994. "Sotsiogenernye otnosheniya v period sotsial'noi transformatsii Rossii" (Sociogender relations in the period of social transformation in Russia). *Sotsiologicheskie-Issledovania* 21, 3: 15–22.

Slovenko, Ralph. 1983. "Psychiatric Postdichting and the Second Opinion on Grigorenko." *Journal of Psychiatry and Law* 11: 387–412.

Smith, Gordon B. 1992. *Perestroika and the Procuracy: The Changing Role of the Prosecutor's Office in the USSR.* Washington, DC: United States Department of Justice.

———. 1997. "The Struggle over the Procuracy." In Peter H. Solomon, Jr. (ed.), *Reforming Justice in Russia, 1864–1996: Power, Culture, and the Limits of Legal Order.* Armonk, NY: M. E. Sharpe.

Solomon, Peter H., Jr. 1974. "Soviet Criminology: Its Demise and Rebirth." *Soviet Union* 1: 122–40.

———. 1978. *Soviet Criminologists and Criminal Policy.* New York: Columbia University Press.

———. 1981. "Criminalization and Decriminalization in Soviet Criminal Policy, 1917–1941." *Law and Society Review* 16: 9–44.

———. 1992. "Soviet Politicians and Criminal Prosecutions: The Logic of Party Intervention." In James R. Millar (ed.), *Cracks in the Monolith: Party Power in the Brezhnev Era.* Armonk, NY: M. E. Sharpe.

———. 1996. *Soviet Criminal Justice under Stalin.* Cambridge: Cambridge University Press.

———. 1997. "The Persistence of Judicial Reform in Contemporary Russia." *East European Constitutional Review* 6, 4: 50–55.

Starikov, Evgenii N. 1996. "The Social Structure of the Transitional Society: An Attempt to Take Inventory." *Russian Social Science Review* 37, 2: 17–36.

Terrill, Richard J. 1997. *World Criminal Justice Systems: A Survey.* 3rd ed. Cincinnati, OH: Anderson Publishing Company.

Tucker, Robert C. 1990. *Stalin in Power: The Revolution from Above, 1928–1941.* New York: Norton.

U.S. Bureau of the Census. 1988. *International Database.* [Online]. Available: http://www.census.gove/cgi-bin/ipc/idbsprd

Williams, James L., and Adele S. Serrins. 1993. "The Russian Militia: An Organization in Transition." *Police Studies* 16: 124–28.

World Bank. 1997. *Annual Report 1997.* [Online]. Available: http://www.worldbank.org/html/extpb/annrep97/chal.htm

World Health Organization. 1995. *1995 World Health Statistics Annual.* Geneva: Author.

Zeldes, Ilya. 1981. *The Problems of Crime in the USSR.* Springfield, IL: Charles C. Thomas.

13

TAIWAN

(Developed Nation-State)

Mayling Maria Chu

PROFILE OF TAIWAN

Taiwan is located about 100 miles off the coast of southeastern China. Taiwan has also been known to Westerners by the name of "Formosa." This name dates back to 1517 (the Ming Dynasty in China) when the Portuguese, on their way to Japan, passed along the coast and called the island "Ilha Formosa" (the beautiful island) (Carrington, 1977; Davidson, 1988; Long, 1991; Copper, 1993; Shepherd, 1993). At present, the Taiwan area (under the sovereignty of the Republic of China) includes the Taiwan island and surrounding small islands (*Taiwan with a View*, 1989). It is one of the most densely populated regions in the world. More than 20 million people live in Taiwan. In 1992 the average population density was 577 persons per square kilometer (approximately 1,900 persons per square mile) ("A Culture," 1993; Yuan, 1993). As of 1991 the island's population was largely composed of Chinese, numbering 20,944,006 (98.3 percent), compared to 357,585 aborigines (*Monthly Statistics of the Republic of China*, 1992). Because of the population composition, Chinese culture is prevalent.

Since the postwar time, economic development has made significant progress. Major economic growth occurred in the 1970s when annual rates of growth averaged 13.35 percent. Since the 1980s, economic growth rates have been stable at around 6.5 percent. The gross national product has continually expanded since the 1960s, and the economic conditions and wealth of residents in Taiwan have improved as well. During this time period, consumer prices have also steadily risen, whereas saving rates have gradually declined (*Social Indicators in the Taiwan Area of the Republic of China*, 1995).

The homogeneity of Taiwan (in terms of population, culture, and religion) is a process of continuous migration and development. This process can be divided into five eras (the tribal society and loose Chinese control, the Western colonization, the Chinese culture as in the migrations and Imperial penal code, the Japanese police state, and the Chinese homogenization), each representing a specific social control mechanism of political power (see Table 13.1). The shifts of power and control affected the establishment of social order and the criminal justice system in Taiwan.

HISTORICAL PERSPECTIVE ON CRIME AND CRIME CONTROL

In spite of its history of colonization by Occidental and Oriental powers, a controlled social structure, either by extralegal (traditional and ideological) or legal forces, has existed in Taiwan for a long time. Indigenous residents (Malayo-Polynesians), the Chinese, the Dutch, the Spanish, and the Japanese have controlled Taiwan at different periods of time. Strict state control was particularly enforced during the period of Japanese colonization (especially the Japanese rule during 1895–1945) and the Chinese rule since 1949. The controlled social condition may be the root of low crime-victim rates and criminal activities in Taiwan (see Tables 13.2 and 13.3).

The Tribal Society and Loose Chinese Control

Historically, Chinese emperors had claimed Taiwan to be under their sovereignties long before Christ was born (ca. 1523–1028 B.C.) (Chiu, 1992). The Chinese settlement on Taiwan had taken place as early as the seventh century (Shepherd, 1993). The population, however, was largely made up of native tribes. The aborigines, who still live in Taiwan today, are descendants of Malayo-Polynesians and have distinct tribal cultures different from the Chinese culture. Although Chinese emperors had practiced imperial penal codes on the mainland since the seventh century (Tang Dynasty, 618–907), they, by and large, ignored Taiwan and left it on its own for centuries (*Taiwan with a View*, 1989; Long, 1991; Lin, 1992). It was not until the sixteenth century that Taiwan could no longer maintain its isolation.

The Western Colonization

During the sixteenth and seventeenth centuries, Occidental sea adventurers traveled in Asia for trading and commercial benefits. In the early sixteenth century, the Portuguese sighted Formosa (Taiwan) but did not settle there (Davidson, 1988; Long, 1991). The Dutch United East India Com-

Table 13.1
Social and Crime Control Mechanisms in Taiwan

Year	Dynasty/State	Social Order
ca. 1523 B.C.—A.D. 1279	Chinese Empires (from Shang to Sung Dynasties)	Loose Chinese control
1279–1368	Mongolian Yuan Dynasty	
1368–1644	Ming Dynasty	
1624–1662	Dutch	Western colonization
1626–1642	Spaniards	Chinese migration
1662–1683	Chengs (Ming loyalists)	
1683–1895	Manchuan Ching Dynasty	Imperial penal codes
1895–1945	Japan	Japanese police state
1945–present	Republic of China (ROC)	Chinese homogenization and liberation in the 1990s

Table 13.2
Crime Rates and Offender Rates, 1963–1992

Year	Cases Known to the Police	Crime Rate[a] (per 1,000 population)	Number of Offenders	Offender Rate[b] (per 1,000 population)
1963	53,086	4.54	30,189	2.58
1964	45,790	3.79	27,749	2.30
1965	48,055	3.86	31,643	2.54
1966	45,969	3.59	32,298	2.52
1967	35,663	2.71	27,924	2.12
1968	37,330	2.77	30,789	2.29
1969	38,280	2.74	34,488	2.47
1970	38,647	2.66	33,685	2.32
1971	36,013	2.43	30,927	2.09
1972	36,911	2.44	30,200	1.99
1973	38,415	2.49	34,328	2.23
1974	41,732	2.66	38,266	2.44
1975	45,824	2.86	40,856	2.53
1976	43,936	2.69	40,818	2.50
1977	47,868	2.87	44,122	2.65
1978	48,640	2.87	39,184	2.31
1979	52,512	3.03	43,585	2.52
1980	52,350	2.97	44,669	2.53
1981	51,292	2.85	43,612	2.43
1982	44,622	2.44	38,285	2.09
1983	51,427	2.77	43,601	2.35
1984	52,168	2.76	49,168	2.61
1985	60,707	3.17	57,408	3.00
1986	93,181	4.81	80,814	4.18
1987	89,468	4.57	87,086	4.45
1988	88,215	4.46	81,503	4.12
1989	90,340	4.52	86,900	4.34
1990	91,770	4.54	86,723	4.29
1991	122,747	6.00	145,442	7.11
1992	139,306	6.75	172,551	8.35

[a]Crime Rate = (cases known to the police/midyear population) × 1,000.
[b]Offender Rate = (total offenders/midyear population) × 1,000.
Source: Adapted from Social Indicators in the Taiwan Area of the Republic of China, 1992, 1993: 220–21.

pany colonized Taiwan in the first quarter of the seventeenth century (*Taiwan with a View*, 1989; Chiang, 1992). In 1626, two years after colonization by the Dutch, Spaniards invaded the island of Taiwan. Taiwan was then divided into two colonies: Dutch in the south and Spanish in the north.

The Dutch fought with the Japanese (who wanted to occupy Taiwan,

Table 13.3
Victim Rates, 1983–1992

Year	Number of Victims	Victim of Violent Crimes[a]	Victim Rate (per 1,000 population)	Victims of Violent Crimes (per 1,000 population)
1983	47,468	5,347	2.55	0.29
1984	45,961	5,248	2.44	0.28
1985	67,668	6,415	3.54	0.34
1986	83,309	7,363	4.30	0.38
1987	73,849	7,283	3.78	0.37
1988	76,428	8,789	3.86	0.44
1989	78,143	10,632	3.91	0.53
1990	78,569	13,987	3.88	0.69
1991	86,542	11,924	4.23	0.58
1992	80,713	8,559	3.91	0.41

[a]Violent crimes include homicide, robbery and forceful taking, kidnapping, intimidation, forcible rape, and gang rape.

Source: Adapted from Social Indicators in the Taiwan Area of the Republic of China, 1992, 1993: 235.

too), expelled Spaniards, and were finally banished by the Chinese, who fled to Taiwan to escape the Manchuan rule on the mainland (J. Chen, 1969; Long, 1991; Huber, 1992). This ended the 38-year Dutch colonial rule. The Dutch rule was largely a story of relations with the aborigines, the majority group before the early nineteenth century (Shepherd, 1993). The Dutch Calvinist missionaries were designated as "legal affairs officers" who intervened in every aspect of aboriginal tribe life. The Dutch organized the Chinese, the minority population at the time, as production units of the United East India Company for trade (Carrington, 1977; Yin et al., 1992). About the same time, Spaniards focused mainly on establishing Christian missions in their short-lived colony. Commercial trades and Christian missions were the social structures during this colonial period.

The Chinese Migration

The Western colonial time coexisted with the Chinese (Ming) Dynasty. The Dutch were driven out of Taiwan by the Chinese Ming loyalists who came to the island to rebel against the Manchuan rule on the mainland. In addition to politics, piracy, banditry, rebellions, and population pressures in southern China were contributing factors to the Chinese migration for decades to come (Tong, 1991). These Chinese people brought with them their culture and literacy. Because of the Chinese rebellion (against Manchus) on Taiwan, Manchuan emperors were reluctant to manage the Taiwanese society, although imperial penal codes were symbolically enforced there. Not until the last years of the Ming Dynasty did the Manchu Court finally recognize the importance of Taiwan and subsequently appoint three administrators to take charge of the civil affairs on the island. The fourth administrator, however, adopted a policy of retrenchment, which halted his predecessors' projects (on transportation, schools, and soothing the aborigines) until Japan seized Taiwan (*Taiwan with a View*, 1989).

Manchuan emperors also forbade free migration between southern China and Taiwan by imposing the death penalty (Copper, 1993). Despite the intimidation of a death sentence, the Chinese migration still proceeded as a result of continuous droughts in southern China and labor needs on Taiwan (*Taiwan with a View*, 1989; Yin et al., 1992). By the early nineteenth century (the late Manchu Dynasty), the Chinese had become the majority in the Taiwan area (Chi, 1991).

The increase of a large number of migrants and the clashes between the Chinese and the aborigines had caused serious social problems. The situation was hardly improved in that officials sent from the mainland "were a byword for incompetence and venality" (Long, 1991: 16). Because of the lack of effective law enforcement, Taiwan relied on kinships, clans, secret societies, and other forms of subversive social organizations for settling societal and interpersonal disputes (Copper, 1990; Long, 1991). The informal social control and sanctions were later replaced by strict state control under the Japanese rule.

The Japanese Police State

Japan took over Taiwan from the Manchus in 1895, according to the "Shimonoseki Treaty" signed after the Sino-Japanese War (Long, 1991). After years of successful suppression of rebellions against the Japanese in Taiwan, Japanese colonial authorities controlled the island and enforced their rule on the Chinese and the aborigines (Balcom, 1993). Under the system of Japanese courts (see Table 13.4), laws enacted only on the Taiwanese were in effect (J. Chen, 1969; Myers and Peattie, 1984; Lai, Meyers, and Wei, 1991). For example, under the "Bandit Punishment Law," any residents in Taiwan who resisted Japanese rule were labeled "bandits" and given the mandatory death sentence (J. Chen, 1969). Taiwan was under Japanese rule for half a century, until the end of World War II when Japan was bombed by the United States.

Comparatively speaking, the Japanese governed Taiwan differently from Chinese emperors and the Dutch. The former ruled Taiwan "with a rod of iron" and installed the *hoko* system of social control, which was derived from the traditional Chinese *bao-jia* (community management) system (Long, 1991; Lin, 1992). The *hoko* system demanded mutual responsibility from

Table 13.4
The Criminal Justice System under the Japanese and Chinese Rules

	Japanese Rule	Chinese Rule
Criminal Laws	Laws Concerning Laws and Regulations to Be Enforced in Formosa (LLR for Formosa)	Constitution
	Law No. 63	Organic and Administrative Law
	Bandit Punishment Law	Commercial Law
	Law No. 31	Civil Code
	Criminal Procedure	Criminal Code
	Law of Court Expenses in Criminal Cases	Code of Civil Procedure
	Procedural Law for Cases of Private Affairs	Code of Criminal Procedure
	Maritime Laws	Martial Law (1949–1991)
		Curfew Law (1949–late 1950s)
		Juvenile Law (1980)
The Court	Colonial Courts	Three-Tier Civil Courts and Military Courts

Note: Six laws include "Organic and Administrative Law," "Commercial Law," "Civil Code," "Criminal Code," "Code of Civil Procedure," and "Code of Criminal Procedure."

Source: J. Chen, 1969: 91–114.

neighborhood members to prevent crime, organize community service, and prevent subversion. The entire neighborhood unit was responsible for the action of individual members. The civil head of the *hoko* group was chosen and approved by Japanese county officials and police (Ballantine, 1952; J. Chen, 1969; Long, 1991). "This was the first time in Taiwan's history that state control has so thoroughly penetrated to the local level" (Long, 1991: 27).

The *hoko* system also served as the backbone of the Japanese police structure in Taiwan. The colonial police had comprehensive roles in every aspect of *hoko* residents' lives. As enforcers of law and defenders of colonial public order, these police censored publications, supervised public rallies, controlled use of firearms and explosives, rendered summary judgment in minor criminal cases, curbed illegal entry of laborers, kept domiciliary records, regulated public health and sanitation matters, managed fire control and prevention, established traffic control of residents island wide, supervised business facilities (such as pawnshops, bathhouses, hotels, restaurants, slaughterhouses), and licensed prostitution (Ballantine, 1952; C. Chen, 1984). The society of Taiwan was transformed to a "Japanese police state" haunted by the brutality and terror of "Tokko" (Special Higher Police), the same situation as that of prewar (before 1945) Japan (Tipton, 1990). Japanese civilians and Occidentals residing in Taiwan were also subject to the jurisdiction of the Japanese police (Ballantine, 1952).

The Chinese Homogenization

Taiwan was freed from the Japanese military/police rule at the end of World War II. The period of Chinese homogenization began with strict state control followed by political liberation in the late 1980s and uncertainty in the 1990s. After being defeated by Chinese communists on the mainland, the Nationalist government and its troops arrived in Taiwan in 1949. In order to ensure national security and public order, the president and leader of the Nationalist government declared a state of emergency. "Martial Law" and "Temporary Provisions" (of the suspended Constitution), which had been previously justified by the civil war against Chinese communists on the mainland, were kept in force. In fact, it was not until the late 1950s that curfews were lifted.

In addition to political and legal control, Nationalist officials introduced their own control mechanism in related spheres, such as the military, educational system, and mass media. Further, to replace the Japanese colonial law, Nationalist officials introduced their Constitution (promulgated in 1947) and six basic laws (including the Criminal Code and the Code of Criminal Procedure), which had been enacted during the civil war on the mainland. The implementation of the Nationalist Constitution, however, has been circumscribed by a series of at least 30 emergency laws, decrees, and judicial interpretations by the Grand Justices who have been appointed by the president (Copper, 1988; Tien, 1989).

The circumscription of laws happened not only to the Constitution but to the Criminal Code. The Code (implemented in 1928 and later revised in 1935) had been accompanied by special regulations that dealt with specific types of crime. These include: "Peace Preservation Measure" (for dealing with serious crime offenders and political criminals); "The Law of Forgery and Check Fraud" (which granted imprisonment as a means of economic control and which was abolished in 1987); "The Regulation of Punishment on Robbers and Burglars" (adopted in 1944 and revised in 1957); "The Regulation of Firearms and Explosives Control"; and "The Regulation of Opiates and Hallucinogens Control" (opium, opium poppy, marijuana, morphine, heroin, and their semisynthetics as well as synthetics) (*The Almanac of Six Codes*, 1992).

All these regulations resulted in more severe punishment than those inscribed or not inscribed in the Criminal Code. They were formulated to control "serious crimes" (see Table 13.5). The category of "serious crimes" was expanded several times during Chinese homogenization to include homicide; piracy; robbery; forcible rape; gang rape; intimidation (violent threat); kidnapping and murder; kidnapping and rape; interference with personal liberty; manufacturing, trading, and trafficking in firearms and explosives; espionage; intentional harm to foreign delegates; sedition; forgery and check fraud; and counterfeiting (the last two were removed from the list in the 1980s). The intent of these legally defined "major crimes" was to control the use of violence against person, of firearms and explosives, of financial means, and of antigovernmental activities (Chaffee et al., 1969; Chiu and Fa, 1981; *Crime and Analysis*, 1991; *Social Indicators in the Taiwan Area of the Republic of China, 1992*, 1993).

The procedures for domiciliary search or arrest required a search warrant or an arrest warrant. Criminal suspects had to be either released or transferred to a civilian court for a hearing within 24 hours after arrest. Civilians facing criminal prosecution were given the right of legal counsel. This right, however, was not always applied to certain lawbreakers, such as political criminals or offenders of serious (major) crimes before the 1990s. Instead, these defendants were sent to military courts where "appeals were handled quickly and without the encumbrances of legal procedures used in civilian courts" (Copper, 1988: 15). Moreover, hearings in the military courts have never been open to the public. The trials of offenders of serious crimes by the military courts were meant to send a message to the general public about the government's style of intervention and determination to control certain types of crimes.

Table 13.5
Selected Serious Crimes and Punishment

Offense	Sentence
Piracy combined with any of the following: arson, rape, kidnapping, or murder	Capital punishment
Rape and killing	Capital punishment
Homicide	Capital punishment, life sentence, or imprisonment for 10 years or more
Attempted homicide	Imprisonment up to 2 years
Kidnapping and murder	Capital punishment
Kidnapping and killing or kidnapping and aggravated assault	Capital punishment or life sentence
Kidnapping and rape	Capital punishment or life sentence
Kidnapping	Capital punishment, life sentence, or imprisonment for 7 years or more
Attempted kidnapping	Imprisonment for up to 2 years
Violent robbery[a] and killing	Capital punishment or life sentence
Violent robbery and aggravated assault	Capital punishment or life sentence
Violent robbery combined with any of the following: arson, rape, kidnapping, or murder	Capital punishment or life sentence

[a]Violent robbery means committing robbery by using violent forces, threats, or narcotics to disable the victim.
Source: *The Almanac of Six Codes*, 1992.

PUBLIC PERCEPTION OF CRIME AND CRIME CONTROL

Until political liberation came in the 1990s, Taiwan had been essentially a police/military state where censorship and tight control of the media and public discourse prevailed. As late as the beginning of the Chinese Nationalist regime in 1949, the Nationalist secret police adopted most of the responsibilities of the Japanese colonial police, such as control of the press, censorship, strikes, public rallies, firearms and explosives, and domiciliary records. These practices did not desist until 1992 (Copper, 1993; *The Republic of China Yearbook*, 1993).

Moreover, the circumvention of the Nationalist Constitution and the declarations of emergency laws and decrees all but suffocated public speech and the free expression of ideas. As for perceptions of crime and crime control, these were well regulated and managed, both civilly and politically. For example, the civil liberties and individual rights common to citizens that are listed in the Constitution (Articles 9–24) succumbed to the authoritarian governmental practices. Those restrained liberties and rights included freedom of speech; formation of political parties other than the Nationalist Party; assembly and association; writing and publication; religious belief; privacy of correspondence; and the right to work, own property, receive education, and hold public office (Copper, 1993; Kaplan, 1992; Tien, 1989).

For those political dissidents who disobeyed, they were picked up by the Nationalist secret agents using as their vehicle of suppression the "Peace Preservation Measure" of the Criminal Code. The measure granted the National secret police agencies comprehensive authority in dealing with ideological and political dissent. Not until 1991 was this act and the "Temporary Provisions of the Constitution" lifted, restricting, for example, military trials and military prisons for soldiers on active duty who violate military laws.

Public perceptions were also tightly controlled throughout the Taiwanese society as a whole. The Conscription Law, for example, was revised in 1959 to stipulate that 19-year-olds be drafted for two years in the army or three years in the navy or air force. Young men in the service were under supervision of superiors with strong Nationalistic patriotism. Also, the "educational system, media and cultural affairs were under the direct and pervasive control of [Nationalist] party leadership and censorship (sometimes self-imposed)" (Gold, 1993: 170).

In other words, it is still a relatively short period after political liberation for public perceptions of crime and crime control to have emerged and solidified, as in those other nation-states with a long history of political democracy and freedom of expression.

CONTEMPORARY CRIME

Concurrent with economic development and educational achievement, Chinese families in Taiwan have experienced dramatic changes in and challenges to their historic, patriarchal relationships. The shrinking size of families, the trend of two-income families, and the increased divorce rates have shaken the traditional Chinese family structure. According to a survey on family life, conducted by the Ministry of the Interior, 18.5 percent of those sampled households were extended families, 55.5 percent were nuclear families, 6 percent were single-parent families, and 3.5 percent were single people living alone (Yuan, 1993). The average family size has been decreasing. In 1980 the average married couple had 3.6 children, and most dwellings housed 4.8 persons; in 1990 the average married couple had 3.1 children, and most homes were composed of 4 persons.

The Ministry of Interior also reported that in 4.4 households out of 10 both the husband and the wife worked. About one third of Taiwan's workforce of 8.6 million is women, and 1 million of them have children under 12 years old; 44 percent of women around the age of 15 are employed, and 70 percent of married women with college degrees have jobs. The trend of two-income families is believed to be linked with the high cost of living associated with industrialization and urbanization. The declining family size and the rise of multi-income families indicate that children have fewer siblings and are spending more time by themselves (Yuan, 1993).

Regarding family relationships, different philosophies on life and leisure seeking have created a huge generation gap between contemporary parents and children. Young adults perceive that "enjoying life" is more important than "working hard" and "saving money," which have been the practices of the previous generations. One editorial ("A Culture of Convenience," 1993) captured this sentiment: "Quick-and-easy has become the standard of life." Youth between the ages of 12 and 24, for example, spend their free time mostly on forms of convenient leisure such as watching television programs and/or videotapes (61 percent); reading newspapers, magazines, and novels (9 percent); and listening to music (8 percent) (*Survey Report of the Youth in Taiwan*, 1994). Renting a book (i.e., comic, romance, novel, kung fu thriller, and science fiction) from commercial bookstores is particularly popular among junior high students (Yuan, 1993). They also spend more free time on ball games, hiking, chats, and social get-togethers than other age groups.

Children and youngsters are the ones profoundly affected by the changed family structure and organization of daily life. One consequence is that juvenile delinquency is on the rise and increases faster than adult crime, especially by the early 1990s (see Table 13.6). However, juvenile delinquency rates in Taiwan are still low compared to Western societies.

According to reports on juvenile delinquency, youngsters between the ages of 12 and 17 who were involved in crime, 1986 through 1990, reported on average (43 percent) that family was the primary cause. During the same period, on average (83 percent), these youths reported that poor child-rearing techniques was the primary contributing factor (*Crime and Analysis*, 1991). In response, many juvenile delinquency prevention and crime control programs in Taiwan have tried to reinforce traditional values associated with strong family functioning (Jan, 1986).

After family dysfunctioning, deviant environment, delinquent peers, juvenile gangs, pornographic and violent books/magazines, and unemployment are revealed to be a second set of influential factors contributing to juvenile delinquency, averaging a 21 percent reporting rate between 1986 and 1990 (*Crime and Analysis*, 1991). Among these social factors, bonding with delinquent peers has been reported to be the most significant factor, averaging 96 percent during this same period of time, yet participation

Table 13.6
Criminal Population Rates by Age Group

	Child Offenders			Juvenile Delinquents			Adult Criminals		
Year	Population under 12 Years Old	Persons	Criminal Population Rate (0/00)	Population between 12 and 18 Years Old	Persons	Criminal Population Rate (0/00)	Population 18 Years Old and Over	Persons	Criminal Population Rate (0/00)
1981	4,595,116	522	0.11	2,324,449	10,080	4.34	11,225,943	46,489	4.14
1982	4,614,912	449	0.10	2,303,648	9,853	4.28	11,539,363	45,672	3.96
1983	4,633,843	497	0.11	2,279,867	10,376	4.55	11,819,228	47,058	3.98
1984	4,629,185	649	0.14	2,240,816	10,925	4.88	12,142,511	53,219	4.38
1985	4,610,494	809	0.18	2,229,099	11,070	4.97	12,418,460	55,628	4.48
1986	4,567,994	911	0.20	2,198,889	12,051	5.48	12,687,727	60,366	4.76
1987	4,505,058	949	0.21	2,180,200	14,695	6.74	12,987,354	68,342	5.26
1988	4,425,509	920	0.21	2,216,426	16,251	7.33	13,261,877	58,360	4.40
1989	4,365,104	963	0.22	2,228,312	18,167	8.15	13,514,024	66,595	4.93
1990	4,312,171	863	0.20	2,268,912	16,955	7.47	13,778,320	67,070	4.87

Note: The above statistics exclude "potential juvenile delinquents" (status offenders) and adult offenders who committed "forgery and check fraud" (the Law of Forgery and Check Fraud was abolished in 1987).

Source: Crime and Analysis, 1991.

in delinquent gangs was rare, averaging less than 1 percent between 1986 and 1990. Schools were reported to have even less influence than delinquent gang participation. However, maladjustment and school absenteeism were reported to have influences on most of the problems in school.

The peak period of prison inmates' age has been between 30 and 39 (34.23 percent), followed by 24 and 29 (23.95 percent), and 18 and 23 (18.11 percent) as of 1990 (*Crime and Analysis*, 1991). Those between 14 and 17 years of age comprise only 4.63 percent of the criminal population, lower than that of the age group between 50 and 59 at 4.76 percent (see Table 13.7). This shows a pattern of later involvement in crime compared with Western societies.

Up to the present, empirical studies have supported the relationships among family bonds, school attachment, and low criminal involvement in Taiwan. The emphases on family ethics and school education are believed to be explanatory (i.e., social control theory) factors of law-abiding attitudes and low delinquency involvement. Longitudinal data also demonstrate that crime and victimization rates have been relatively flat (see Tables 13.2 and 13.3).

CONTEMPORARY CRIME CONTROL

The year 1990 marked the end of the "Temporary Provisions to the Constitution." The "Period of Mobilization" was terminated the next year, discontinuing the state of war with mainland China. In 1992, the Sedition Law (Article 100 of the Criminal Code) was revised to make it no longer a crime to discuss Taiwan's independence of communism. Between 1991 and 1997, the Constitution was revised four times (Overseas Chinese Scholars, 1998).

Furthermore, after the end of the "Period of Mobilization," not only were some laws abolished, but others were revised. Laws focusing on robbery, illegal drug use, smuggling, and organized crime were revised to grant the police department authority in dealing with these types of crime. Before these laws were modified, the Taiwan Garrison Command of the Department of Defense had the power to use secret agents and secret witnesses in arresting or imprisoning "lawbreakers." Strict sentences for these kinds of crimes were also shortened, in order to be comparable with the content (civil seriousness versus civil nonseriousness) of offenses. The social movement for liberation, which had been perceived as a threat to the order and security of the Chinese Nationalist regime before the 1990s, gradually became more "acceptable" and handled, for example, by civil procedures rather than by draconian and repressive measures of political control (Overseas Chinese Scholars, 1998).

The legal responsibility of individuals in contemporary Taiwan is defined according to age and competence in the Criminal Code. By definition, a lawbreaker under the age of 14 is not subject to legal punishment; those

Table 13.7
Prison Inmates' Age at the Time of Imprisonment

Year		Total	14–17	18–23	24–29	30–39	40–49	50–59	60–69	70–79	80 and older
1986	N	23,453	835	4,074	5,758	7,525	3,166	1,541	489	60	5
	%	100	3.56	17.37	24.55	32.09	13.50	6.57	2.09	0.25	0.02
1987	N	19,240	541	3,312	4,884	6,404	2,492	1,190	360	55	2
	%	100	2.81	17.21	25.38	33.28	12.09	6.19	1.87	0.29	0.01
1988	N	13,886	453	2,517	3,430	4,643	1,769	773	270	29	2
	%	100	3.26	18.12	24.70	33.44	12.74	5.57	1.94	0.21	0.01
1989	N	19,375	729	3,407	468	6,642	2,586	992	300	38	—
	%	100	3.76	17.58	24.16	34.28	13.35	5.12	1.55	0.20	—
1990	N	21,123	979	3,825	5,058	7,231	2,636	1,005	330	58	1
	%	100	4.63	18.11	23.95	34.23	12.48	4.76	1.56	0.27	0.01

Source: Crime and Analysis, 1991.

who are over 14 but under 18 are eligible for reduced sentences; mentally ill and mentally incompetent lawbreakers are either unaccountable or receive reduced sentences for their offenses. Repeat offenders receive stricter punishment than nonrepeat offenders. Juvenile delinquents, 12 to 17, are subject to "Laws and Regulations Concerning the Management of Juvenile Matters" (*Juvenile Law*, 1981). The Juvenile Law is also applicable to minors under 12 who commit crimes. Juvenile offenders and "potential offenders" (similar to "status offenders" in the United States) are under the jurisdiction of the juvenile courts that operate at the local levels. Procedures of the juvenile courts are identical to those of adult courts, but juvenile trials are not open to the public.

Juvenile offenders by law are not sentenced to the death penalty or life imprisonment, unless they are involved in killing a lineal relative (*Juvenile Law*, 1981). Juvenile offenders who receive prison sentences for at least five years are kept in the juvenile prison (there is only one in Taiwan). Juvenile burglars are sentenced to reformatories, and first-time offenders to probation. Juvenile offenders who have behavioral problems or who have consumed significant amounts of alcohol or drugs are accommodated in reformatories. Leaders of delinquent gangs receive extended sentences for the offense they commit. Status offenders in Taiwan mostly are involved in littering or drug-related offenses. Juvenile offenders who have drug-related offenses are sent to reformatories. Other types of status offenders usually receive a stern lecture by the judge (regarding law and responsible behavior) or supervision by a legal guardian (Jan, 1986; *Crime and Analysis*, 1991).

Within the current law enforcement structure, each police department has a juvenile corps unit. The "Project on Juvenile Delinquency Prevention" was first established in the capital city in 1981. Four years later, the "Juvenile Guidance Section" under the project was stationed in the city's local police departments. The Juvenile Guidance Section targets youngsters between 12 and 18 years of age; it offers services such as individual and group counseling, programs for prevention and treatment of juvenile delinquency, programs for enhancing parent-child relationships, cultural and recreational activities suitable for youth, and referral services (*Introduction of Juvenile Guidance Sections*, 1991).

The judicial system, prescribed in the Constitution, is three-tier (the Supreme Court, High Courts, and District Courts) and operated by the rule of "three levels and three instances" (Kaplan, 1992; *The Republic of China Yearbook*, 1993). The court system is based on the Continental Code. The Chinese procurator (legal delegates) conducts the preliminary investigation of a legal claim to determine whether prosecution is necessary. After the procurator has brought a case to court, the records and dossiers are forwarded to the judge, who is expected to study these materials thoroughly in advance of the trial in order to carry out the responsibility of interrogation (Chiu and Fa, 1981). Victims of crimes may bring a "private prosecution" to the court, unless the prosecution is directed against a lineal relation or a spouse (Chiu and Fa, 1981).

A civil trial begins with the interrogation of the accused. The trial is open to the public and is generally heard through several brief court sessions. There is no jury or cross-examination for a criminal case. Normally, a panel of three judges sits for a case. The panel directs the trial, questions the witnesses, and renders a verdict. The defendant may not take the witness stand. Witnesses are put under oath, and they testify in response to questions issued by the judge. It is believed that the pretrial investigation and discovery, the dominant role of the judge at trial, and fewer means for the defendant to delay the process of justice (of the Continental system) shorten criminal trials in Taiwan (and other civil law countries) when compared to those countries that ascribe to the Anglo-Saxon common law traditions (Chiu and Fa, 1981; Kaplan, 1992).

FUTURE OF CRIME AND CRIME CONTROL

The society of Taiwan has a history of continued migration and shifts among political powers of repression. These two factors have caused twists and turns in the constitutional and political regulations of "criminal justice" that have served to control "crime" in the undemocratic periods of the Taiwanese past. In the rigidly controlled society or "police state" with its highly structured social and cultural environment, Taiwan has experienced relatively low criminal and victimization rates. At the same time, empirical studies suggest that the cultural homogeneity as well as the traditional social and familiar bonds have contributed to the low rates of delinquency involvement.

In addition, certain important attributes and opportunities of rapid economic development in Taiwan should be taken into consideration. These include the successful family planning programs and declining birthrates/family sizes; two-income families; high rates of literacy, education, employment, and consumption of goods and services; and a markedly absent pervasiveness of political-legal surveillance. Moreover, as Taiwanese society becomes more open and democratic, it appears that contemporary youth (and future generations) are experiencing a "Westernization" in their values and attitudes toward work and leisure.

Youth of today and tomorrow in Taiwan, in other words, have more access to opportunities, both legal and illegal. They also have less nurturing (or protection) from their primary networks, as family control continues to atrophy. In order for Taiwan to be effective in preventing and controlling criminal activities in the future, its mechanisms of crime control will need to address the multidimensional aspects of political, economic, and social development as these impact the family, school, and wider society.

REFERENCES

The Almanac of Six Codes (in Chinese). 1992. Taipei, Taiwan: Wu-Nan.

Balcom, J. 1993. "Overcoming the Language Barriers." *Free China Review* 43, 7: 42–53.

Ballantine, Joseph B. 1952. *Formosa: A Problem for the United States Foreign Policy.* Washington, DC: Brookings Institution.

Carrington, George W. 1977. *Foreigners in Formosa, 1841–1874.* San Francisco, CA: Chinese Materials, Inc.

Chaffee, Frederick H., G. E. Aurell, H. A. Barth, A. S. Cort, J. H. Dombrowski, V. J. Fasana, and J. O. Weaver. 1969. *Area Handbook for the Republic of China.* Washington, DC: U.S. Government Printing Office.

Chen, C. C. 1984. "Police and Community Control System in the Empire." In R. H. Meyers and M. R. Peattie (eds.), *The Japanese Colonial Empire, 1885–1945.* Princeton, NJ: Princeton University Press, 213–39.

Chen, J. L. 1969. *Japanese Colonization in Korea and Formosa: A Comparison of Its Effects upon the Development of Nationalism.* Ann Arbor, MI: Microfilm, Inc.

Chi, J. L. 1991. *The Taiwanese History, 1600–1945* (2 vols. in Chinese). Taipei, Taiwan: self-published.

Chiang, S. S. 1992. "Taiwanese Historical Studies during the Dutch Period." In Y. C. Chang (ed.), *History, Culture and Taiwan: Taiwanese Studies Seminar Proceedings* (in Chinese). Vol. 2. Taipei, Taiwan: self-published.

Chiu, Hongda. 1979. "Republic of China: Editorial Note." In L. W. Beer (ed.), *Constitutionalism in Asia: Asian Views of the American Influence.* Berkeley: University of California Press, 35–38.

Chiu, H., and J. P. Fa. 1981. "Law and Justice since 1966." In James Chien Hsiung (ed.), *The Taiwan Experience, 1950–1980: Contemporary Republic of China.* New York: Praeger, 314–30.

Chiu, S. A. 1992. *The Historical Notes of Taiwan* (Taiwan shi nwa [in Chinese]). Taipei, Taiwan, Republic of China: Li-Ming.

Copper, John F. 1988. "Ending Martial Law in Taiwan: Implications and Prospects." *Journal of Northeast Asian Studies* 7, 2: 3–19.

———. 1990. "Society and Culture." In John F. Copper (ed.), *Taiwan: Nation-State or Province.* 2nd ed. Boulder, CO: Westview, 33–51.

———. 1993. *Historical Dictionary of Taiwan.* Metuchen, NJ: Scare Crow.

Crime and Analysis (in Chinese). 1991. Taipei, Taiwan: Ministry of Justice.

"A Culture of Convenience" (editorial). 1993. *Free China Review* 43, 7: 1.

Davidson, James W. 1988. *The Island of Formosa, Past and Present: History, People, Resources, and Commercial Prospects.* Oxford, England: Oxford University Press.

Gold, Thomas B. 1993. "Taiwan's Quest for Identity in the Shadow of China." In Steven Tsang (ed.), *The Shadow of China: Political Developments in Taiwan since 1949.* Honolulu: University of Hawaii Press.

Huber, J. 1992. "The Dutch Literature Regarding Taiwanese History." In Y. C. Chang (ed.), *History, Culture and Taiwan: Taiwanese Studies Seminar Proceedings* (in Chinese). Vol. 1. Taipei, Taiwan: self-published.

Introduction of Juvenile Guidance Sections (in Chinese). 1991. Taipei, Taiwan: Republic of Taiwan.

Jan, L. A. 1986. "Corrections in Taiwan (Republic of China)." *International Journal of Comparative and Applied Criminal Justice* 12, 1: 95–100.

Juvenile Law (in Chinese). 1981. Taipei, Taiwan: Republic of Taiwan.

Kaplan, D. E. 1992. *Fires of the Dragon: Politics, Murder, and the Kuomingtang.* New York: Atheneum.

Lai, Tse-Han, Raymon H. Meyers, and Wou Wei. 1991. *A Tragic Beginning: The Taiwan Uprising of February 28, 1947.* Stanford, CA: Stanford University Press.

Lin, C. C. 1992. "The Ching Dynasty and the Japanese Government in Taiwan before 1945." In Y. C. Chang (ed.), *History, Culture and Taiwan: Taiwanese Studies Seminar Proceedings* (in Chinese). Taipei, Taiwan: self-published, 3: 47–79.

Long, Simon. 1991. *Taiwan: China's Last Frontier.* New York: St. Martin's Press.

Meyers, R. H., and M. R. Peattie (eds.). 1984. *The Japanese Colonial Empire, 1895–1945.* Princeton, NJ: Princeton University Press.

Monthly Statistics of the Republic of China (in Chinese). 1992. Taipei, Taiwan: Department of Civil Affairs, October.

Overseas Chinese Scholars. 1998. *Report on the Constitution.* Taipei, Taiwan: Department of Education.

The Republic of China Yearbook. 1993. Taipei, Taiwan: Government Information Office.

Shepherd, John R. 1993. *Statecraft and Political Economy on the Taiwan Frontier, 1600–1800.* Stanford, CA: Stanford University Press.

Social Indicators in the Taiwan Area of the Republic of China, 1992. 1993. Taipei, Taiwan: Directorate-General Budget, Accounting and Statistics, Executive Yuan.

Social Indicators in the Taiwan Area of the Republic of China, 1994. 1995. Taipei, Taiwan: Directorate-General Budget, Accounting and Statistics, Executive Yuan.

The Survey Report of the Youth in Taiwan. 1994. Taipei, Taiwan: Directorate-General Budget, Accounting and Statistics, Executive Yuan.

Taiwan with a View. 1989. Taipei, Taiwan: Independence Evening Post.

Tien, Hong-mao. 1989. *The Great Transition: Political and Social Change in the Republic of China.* Stanford, CA: Hoover Institute, Stanford University.

Tipton, Elise K. 1990. *The Japanese Police State: The Tokko in Interwar Japan.* Honolulu: University of Hawaii Press.

Tong, James W. 1991. *Disorder under Heaven: Collective Violence in the Ming Dynasty.* Stanford, CA: Stanford University Press.

Yin, Y. F., P. Yi, W. C. Chou, S. Li, and C. W. Lin. 1992. *Discover Taiwan.* Vols. 1–2. Taipei, Taiwan: The Commonwealth.

Yuan, Y. 1993. "Small Is Still Big." *Free China Review* 43, 11: 8–12.

14

UNITED KINGDOM

(Developed Nation-State)

Nic Groombridge

PROFILE OF THE UNITED KINGDOM

The total population of the United Kingdom in 1994 was 58.3 million, with the bulk (48.7 million) to be found in England. The population of Wales was 2.9 million; Scotland stood at 5.1 million, and Northern Ireland at 1.6 million. The percentage of the population under 16 was 20.7 percent, a fall over the last 20 years from 25.2 percent. The ethnic minority population of Great Britain was 3.2 million, mostly located in the large urban communities of London, Birmingham, Manchester, and Glasgow (Office of National Statistics, 1996).

The economic base of the United Kingdom has moved sharply away from manufacturing toward the service and information sectors. This has been a particular problem for the English regions and the "Celtic" fringe. The legacy of Mrs. Thatcher's term as prime minister can be seen in new Labour's promise to the electorate to remain within the previous administration's spending limits. Britain is now very much a free market economy. One example is the privatization of utilities such as gas, water, transport, and electricity. As we shall see, these trends have their echo in crime and crime control. Another trend is the "demutualizing" of formerly membership-owned financial institutions such as building societies (savings and loans). Other significant areas of growth are the cultural industries of music and design. Thus, "Britpop" and "dance music" are seen as significant export earners.

It is clearly too early to write the history of the politics of the late 1990s

United Kingdom. But just as the election of Margaret Thatcher in 1979 can be seen as a milestone, so many liberal and progressive commentators hoped that Labour's election on May 1, 1997, would mark another milestone. This may be the case, but continuity with previous policies—particularly crime and crime control—has been notable, and the greatest change has been that of style—a caring style linked to the perceived need to make "tough" decisions, to prioritize spending. A major plank is Labour's reform of welfare with a "New Deal" that presumes that all those capable of working will seek work. The budget speech for 1998 emphasized the need to "make work pay" yet also increased funding for transport, education, and health services.

However, while the budget made great play of the extra amounts to be awarded to areas of need, less emphasis has been given to the Home Secretary's determination that the criminal justice system, especially the provision of prison places, be "demand-led." The Secretary sees his job as providing sufficient cells for those given into custody. Projections based on current trends suggest that the prison population in England and Wales could reach a population of 92,600 by 2005 (Home Office, 1998c). This kind of growth will place a strain on case-limited budgets such as crime prevention and community services. Although these modern problems of crime control finance and administration have global resonances today, and may in fact be connected to "globalization," they can also be traced back to historical practices.

HISTORICAL PERSPECTIVE ON CRIME AND CRIME CONTROL

While the traditions of "Old England" may now be played down by the politicocultural marketeers, they retain a firm grip on the style of the criminal justice system. The United Kingdom has a long history, and its empire and former colonies have been marked by that history—if only in rejecting it. Therefore, the brief histories of policing and prisons set out below form part of the prehistory of the United States' policies on crime and crime control, though lately, Britain has been very welcoming of the U.S. "crime control" policies and technologies.

The United Kingdom comprises the three jurisdictions of Scotland, Northern Ireland, and England and Wales. Although legislation for each is enacted by Parliament in London, different historic traditions as well as contemporary problems mean that it is not appropriate to speak of UK law or of a common crime control policy. Scotland's historical connections with the continent of Europe have led to a very different tradition that owes something to both the United States and European practice. For instance, Procurators Fiscal instruct the police, lay sentencers are unknown, and children are dealt with in a "welfarist" rather than a "justice" fashion. Moreover, juries are allowed a third verdict of "not proven." In England and Wales, the common law tradition still holds sway—with judicial independence fiercely guarded, most recently against the extension of mandatory sentencing to repeat drug dealers or sex offenders—and the Crown Prosecution Service is only able to advise the police or discontinue the case. Hence, legislation liberalizing homosexual acts and abortion lags behind that of England and Wales; yet religious discrimination is unlawful. In the rest of the United Kingdom, religious minorities have to prove a racial motive to any discrimination. However, much of what follows relies on the English model, and figures are from the Home Office Web site at www.homeoffice. gov.uk, as updated. However, where significant differences add useful "within-nation" comparisons, these are discussed.

A historic overview of crime and crime control in the United Kingdom might start in the thirteenth century (long before the kingdoms of England, Scotland, Ireland, and Wales were united), when the eleventh-century invention of constables was fully implemented, or in the fourteenth century, when Justices of the Peace (JPs) were established. There is an argument among historians as to whether the JPs forced a decline in the use of constables, which required their reinvention 400 years later with Sir Robert Peel's Metropolitan Police Act of 1829. Others might point to the influence of Patrick Colquhoun's *Treatise on the Police of the Metropolis* (1800) or to Peel's experiences in Ireland before he became Home Secretary.

These historical observations are included to establish the United Kingdom as the origin of early innovation in crime control in contrast to the position that finds the United Kingdom importing policy from elsewhere, such as "three strikes," "zero tolerance," private provision of criminal justice services, and even HM *Prison Weare* (formerly the New York prison ship *Resolution*). These and other innovations will be discussed later, but it should be noted that the United Kingdom's early preeminence was related to its early industrialization and imperial power rather than any unique creativity or the gravity of its crime problems. Now the United States predominates in world markets, world politics, and in the sheer scale of its policy and academic output on crime and its control. Arguably, Japan ought now to have a greater share in the market for penality, and its absence from this market needs as much explanation as its low recorded crime rate.

PUBLIC PERCEPTION OF CRIME AND CRIME CONTROL

Not since Beatlemania or the heyday of punk has there been so much emphasis on the popular cultural aspects of life in Britain. Preparations for the millennium occasioned much debate about the meaning of "Britishness," particularly how it differs from "Englishness." Others were concerned about the London focus of the planned celebrations. Some argued that under the new Labour government, Britain was being "rebranded" like a soap powder or cola—"Cool Britannia." Indeed, in April 1998, the Foreign Office launched Panel 2000 to advise diplomats on marketing Labour's "new Britain." Traditionalists bemoan the extent to which the national flag is being played down—for example, British Airway's decision to remove the Union Flag from their airplanes. Yet some supporters in the popular cultural industries believe Labour has already abandoned radical promises and is simply retailing the previous Conservative administration's policies.

Crime and crime control are important elements in popular culture and are dealt with by politicians and media in populist fashion. The success of *The Full Monty* is illustrative of some of the issues raised in this chapter. While it is the story line and humor that made it a worldwide hit, the background of deindustrialization, changing gender roles, and petty theft are highly relevant. One of the leitmotifs of the film is the availability of jobs in the private security industry or in "women's work." Employment as a security guard is decisively and criminally rejected by one of the characters and parodied when all the men dress as security guards for the final strip show. However, "the most successful British film ever made" could not have been made without U.S. venture capital.

The exigencies of electoral politics are such that Labour was perceived to be "soft" on crime. For example, the British Crime Survey taken in 1998 revealed that the public believes that sentencing is too "soft." They were mistaken, however, about the outcomes of trials; for instance, half of those polled believed that only half of all rapists were sent to prison; the true figure is 97 percent (Hough and Roberts, 1998).

So when Tony Blair, at the time Labour's spokesman on Home Affairs, declared himself "tough on crime, tough on the causes of crime," many thought the toughness was merely rhetorical and that behind the rhetoric lay a social democratic positivism that would emphasize causes such as bad housing, poor education, and income inequalities. However, his moralizing stance, and that of his Home Secretary Jack Straw, currently emphasizes "zero tolerance" of crime and focuses on dysfunctional families and their failure to socialize or control their children. Parenting orders are to be introduced by the government's Crime and Disorder Bill, and there are proposals to cut the benefits of parents who allow their children to be truant. Yet at the same time, "restorative justice" is increasingly spoken of as informing the bill's plans for "reparation orders" and the policies of a number of police forces.

CONTEMPORARY CRIME

Between 1992 and 1997 the recorded crime figures fell every year (although violent crime and sex crimes rose again). Although the British Crime Survey (BCS) figures show higher levels of unreported crime, it is not seriously argued that the drop is totally illusory. The work of Field (1990) anticipates falling property crime (and therefore the near-congruent recorded crime) during an economic boom. However, a recession can be expected soon, and the number of young men in the population is expected to grow again. The number of recorded offenses in England and Wales for 1997 were 4.6 million (Home Office, 1998a), and the number of crimes in Scotland for 1996 was 451,956 (Scottish Office, 1997b). Both jurisdictions show a fifth in annual decline. The picture for Northern Ireland is more mixed, but 68,808 crimes were recorded (Brewer, Lockhart, and Rodgers, 1997).

The British and Scottish Crime Surveys and Northern Ireland's contribution to the International Victimization Study (Van Dijk, Mayhew, and Killias, 1990) tell a slightly different story. Such surveys reveal greater levels of crime and fear than the recorded figures and certainly suggest Northern Ireland is a generally peaceable place; however, Brewer et al. (1997) would point to the complexities caused by criminal activities *and* the crime control activities of the paramilitaries and the concentration of the police on security issues. The Scottish Crime Survey for 1996 suggests that crimes run at 1 million and that rates of victimization were lower than for England and Wales (Scottish Office, 1997a). The main points arising from the 1996 BCS are: Since 1981 (when the surveys began), recorded crime rose by 91 percent, whereas crimes recorded by the BCS rose only 83 percent; in addition, behind the fall of recorded crime figures between 1993 and 1995 of 8 percent, there was a 2 percent rise, but this was the smallest ever rise recorded by the survey (Home Office, 1996).

There is argument about the extent to which such surveys can reveal hidden crimes against women, but 1.3 percent mentioned one or more incidents of domestic violence. Extensive victimization of ethnic minorities has been shown, and section 95 of the Criminal Justice Act of 1991 now requires the Home Secretary to publish information about discrimination. Thus, black people were four times as likely to be stopped and searched by the Metropolitan Police, and they were overrepresented in prison by a ratio of 2 to 1 (Home Office, 1997), although the greater vulnerability of Asians and Afro-Caribbeans to violent crime was largely due to demographic/social and area affects (Home Office, 1993). However, the political pressure to disprove discrimination and to act against racist violence has continued, and the Crime and Disorder Bill seeks to introduce offenses of racially aggravated assault, public order offenses, and harassment.

CONTEMPORARY CRIME CONTROL

The Crime and Disorder Bill is a portamento measure in the now-established tradition of near-annual Criminal Justice Bills. Among many other things, it puts a duty on the police and local authorities to cooperate in formulating and implementing a crime and disorder strategy that includes the collaboration of all relevant agencies in dealing with youth crime by means of Youth Offending Teams. It would enable these teams to seek antisocial behavior orders against individuals and place children below the age of criminal responsibility (10 in England and Wales) under supervision. It allows for the making of curfew orders for those under 10 in certain areas. It also abolishes the current presumption (*doli incapax*) that a child under 14 is incapable of criminal intent (rebutted in the case of the killers of James Bulger). It also ends the extrastatutory practice of cautioning by the police— which allowed for multiple cautions—by instating a system of reprimands and warnings. It provides for extended periods of supervision for sex of- fenders and a drug treatment and testing order. Various measures are pro- posed to speed young offenders' proceedings and for the Court of Appeal to give guideline sentences advised by a sentencing panel. Trials of electronic tagging of offenders on community sentences have been declared a success and are to be extended to the early release of prisoners on license. The toughness of some of these measures has dispelled any notion that Labour's preelection pronouncements were merely electoral window-dressing and has raised human rights issues that remain unresolved at the time of this writing, such as the public inquiry into the racist murder of Stephen Lawrence in South East London while waiting at a bus stop in 1983.

At the same time, the Thames Valley Police (TVP) are in the forefront of using family group conferences in the United Kingdom in dealing with youth crime. Although the origin of these conferences is cited as New Zea- land's 1989 Children and Young Persons Act, the police involvement is more reminiscent of the Australian model. TVP's work calls specifically upon restorative principles, but there is also concern that it is the effectiveness and efficiency of the process that attract politicians rather than its philoso- phy. That philosophy can be traced through a number of religious, cultural, and political routes. Mennonites in the United States and Quakers in the United Kingdom have been influential, as have aboriginal practices; and both communitarian and anarchist roots can be identified, too. Currently, interest in restorative justice is growing but is largely seen to be a minority interest or adjunct to criminal justice. For instance, victim-offender media- tion is still poorly funded, and only two small schemes operate in London. However, many existing programs of community supervision, and even cus- tody, often incorporate elements of it.

Meanwhile, the Probation Services in England and Wales have been sub- ject to many of the effects of managerialism that have buffeted the police but without the same capacity to protect themselves. They are a smaller service (though supervising 169,000 in 1996) and are seen to be less polit- ically useful—or even potentially dispensable. In a hundred years, they have moved from voluntary Church of England missionaries concerned about drunkenness to a therapeutic social service with strong local links to a na- tionally standardized, but still locally organized, "correctional" organization for the delivery of "punishment in the community." When the trials for electronic monitoring are carried out by private contractors, it seems likely that this form of supervision will affect the way that probation does its work even if the full implementation is expected to contract to or work with the "independent" sector. While this could be private firms, the bulk of the work is done by the "voluntary" sector, that is, not-for-profit organizations delivering courses or modules as diverse as anger management, drug treatment and advice, housing, or job training. Indeed, given the difficulties in finding employment for those on release from prison or under supervision in the community, the Home Secretary has already made clear his expectation that probation officers will work closely with Employment Services in delivering "Welfare to Work."

However, the greatest "threat/opportunity" facing the 54 probation areas in England and Wales is the current prisons/probation review that is expected to report in 1999. It is considering the extent to which local services might be merged and whether a single corrections agency might be formed from prisons and probation, as in some other countries. In the Home Office, there has been a tradition of different ministers being responsible for each service, but now they are both responsible to the same minister. The overarching context of the review is disparities between the boundaries of the different criminal justice agencies. In England and Wales, prison is provided and run nationally; the police have 43 areas—though with significant regional groupings for serious crime, national intelligence for drugs, and soccer hooliganism. The Crown Prosecution Services is run nationally, but there are now proposals to align its administration with police forces and provide district attorneys.

Some have suggested that managerialism in the probation service and its possible absorption by prison may lead to a "return to mission" whereby the former evangelical intentions of its founders might be revived, as no one is left "to advise, assist and befriend" the offender. It is less clear who would lead this, but some churches have shown a renewed interest in evangelizing in prisons. The Church of England Temperance Society still exists as the National Council for Social Concern. It retains links with the probation service and has been instrumental in establishing the Restorative Justice Consortium. Although it would run counter to the managerialist and correctionalist trends, Nellis (1995) has proposed that the probation service embrace restorative justice principles. In Scotland, probation is provided by social services, and its areas match local authority boundaries. In Northern Ireland there is one probation service, one prison service, and one police service.

Just as there is a politicohistorical argument about the purpose of prison, so there is an ongoing argument about whether there is a crisis in prisons and the nature of that crisis (Ruggiero, Ryan, and Sim, 1995). Although the numbers in prison continue to rise, the prison service itself is subject to increased cash limits upon what each governor can spend. Thus, increased numbers have meant the prioritization of security and control over educational and rehabilitation programs. The new Labour government has decided to retain the previous government's plans for secure training orders for 12- to 14-year-olds and, despite opposing them in Opposition, have sanctioned the ongoing use of private prisons and escort services. At the same time, they have closed the "boot camp" based at the Military Prison.

On June 30, 1997, there were 61,141 prisoners. There were marked rises in the numbers (3,053) of women in prison (up 19 percent) and sentenced 15- to 17-year-olds (up 32 percent) (Home Office, 1998b). Further attention might be expected to be paid to this, as the United Kingdom's longest-running soap opera, *Coronation Street*, recently incarcerated one of its leading female characters. In a hyperreal twist, tabloid newspapers campaigned for her release.

The number of offenders sentenced by courts for indictable (the most serious) offenses in 1996 was 302,000 (about two thirds by the lay magistrates who deal with about 96 percent of all criminal cases). The fine continued to be the most used sentence for all offenses (75 percent), and even indictable offenses were dealt with by community penalties such as probation or community service. The use of immediate custody in 1995 for all indictable offenses was 20 percent for all courts (the highest in 20 years). It is the continued growth in the use of immediate custody that accounts for the expansion of the numbers in prison.

FUTURE OF CRIME AND CRIME CONTROL

As we have shown, the United Kingdom is at a crossroads in its crime control policies. There are hints of both liberalism and conservativism. Directions in criminal justice policy are also reflecting pressures local, national, European, and global in scope. Thus, the few issues discussed in closing stem mostly from known announcements, but their impact must remain speculative.

For example, one of the successes to date of the new Labour administration has been with "big tent" politics or what might have once been called "broad church." For the millennium celebrations in Northern Ireland and at the recent Earth Summit former Conservative ministers have been involved. This inclusiveness can be seen in Labour's pledges to get people back to work and for a minimum wage. Mrs. Thatcher famously remarked that there was no such thing as society. However, Tony Blair clearly believes in society. Nevertheless, it is clear that his version of society is both broadly drawn and tightly bound. Labour MPs (members of Parliament) now have pagers to keep them "on message." Similarly, parents are to be given pagers to keep in contact with their children at school. Elsewhere, "electronic tags," closed-circuit TV, and curfew orders offer further "techno-fixes."

On other fronts, one result of the Irish peace talks is a review of the Royal Ulster Constabulary by former Conservative minister Chris Patten. This review and the release of paramilitary prisoners pose obvious political difficulties and offer significant criminological research opportunities into criminal and political controls. However, as of the spring of 1998, those detained under the emergency powers legislation have no right to lawyers, audio taping of interviews, or a jury trial. The United Nations Human Rights Commission has called for an end to these practices as well as to the harassment of defense lawyers by the police.

A related aspect of the peace agreement was the proposal for a Council of the Isles whereby representatives of the newly devolved Scottish and Welsh Assemblies could meet. And in the epicenter of the United Kingdom, London, the electorate in early 1998 approved plans for an elected mayor and a police authority for Greater London. The plans propose, for the first time, that the metropolis should have a partially elected Police Authority.

Previously, the Metropolitan Police were seen to require special arrangements that precluded democratic representation. The proposed 23-member Authority will have 11 appointees by the Home Secretary (probably magistrates and businesspeople) and 11 appointees from the GLA (including the deputy mayor). The final appointee is to represent areas outside of London but within the area currently policed by the Metropolitan Police. The Authority is expected to set the crime control strategy and call the Commissioner to account, although the Home Secretary will appoint the Commissioner and have a majority control of finances.

Most of the media interest to date has been about who will become the mayor in the election of May 2000. Several high-profile names have entered the race, including novelist and conservative politician Jeffery Archer, actress Glenda Jackson, and the Transport Minister. Polls say that the front-runner is socialist backbencher Ken Livingstone, formerly leader of the Greater London Council (abolished by Mrs. Thatcher). Today, the ancient post of Lord Mayor of the City of London is largely ceremonial, as is the anomalous position of the City of London Police. Thus, with the introduction of the proposed GLA, attention must turn to the powers of the mayor with respect to the police and the nature of accountability. If the mayor of London is seen to be a success, other provincial towns will seek to elect one. However, running contrary to this localization is a new national police squad against crimes such as drugs, money laundering, and pedophiles.

The effect of these very different "devolutions" in the Celtic fringes and in London on crime control cannot be foreseen, yet expectations seem likely to outrun the formal powers given to them. At the same time, European and other transnational legislation and crime control seem likely to be pulling in still another direction (Taylor, 1999). And far from operating "big tent" politics, Labour seems intent on operating a more limited, "Millennium Dome" politics, in which the external image of "Cool Britannia" rests upon the authoritarian exclusionism of "Cruel Britannia"—the cruel policies consisting of those in which single mothers and young people (as well as failing schools, hospitals, and so on) get one chance in the free enterprise system to enter the Dome (Ark?) before being cast out. Labour's policies, in other words, run the risk of creating new "outlaw" classes.

REFERENCES

Brewer, J. D., B. Lockhart, and P. Rodgers. 1997. *Crime in Ireland 1945–95: Here Be Dragons.* Oxford: Clarendon Press.

Field, S. 1990. "Trends in Crime and Their Interpretation: A Study of Recorded Crime in Post-war England and Wales." *Home Office Research Studies,* 119. London: HMSO.

———. 1993. "The 1992 British Crime Survey." London: HMSO.

———. 1996. "The 1996 British Crime Survey: England and Wales." *Home Office Statistical Bulletin* 19/96.

———. 1997. *Race and the Criminal Justice System.* London: HMSO.

———. 1998a. "Notifiable Offences 1997." *Home Office Statistical Bulletin* 7/98.

———. 1998b. "The Prison Population in 1997." *Home Office Statistical Bulletin* 5/98.

———. 1998c. "Revised Projections of Long Term Trends in the Prison Population to 2005." *Home Office Statistical Bulletin* 2/98.

Hough, M., and J. Roberts. 1998. "Attitudes to Punishment." London: Home Office.

Nellis, M. 1995. "Probation Values for the 1990's." *Howard Journal for Criminal Justice* 34: 19–44.

Office of National Statistics. 1996. *United Kingdom in Figures.* London: HMSO.

Ruggiero, V., M. Ryan, and J. Sim. 1995. *Western European Penal Systems.* London: Sage.

Scottish Office. 1997a. "The 1996 Scottish Crime Survey: First Results." *Crime and Criminal Justice Research Findings.* No. 16. Scottish Office: Edinburgh.

———. 1997b. "Recorded Crime in Scotland, 1996." *Statistical Bulletin* CrJ/1997/3.

Taylor, I. 1999. *Crime in Context: A Critical Criminology of Market Societies.* Cambridge, United Kingdom: Polity Press.

Van Dijk, J.J.M., P. Mayhew, and M. Killias. 1990. *Experiences of Crime across the World.* Deventer, Netherlands: Kluwer Law.

15

UNITED STATES

(Developed Nation-State)

Gary Feinberg

PROFILE OF THE UNITED STATES

The United States logs into the postmodern world of the twenty-first century with a population of about 276 million. By race, 83 percent are white, 12.5 percent are black, and 4.5 percent are American Indian, Alaskan Natives, and Pacific Islanders. Approximately 18 percent of whites claim Hispanic origin. It is also a rapidly aging population, going from a median age of 28 in 1970 to 34 in 1995. Of special relevance to criminologists, the proportions of those ages 14 to 17 and 18 to 24 are declining. In 1970 they made up 7.8 percent and 17 percent of the population, respectively. By 1994 the comparable figures had fallen to 5.5 percent and 9.7 percent. This trend is especially salient because it describes the nation's highest crime-prone age groups (U.S. Department of Commerce, Economics, and Statistics Administration, 1995).

The definition of *family* in the United States is undergoing significant reconstruction today, replete with fragmentation and pluralism. People living here report (1) never being married, (2) marrying for the first time at older ages, (3) postponing having children, (4) preferring smaller families, (5) divorcing despite the presence of children, and (6) living together prior to marriage (Knox and Schacht, 1997). Criminologists, in turn, have directed their research attention especially to the dramatic upsurge in the number of broken homes (almost 50 percent of all marriages end in divorce), the decline of the nuclear family as the dominant form of family life in America, the increase in working mothers so that 75 percent are in the labor force, and the fact that 27 percent of all American children under age 18 live with one parent. These are matched by the growing prevalence of single female head of households with no spouse present and one or more children, as well as the dual-career/dual-worker family (U.S. Department of Commerce, Economics, and Statistics Administration, 1995).

As of 1994, the United States has had a workforce of 123 million, including 34 million who are classified as managers or professionals. Of these, 48.1 percent are females, 7.1 percent are blacks, and 4.5 percent are Hispanics. These figures represent significant growth in each instance since 1983. At the same time, females, blacks, and Hispanics continue to be heavily associated with service occupations, whereas Hispanics are gaining especially in the agricultural and fishing occupations. In addition, technical and administrative jobs have increased from about 31 million in 1983 to 37 million in 1994; however, there has been little change in the number of people employed in precision production and repair work or as fabricators, operators, or laborers. Agriculture continues to employ only about 3.7 million people. The major and most portentous change in workforce participation over the past 20 years has been the increasing presence of women. In 1970, for example, 42.6 percent of white women ages 16 and over were in the workforce. By 1994 they constituted 58 percent of this group. The fastest-growing occupations are home health care aides, human service workers, and computer engineers (U.S. Department of Commerce, Economics, and Statistics Administration, 1995).

Since 1980, unemployment in the United States has been in the single digits, varying from about 5.3 percent to 9.6 percent. It is often twice as high for blacks as it is for whites. Median household income in 1993 was $31,241. Controlling for race, it was about $32,845 for whites, $19,533 for blacks, and $22,886 for Hispanics. This same year, over 39 million Americans, 15 percent of the total population, lived at or below the poverty line. By race this translates unevenly: 33.1 percent of blacks live in poverty as compared to 12.2 percent of whites and 30.6 percent of Hispanics. From 1970 forward, the proportion of whites living in poverty has increased about 25 percent, whereas it has remained relatively stable for blacks. Correspondingly, incomes of blacks and Hispanics have improved more rapidly than those of whites (U.S. Department of Commerce, Economics, and Statistics Administration, 1995).

HISTORICAL PERSPECTIVE ON CRIME AND CRIME CONTROL

In the early years the American colonies served England as an important outlet for disposing of its unwanted criminals, vagabonds, and derelicts. Literally tens of thousands of these social outcasts were loaded onto convict ships and banished to their shores. One estimate suggests that transported convicts composed perhaps a quarter of British immigrants to colonial America during the eighteenth century (Ekirch, 1991). Nevertheless, court records, newspaper accounts, diaries, letters, and similar documentary resources indicate that throughout most of seventeenth- and eighteenth-century New England, crime remained relatively low (Flaherty, 1991b). When colonialists complained about crime, it was mainly moral offenses (e.g., fornication, misbehavior on the Sabbath, idleness, illegal sale of liquor), as well as petty theft that concerned them. Crimes against the person were relatively rare (Flaherty, 1991a). The major exception was New York, which winked at moral offenses but which suffered a great deal of serious crime, low conviction rates (under 45 percent), and law enforcement officials who were notorious for neglecting their duties (Greenberg, 1991).

By the turn of the nineteenth century there emerged in the United States an expanding population of criminals all along the Eastern Seaboard. Rampant street crimes including rape, kidnapping, theft, prostitution, counterfeiting, muggings, armed robbery, and assaults became a daily part of the American landscape. Especially disturbing was the mounting toll of crimes against private property. Evidence suggests that the post-Revolutionary spirit of America was one in which the fever for freedom and equality was eclipsed by growing class divisions between wealthy merchants, artisans, and politicians, on one side, and a growing lower class of slaves, immigrants, and laborers, on the other. Materialism ascended as a guiding principle of American purpose and American justice. The law acquired at this time a select new function: protecting private property. No longer is safeguarding one's home and personal property simply a matter of civil law enforced by court orders. Instead, it is the object of criminal law, and violations are now interpreted as threats to the well-being and authority of the state. By 1800, the prosecution of assaults on private property in the United States had become the primary activity of the courts. Middlesex records show that 47 percent of all prosecutions were for theft during those two decades (Browning and Gerassi, 1980). At this stage in American history, crime and its concomitants of poverty and inequality were not only significant for themselves, but they also evidenced an ideological failure, that is, the despoiling of the American dream of a new, more progressive and humane society.

Another major nineteenth-century development in America's crime culture was the rise of a new breed of criminals who collected together to form gangs. Unlike traditional criminals who were essentially individual entrepreneurs or desperate men, these offenders were more professional, organized, and mature. They also added an important new dimension to criminality, that is, political patronage. They provided votes, political support, and when necessary, coercive muscle for many local politicians and ward bosses, forming an enduring unholy alliance and symbiotic relationship. Therefore, while they robbed, stole, extorted, assaulted, and even murdered, they were protected at city hall. Among New York City's famous and often colorful gangs were the Plug Uglies, Daybreak Boys, Dead Rabbits, and the Bowery Boys (Browning and Gerassi, 1980).

This period in American criminal history was also one of extensive civil unrest. Riots accompanied by arson, looting, vandalism, assaults, and even lynchings were common. For example, from 1834 through 1835 there were 16 national riots, costing 61 lives. Most of these riots were caused by economic stress, unemployment, Protestant nativist hatred toward Catholic immigrants, and Irish working-class resentment of wealthy abolitionists and freed blacks, who they feared would take their jobs. Since these riots often resulted in personal injury and the destruction of private property, the ruling classes defined them as crimes deserving penal sanction. By the mid-1830s the courts quite openly sided with employers, and union advocates were quickly condemned as criminals. Strikers typically were imprisoned with murderers, thieves, and other common criminals as the propertied ruling class exploited the criminal law to contain any challenge to their influence (Browning and Gerassi, 1980).

Meanwhile, corruption in government was epidemic. Police officers were often little more than tools of ward politicians who used them to protect their own interests and those of their supporters. In many instances the police would undertake an arrest not because it was their job but because of a fee or reward they might receive from the victim.

Given the gang crime, incendiary violence, civil riots, heavy toll of crimes against property, rising rates of murder and assault, and a corrupt, often ineffective crime control system, there came a clarion call to create a full-time professional police force that would provide better preventive protection to the general citizenry. In 1838, Boston became the first city to establish such a police department, followed by New York City in 1844 and Philadelphia in 1854. These were modeled after the Metropolitan Police in London, England. By the 1870s every major city had its own professionalized police department. However, *professional* at this time simply meant that the police donned uniforms and that their work was a full-time occupation rather than a volunteer service or part-time fee-based position. They were frequently recruited without regard to health, age, or moral standard. Nor did they receive much training or supervision. Alternatively, corruption was rampant and rife with physical brutality. The general public tolerated them mainly because the immediate victims of their abusive behavior were usually the powerless and the social outcasts, for example, the poor, the immigrants, and the unemployed (Adler, Mueller, and Laufer, 1998).

Crime in early twentieth-century America, like many other major industries, underwent a significant metamorphosis and entered the age of mass production. No longer was it simply the craft of men who were either desperate, evil, or social misfits. Notorious gangsters such as Al Capone, Frank Costello, Lucky Luciano, Bugsy Siegel, and Johnny Torrio emerged and began to dominate the criminal world. These figures of the underworld came to realize that far more money could be made by streamlining their enterprises, by corporate mergers, and by organizing their businesses along product lines: one operation for running brothels, another for gambling, another for selling whiskey, and so on. Each, in turn, would be conducted on a citywide or statewide basis and judged according to its profits. Protecting the administration meant bribes to the police and politicians, along with coercive muscle and negotiation with competing administrations and independent gangs. In this way, American gangsters insinuated themselves into the city's normal political and social life.

Criminals were now rich, debonair, articulate architects and managers of large, nationwide criminal cartels. Among the profitable criminal enterprises they organized were liquor sales, gambling, prostitution, loan sharking, and eventually narcotics. They also used extortion, physical violence, and other illegal means to gain control over such legitimate businesses as laundries, restaurants, bars, dock works, movies, entertainment, garment manufacturing, as well as unionizing and strikebreaking. Aiding their rise to fame and power as criminals was a press that turned them into Faustian heroes who by deviant means had achieved the American dream.

The 1920s are also associated with the ascendancy of three common forms of criminality: (1) auto theft, (2) kidnapping, and (3) armed robbery. Auto theft was probably contrived shortly after the invention of the automobile at the turn of the previous century, but it came into its own in the Roaring Twenties. From 1918 to 1929 auto theft quadrupled. Moreover, not only were automobiles stolen for the purposes of resale, but they were also conscripted into service as getaway cars when gangland slayings and bank robberies were daily headline grabbers during the days of Prohibition. As car ownership democratized, so too did appropriating cars without criminal intent for purposes of "joy riding." This was primarily popular among teenagers who were too young or poor to buy their own cars.

Dramatic cases of kidnapping frequently made newspaper headlines in the 1920s and early 1930s. The most celebrated of these was the kidnapping and murder of Bobby Franks by Nathan Leopold and Richard Loeb, two upper-class, well-educated young men from fine families whose ultimate goal was to commit "the perfect crime." A few years later, the infant son of America's great hero Charles Lindberg was kidnapped and murdered. A public outraged, sympathetic, and anguished saw to the advancement of several laws to combat the growing kidnapping problem. One of these elevated the crime into a federal offense, thereby allowing the Federal Bureau of Investigation (FBI) to intercede with its superior resources.

Armed robbery also modernized in the 1920s. The lead pipe and blackjack were replaced by the more efficient machine gun, the horse by the speeding getaway car, and the lone victim on the roadway by banks, gas stations, and mail trucks. By 1925 there were 125,000 "holdups" annually. The relatively rich rewards and low risks of capture by an inefficient, inadequately staffed and equipped, politically confounded, and corrupted police force made armed robbery an attractive alternative criminal career.

The twentieth century ushered in the Progressive Era, named for the educated middle- and upper-class citizens who dedicated themselves to cleaning up dishonesty in government wherever it existed, including police corruption and related political patronage. A by-product of their efforts was the inauguration of various commissions to investigate the nature and extent of America's crime problem, along with the ability of the police to control it. The most famous of these was the 1931 Wickersham Commission. It found that police service in general was grossly inadequate and criticized such police shortcomings as failing to screen out incompetents, insufficient education, poor training, disregard for discipline, political interference and corruption, inferior equipment, and administrators unsuited for their positions.

Dedicating themselves to remedying these widespread inadequacies were two leaders in police reform, August Vollmer and Orlando W. Wilson. Vollmer, a former police chief of Berkeley, California, championed the importance of formal education as a prerequisite to good police service. His efforts resulted in the first baccalaureate program in the United States with a minor in criminology. He advocated training the police in such liberal studies as sociology, psychology, political science, law, and public administration. He also emphasized the importance of incorporating technological advances in communications, transportation, forensic science, and criminalistics to the advantage of the police. Wilson, in turn, brought many of Vollmer's ideas about educating police officers to Wichita, Kansas, and later to Chicago, Illinois. He promoted a new model of policing that emphasized police service as a profession. It was characterized by a "tight quasi-military organization, rigorous discipline, a streamlined chain of command, higher recruitment standards, a lengthy period of preservice training, the allocation of available personnel according to demonstrated need, and extensive use of vehicles, communications, and computer technology" (Reid, 1987: 318).

Improvements in police education and training during the 1930s were probably the most important achievements for elevating law enforcement in general. By the end of the decade, almost every state had its own police force. These led the way in implementing progressive training programs, most of which were at least three months in duration. Correlatively, New York established the first police academy, followed closely by Pennsylvania and Michigan. Augmenting these educational developments, in 1935 the FBI created its own National Academy training center in Quantico, Virginia (Bopp and Schultz, 1972). Encouraged by the Wickersham Reports, other major progressive efforts in police service during the 1930s included the introduction of the first merit promotion system, improved retirement plans, the creation of a police credit union, and the placement of certain departments under civil service administration, thereby checking political interference. The deployment of technological advancements on behalf of police work also instituted during this period include the implementation of modern police labs boasting x-rays, polygraphs, and ballistics equipment, the installation of two-way radios in patrol cars, call boxes teletype, recall systems, and other communication improvements.

PUBLIC PERCEPTION OF CRIME AND CRIME CONTROL

Some might claim that contemporary America is obsessed with crime or crime phobic. The *National Law Journal*'s poll of public attitudes about crime reports 82 percent of all Americans are extremely concerned about crime and personal safety (Sherman, 1994). Moreover, a Public Opinion and Demographic Report published in 1993 finds that Americans rank crime the nation's number-four problem, just behind health care, the economy, and unemployment ("Public Opinion," 1999). Fear of crime has changed how Americans live, work, and play. It constitutes a major reason for dissatisfaction with one's area of residence (Wagner, 1995), results in people closeting themselves away in veritable fortresses (Skogan and Maxfield, 1981), spawns fear of being out alone at night (Hindelang, Gottfredson, and Garafolo, 1978), forces the avoidance of certain parts of the city (Warr, 1985), and generates vigilante justice (Beirne and Messerschmidt, 1991).

The position taken here is that while crime is a serious problem in the United States, some of the concern is based upon exaggerated conceptions of its real scope and direction. In the parlance of the times, the problem is more apparent than real. What the United States is experiencing is not a crime wave but a media-induced and -constructed crime wave precipitated by the media's romance with crime and police shows. More and more crimes, and especially violent crimes, are being depicted on television, the news, and in the movies. As a result the public has developed a false consciousness about crime (Skogan and Maxfield, 1981; Lacaye, 1994). What seems the more salient reality is that Americans feel highly vulnerable to crime and believe that it is rising and growing more serious and that offenders are becoming more resilient to crime control efforts. There is much evidence that these popular public perceptions, beliefs, and fears about crime are often distorted, ill conceived, and somewhat exaggerated. Equally, there has been much research aimed at explaining the origins and causes of these misinformed fears (Staley and Ashkins, 1981). Yet there is little doubt that a soaring fear of crime has emerged over the past 30 years. While it might be somewhat ill founded and overestimated, this fear of crime, real or imaginary, has produced a kind of mass paranoia. It has wealthy people buying expensive security devices, concerned citizens pressuring for more police, judges, and prisons, and legislators allocating huge fiscal investments for crime control as the United States tries to spend itself into a safe society.

Similarly, the public also possesses many ideas on how to control crime.

This, too, contributes to the fiscal crises in state and local governmental bodies. For example, there is often heard a groundswell of advocates and supporters for more police and prisons, speedier trials, and stricter and longer sentencing schemes. Expenditures for such activities divert funds from other needed areas such as education, counseling, medical research, housing, aging services, and refurbishing decaying urban infrastructures.

CONTEMPORARY CRIME

Is the American fear of crime justified? According to the nation's major crime data source, the Uniform Crime Report (UCR), compiled annually by the FBI, there are about 14.4 million known or reported incidents of Index Crimes (murder, rape, robbery, aggravated assault, burglary, larceny, auto theft, and arson) per year. So extensive is this volume that in 1990 it exceeded comparable data found in such equally modern countries as France (3,492,712), the United Kingdom (5,559,827), Japan (1,726,188), the Netherlands (1,141,272), Spain (1,054,551), and Sweden (1,218,829) combined, although its total population is somewhat less (Reddy, 1994). Murder is especially common in the United States, averaging about 25,000 known or reported cases annually. By comparison, countries such as Denmark, Norway, Japan, Sweden, Holland, Finland, and even France and the United Kingdom register their murders in the fifties or low hundreds. Other indications of the seriousness of crime are reflected in rising rates of stranger murders, increased juvenile involvement in some forms of violence (up as high as 100 percent between 1983 and 1993), greater prevalence of guns, and new forms of crime (Gest and Friedman, 1994; Cortese, 1995). Furthermore, statistics show that from one fourth to one third of all U.S. households suffer crime victimization annually (U.S. Department of Justice, 1992). Related research suggests that almost 90 percent of all Americans can expect to suffer crime victimization at least once during their lifetime (Kornblum and Julian, 1995).

Not only is crime in the United States discouraging in absolute numbers and rates, but UCR data reveal longitudinal trends that suggest it is rapidly growing worse. For instance, from 1973 to 1992 the rate of Index Crimes increased by 36.2 percent, going from 4,154.4 to 5,660.2 per 100,000 inhabitants. Violent crime especially rose during this period, going from a low of 417.4 to a high of 757.5 per 100,000 inhabitants, an 81.5 percent increase. Similarly, high rate increases over the same period occur for forcible rape (+74.7 percent), robbery (+42 percent), aggravated assault (+120 percent), larceny (+49.8 percent), and motor vehicle theft (+42.7 percent). Needless to say, some of the volume increases for these offenses are astronomical. Index Crimes by volume are up 65.6 percent, and violent crime rose 120.6 percent, aggravated assault increased by 168 percent, and robbery declined by 75 percent. Meanwhile, the general population grew only a nominal 21.5 percent (U.S. Department of Justice, 1995).

However, not everyone agrees that crime in the United States is increasing. Indeed, some interesting recent findings suggest that crime is actually decreasing. Those holding this position typically cite data from the National Crime Survey (NCS). The NCS polls representatives from tens of thousands of households and asks if they have been victims of various crimes within the given year. These crime categories are roughly comparable to those in the UCR. According to NCS data, there is a sharp decline in criminal victimization from 1973 to 1990. For example, the rate for crimes of violence according to victims dropped from a high of 35.3 in 1981 to 31.7 in 1990. Similarly, the rate for personal theft victimization declined from 97.3 in 1977 to a low of 68.3 in 1990, and the rate of household crimes tumbled from 217.8 in 1973 to 161.0 in 1990 (Table 15.1). Individual crime such as forcible rape, robbery, aggravated assault, and burglary all evidence significant declines in rates and often by volume as well ("Less of It," 1993).

Further support for the belief that crime is actually down in the United States may even be found in the UCR. For example, the UCR shows that the total number of crimes in 1992 fell 3 percent below what it was in 1991. This especially reflects decreases in property crime. Also down is the rate of increase in violent crimes. Whereas such crimes averaged a 6 percent annual increase from 1983 to 1991, between 1991 and 1992 they increased by only 1.1 percent (U.S. Department of Justice, 1995).

How do we resolve the disparity between UCR statistics, which suggest we are experiencing a so-called crime wave, and NCS data, which suggest that the flow of crime is on the ebb? Although there are some significant difficulties in making comparisons between UCR and NCS data, and caution needs to be applied, the general polemic pattern just described remains cogent. It also results in an important explanatory thesis. Specifically, some contend that crime only appears to be increasing (as per UCR data), whereas in reality it is decreasing (as per NCS data). Those pledging allegiance to this thesis offer that although fewer crimes are occurring, a greater proportion of this reduced number is becoming known or reported to the police. The "crime wave" implied by the UCR is really only a paper increase. This latter, in turn, is the result of the fact that there are more and better trained police on the job to observe officially reported crimes, more public confidence in the police, changing definitions of what needs to be reported to the police and what is deemed a private affair, and so on (Davey, 1994). Table 15.2 provides a comparison of crime trends as indicated by UCR statistics and parallel trends in crime according to NCS data. As evidenced by this table, from 1973 to 1990, according to NCS data, crime victimizations declined, especially after the mid-1980s. However, crimes officially known or reported to the police for this same period have increased.

Table 15.1
Trends in Personal and Household Crime Victimizations, 1973–1990

		All Crimes	NCS Victimizations Crimes of Violence	Personal Theft	Household Crimes
Year					
1973	Number	35,661,030	5,350,550	14,970,570	15,339,910
	Rate		32.6	91.1	217.8
1974	Number	38,411,090	5,509,950	15,889,010	17,012,130
	Rate		33.0	95.1	235.7
1975	Number	39,266,130	5,572,670	16,293,720	17,399,740
	Rate		32.8	96.0	236.5
1976	Number	39,317,620	5,599,330	16,519,380	17,198,910
	Rate		32.6	96.1	229.5
1977	Number	40,314,380	5,901,510	16,932,910	17,479,960
	Rate		33.9	97.3	228.8
1978	Number	40,412,370	5,941,080	17,050,240	17,421,050
	Rate		33.7	96.8	223.4
1979	Number	41,249,320	6,158,790	16,382,170	18,708,360
	Rate		34.5	91.9	235.3
1980	Number	40,251,630	6,130,060	15,300,240	18,821,330
	Rate		33.3	83.0	227.4
1981	Number	41,454,180	6,582,310	15,862,850	19,009,020
	Rate		35.3	85.1	226.0
1982	Number	39,756,400	6,459,020	15,553,030	17,744,350
	Rate		34.3	82.5	208.2
1983	Number	37,001,200	5,903,440	14,657,300	16,440,460
	Rate		31.0	76.9	189.8
1984	Number	35,543,500	6,021,130	13,789,000	15,733,370
	Rate		31.4	71.8	178.7
1985	Number	34,863,960	5,822,650	13,473,810	15,567,500
	Rate		30.0	69.4	174.4
1986	Number	34,118,310	5,515,450	13,235,190	15,367,670
	Rate		28.1	67.5	170.0
1987	Number	35,336,440	5,796,070	13,574,720	15,965,650
	Rate		29.3	68.7	173.9
1988	Number	35,795,840	5,909,570	14,056,390	15,829,880
	Rate		29.6	70.5	169.6
1989	Number	35,818,410	5,861,050	13,829,450	16,127,910
	Rate		29.8	70.2	169.9

Table 15.1 (*continued*)

		NCS Victimizations		
Year		*All Crimes*	*Crimes of Violence*	*Personal Theft*	*Household Crimes*
1990	Number	34,403,600	6,008,790	12,975,320	15,419,490
	Rate		31.7	68.3	161.0

Note: Rates for crimes of violence and personal theft are the number of victimizations per 1,000 persons ages 12 or older; rates for household crimes are per 1,000 households. Detail may not add to total because of rounding.

Source: U.S. Department of Justice, Bureau of Justice Statistics, 1993.

CONTEMPORARY CRIME CONTROL

As of 1998, the United States was supporting more than 20,000 separate law enforcement agencies. Only about 50 were at the federal level; an additional 200 were at the state level, but the vast majority were local agencies, including towns, cities, and counties. The number of officers in each varies from only 1 to over 35,000. Most of these agencies employ fewer than 10 full-time officers, and only 5 percent employ 100 or more officers. Over 900,000 full-time law enforcement personnel, including more than 664,000 sworn officers, are employed to carry out the protean responsibilities of these agencies. This translates into 25 sworn and 10 nonsworn employees for every 10,000 residents (U.S. Department of Justice, 1998).

A defining dimension of U.S. policing is that it is decentralized. Divisions between federal and state policing are clearly drawn. Moreover, within each state it is the local police agency that controls crime, and the autonomy of each agency within its geopolitical jurisdiction is strictly guarded and respected. Cooperation does occur; for example, information may be shared, a crime lab may be supported by several municipalities, and jurisdictions may work together where a crime transcends local or state borders. Indeed, in very large or important cases, federal, state, and local police agencies may collaborate and work both individually and collectively on their investigation and resolution.

Federal Law Enforcement

The FBI is probably the most identifiable of all federal agencies with police powers and certainly one of the largest. Its main offices are in Washington, D.C., but each state has at least one branch office. An additional 16 offices are located throughout the world. The FBI employs over 10,000 special agents, plus 13,000 support personnel. The responsibilities of its nonuniformed service include investigating all federal criminal law violations, including the theft or destruction of any federal property, kidnapping, bank robbery, counterfeiting, and using the mails or media to defraud. The jurisdiction of the FBI also includes any instance where two or more states

Table 15.2
Comparing Trends in Crime Using NCS Victimization Data and UCR Data,
1973–1990

Year		UCR Index Crimes	NCS Victimizations All Crimes	Crimes of Violence	Personal Theft
1973	Number	8,718,100	35,661,030	5,350,550	14,970,570
	Rate	4154.4		32.6	91.1
1974	Number	10,253,500	38,411,090	5,509,950	15,889,010
	Rate	4850.4		33.0	95.1
1975	Number	11,292,400	39,266,130	5,572,670	16,293,720
	Rate	5298.5		32.8	96.0
1976	Number	11,349,700	39,317,620	5,599,330	16,519,380
	Rate	5287.3		32.6	96.1
1977	Number	10,984,500	40,314,380	5,901,510	16,932,910
	Rate	5077.6		33.9	97.3
1978	Number	11,209,000	40,412,370	5,941,080	17,050,240
	Rate	5140.3		33.7	96.8
1979	Number	12,249,500	41,249,320	6,158,790	16,382,170
	Rate	5565.5		34.5	91.9
1980	Number	13,408,300	40,251,630	6,130,060	15,300,240
	Rate	5950.0		33.3	83.0
1981	Number	13,423,800	41,454,180	6,582,310	15,862,850
	Rate	5858.2		35.3	85.1
1982	Number	12,974,400	39,756,400	6,459,020	15,553,030
	Rate	5603.6		34.3	82.5
1983	Number	12,108,600	37,001,200	5,903,440	14,657,300
	Rate	5175.0		31.0	76.9
1984	Number	11,881,800	35,543,500	6,021,130	13,789,000
	Rate	5031.3		31.4	71.8
1985	Number	12,431,400	34,863,960	5,882,650	13,473,810
	Rate	5207.1		30.0	69.4
1986	Number	13,211,900	34,118,310	5,515,450	13,235,190
	Rate	5480.4		28.1	67.5
1987	Number	13,508,700	35,336,440	5,796,070	13,574,720
	Rate	5550.0		29.3	68.7
1988	Number	13,923,100	35,795,840	5,909,570	14,056,390
	Rate	5664.2		29.6	70.5

Year		UCR Index Crimes	All Crimes	NCS Victimizations Crimes of Violence	Personal Theft
1989	Number	14,251,400	35,818,410	5,861,050	13,829,450
	Rate	5741.0		29.8	70.2
1990	Number	14,475,600	34,403,600	6,008,790	12,975,320
	Rate	5820.3		31.7	68.3

Note: Rates for UCR Index Crimes are reported per 100,000. Rates for victimizations of violent crimes or personal theft are reported per 1,000 persons ages 12 or older. Rates for household crimes are reported per 1,000 households.

Source: U.S. Department of Justice, Bureau of Justice Statistics, 1993.

are involved in carrying out any criminal law violation, for example, transporting stolen cars, trafficking drugs, or operating a burglary ring across state borders. Alternatively, the FBI normally does not pursue traditional criminal cases such as domestic violence, small-scale drug sales, or home burglaries.

Other major federal law enforcement agencies include (1) the Drug Enforcement Administration (DEA), whose 3,000 agents investigate and pursue the arrest of large major violators of laws controlling the manufacture, sale, and possession of narcotics and other controlled substances; (2) the Immigration and Naturalization Service (INS), which polices the admission, naturalization, exclusion, and deportation of aliens, together with the hiring of illegal aliens by unscrupulous employers who seek to circumvent fair wage laws and related responsibilities to laborers (Abadinsky and Winfree, 1992); (3) the U.S. Customs Service, which is mandated to collect duties on imported goods and to prevent smuggling, the illegal movement of money across borders, cargo thefts, and criminal fraud against the Internal Revenue Service; (4) the Secret Service, a small elite agency originally created by Congress in 1865 to investigate cases of counterfeiting and the forgery of government bonds, checks, and other securities, which today is responsible for protecting the president, vice-president, and visiting heads of state; and (5) the Bureau of Alcohol, Tobacco, and Firearms (ATF), which oversees regulations governing the liquor and tobacco industries and, most important today, the illegal trafficking in firearms and explosive devices, especially as these are linked to terrorism and organized crime.

State Law Enforcement

In the United States, every state has its own police force, and there are 52,000 sworn state officers throughout the country, most of whom are males. Pennsylvania established the first such agency in 1905. Pennsylvania's force, based on a paramilitary model, became the model for the creation of other state police departments. Their duties came to focus on maintaining order on the nation's growing system of highways. Indeed, contemporary state police today patrol the state highways, enforce traffic laws, license motorists, investigate auto accidents, and monitor highway conditions, emission control standards, and other matters related to highways, cars, and trucks, including the use of the highways for emergency aid or evacuation. Some state police agencies, however, are really full-service systems. They provide all of the services described and many others, such as investigating statewide criminality, patrolling state-owned universities, and securing major sports events (Abadinsky and Winfree, 1992).

Local Law Enforcement

The bulk of law enforcement in the United States occurs at the local level. There are three types of local police agencies: (1) municipal police; (2) county police; and (3) constables. The municipal police are found in incorporated urban areas and towns ranging from 10,000 to several million residents. In all, there are about 17,000 municipal police departments in the United States. These departments are generally headed by a police chief (also known as a director, superintendent, or commissioner, depending upon the community). Municipal police departments are responsible for maintaining law and order in their jurisdictions and have general arrest and investigatory powers over all traditional forms of crime. The workhorses of the law enforcement system, these officers are normally recruited, trained, paid, managed, and disciplined by the city or town in which they work. This is a highly decentralized system with no overreaching authority. Individual municipal police departments are totally autonomous and independent of each other. However, they are responsible to the city council or its equivalent body.

Policing the unincorporated areas of the United States is usually the work of the sheriff's office. Responsibilities typically include daily security patrol and crime control, with its correlates of arrest and investigatory powers. In addition, the sheriff's office runs the county jail, provides security and bailiff assistance at the county courthouse, and serves subpoenas, levies, and eviction notices. Sheriffs and their deputies also work traffic accidents in unincorporated areas, assist in riot control, and in some places collect taxes. Sometimes sheriffs are limited to only a few of these control measures. This tends to be true more in eastern states than in those in the South and West.

One can still find constables in some smaller U.S. communities. The constable's role usually is relatively minor, and their police powers are limited. Although their responsibilities vary by jurisdiction, they tend to concentrate on enforcing local traffic ordinances, collecting local taxes, distributing election notices, and occasionally performing some patrol duties. It is not unusual for constables to be part-time employees who are paid on the basis of a fee system, their earnings being a proportion of the revenues they generate.

Stages in the Criminal Justice Process

Apprehending Suspects

With respect to arresting persons, policing involves a number of distinctive characteristics. Four of the more salient entail the rules and restrictions regarding (1) stop and frisk, (2) detention, (3) search and seizure, and (4) use of deadly force.

A major technique used in aggressive police patrol work is to stop and frisk those suspected of a crime. However, police officers cannot stop an individual simply on a whim or conjecture that he or she "must be up to some criminal act." Reasonable suspicion that the individual stopped has committed a crime or is about to do so must exist. What constitutes reasonable suspicion is always a question of fact. Failure to have reasonable suspicion can result in criminal penalties levied against the police officer for illegal detention.

Concomitant with stopping suspicious persons, the police have the right to frisk them. This means patting the suspect down specifically and solely for weapons. The main justification is to ensure that the police officer or others in the vicinity are not in danger of bodily harm by a weapon. It does not mean that the police officer can search the suspect to locate contraband, stolen merchandise, or comparable evidence that he or she has committed a crime or is about to do so. The police can arrest for suspicious behavior, but failing to respond to questions cannot be used as evidence of suspicious behavior. Other material facts prior to the stop would need to be cited to justify the stop in the first place.

The police cannot make a legitimate arrest without probable cause. This means that there is articulated evidence that would make a reasonable person believe that a crime had been committed and that the suspect likely did it. Immediately upon making such an arrest they must inform the accused of his or her "Miranda Rights" (i.e., that they are entitled to a lawyer, that a lawyer will be provided if they cannot afford one, and that anything they say may be used against them in a court of law). Nor can they interrogate a suspect without the defense attorney being present once the suspect has requested one. At the moment of arrest, the accused must also be informed of the specific charges.

The police have the authority to examine or inspect a location, vehicle, or person in order to locate objects related to, or believed to be involved in, criminal activity. They also have the authority to seize and take into custody any such evidence. However, before either of these actions can be done lawfully, they must be done with "probable cause." What constitutes probable cause often entails a complex factual determination. Among the guidelines used are the following: Was there a valid search warrant? Was the search incidental to a valid arrest based on probable cause? Was the evidence in plain view? Did the suspect voluntarily consent to the search?

The U.S. police have the right to carry guns. However, the laws of most states strictly limit their authority to use them. Generally, before a police officer can draw his or her weapon, one of three conditions must be met: (1) The suspect is resisting arrest, and the officer's life or those of other persons in the vicinity are in danger; (2) the suspect is committing a forcible felony (e.g., armed robbery); or (3) the suspect is fleeing from the scene of a forcible felony and continues to carry a weapon, posing a danger to others. Alternatively, the police are not justified in shooting someone committing a misdemeanor or a nonforcible felony or even fleeing the scene of a forcible felony after discarding the weapon.

Arraignment and Bail

A suspect who has been arrested cannot be held incommunicado. He or she must be arraigned before a judge, usually within 24 hours, so that the court can determine the legitimacy of the detention. Failure to do so can ultimately result in a contempt of court proceeding and incarceration of those agents refusing to bring the defendant to court. The objective here is to use the court as a neutral and independent authority to check the arrest and detention powers of the police and prevent the loss of individual liberty without due process.

At the arraignment a judge informs the accused of the charges and advises him or her of the constitutional rights to which he or she entitled (e.g., the right to an attorney, the right to court-appointed counsel if he or she is indigent, the right to a public hearing or trial). The accused must enter a plea at this time. One of the most important decisions made here is whether the accused should be incarcerated or released on bail. The main purpose of bail is to ensure the accused returns for trial. The amount of bail is fixed by the seriousness of the charges, the defendant's economic position, and the likelihood of flight.

The Preliminary Hearing

In felony cases a preliminary hearing, also known as probable cause hearing, follows the arraignment. Its purpose is to determine if a crime has been committed and if there is probable cause for the defendant to be charged with it. This stage functions as a screening process to safeguard against unwarranted prosecutions. Both the state and the defendant are actively represented by counsel at this hearing. Evidence of probable cause is presented, and witnesses may be examined and cross-examined for this purpose. The prosecutor need only demonstrate probable cause and does not have to introduce all the evidence at this time. The defense, in turn, can motion for dismissal of the charges or offer evidence on its own behalf.

The judge must then make one of four decisions: (1) dismiss the case; (2) find probable cause that a crime was committed and that the defendant should be charged with it and remand him or her over for trial; (3) find probable cause that a lesser crime was committed by the defendant and bind him or her over to the appropriate court for trial; or (4) find probable cause that a crime was committed but that the defendant did not do it and should be discharged. Once the judge decides that there is probable cause to continue a case against the defendant, one of two things can happen, depending upon the jurisdiction. In some states the prosecutor files the case with the appropriate trial court by means of a formal accusation of the crime against the defendant known as "an information." In other states the prosecutor seeks "an indictment" (formal accusation) against the defendant by presenting the evidence against him or her before a grand jury.

Plea Bargaining

Practically speaking, more than 90 percent of all defendants plead guilty to some crime in the United States and never receive a trial. These guilty pleas are the result of an intricate and highly disputed legal process known as plea bargaining. It is also one of the most crucial, given the administrative, economic, social, and psychological pressures of having to address tens of thousands of criminal cases annually.

Plea bargaining is a negotiated agreement by the defendant to plead guilty for special concessions granted by the prosecutor. These considerations take one or more of six forms. The prosecutor may agree to: (1) charge the defendant with a less serious offense; (2) charge the defendant with an offense carrying a less severe penalty; (3) reduce the number of charges against the defendant; (4) charge the defendant with a less stigmatizing crime (e.g., "sexual assault against a minor" devolves into "sexual assault"); (5) avoid prosecuting the defendant under statutes that compound the conviction, sentence, or both; and (6) recommend probation. The plea bargain is made with the input of both the prosecutor and the defendant. It may be initiated by either party, but typically it is done by the one with the weaker case. Fear of losing, for whatever reason, such as inadequate exculpatory evidence, unreliable witnesses, and damning motive and opportunity, is what drives the negotiation.

There are admittedly numerous difficulties with the plea bargaining system of criminal justice. Prosecutors may overcharge or recommend more severe sentences than they really have a case for so as to bully defendants into pleading guilty. It also (1) abrogates the defendant's constitutional right to have a public trial by a jury of disinterested citizens; (2) frustrates the police and crime victims to see the defendant receive a lesser sentence for a crime of lesser significance; (3) results in prosecutors superseding judges as the central decision makers in criminal cases; and (4) produces much distrust, confusion, and contempt for justice, especially among the poor and minorities who likely have court-appointed attorneys who are less able to be as aggressive in negotiating a fair deal for their clients.

Trials

Trials in the United States are unabashedly adversarial proceedings. The state and defendant offer point and counterpoint arguments in a self-serving, often biased manner. In their dynamic polemic it is hoped that the truth will emerge. The chief role players are the prosecutor, the defense counsel, and the judge. In relatively rare instances, there are also juries, generally composed of 6 or 12 peers, chosen with equal input and approval by both the prosecutor and the defense through a process of selection known as the *voir dire*. The state, through the prosecutor, always begins the trial process by presenting its case against the defendant, aggressively slanting its argument. Witnesses are called and evidence presented according to strict rules of procedure. The burden of proof is entirely with the state. The defendant is always presumed innocent. Moreover, in criminal trials the level of proof is very strict. Prosecutors must prove guilt beyond a reasonable doubt, that is, beyond what any reasonable person could possibly question. It is a much higher level of proof, for example, than claiming that the majority of the evidence points in the direction of guilt. Alternatively, the defendant need not say or do anything. It is quite possible for the prosecutor to present the state's case only to have the defense ask the judge for a "directed verdict" or to dismiss the case for having failed to meet the state's burden of proof.

Many suggest that the main task of the defense counsel is not to prove the defendant innocent or not guilty but rather to ensure that the prosecutor follows all the rules and procedures to make a case against the accused and to challenge any errors. Here due process clearly has precedence over questions of fact. Prosecutors, generally speaking, have an "uphill battle" to prove their cases. The defense can call its own witnesses, produce its own evidence, cross-examine state's witnesses, and refute its evidence in a manner distinctly biased in its own favor. Once the defense has presented its side, the prosecution can rebut, and in turn, the defense can reply to the rebuttals, all within strict procedural guidelines.

After opening statements and arguments have been made, then the defense and the state are each given an opportunity to speak directly to the jury, positioning the major facts in a light most favorable to their side and forcefully reasoning with the jury as to why their side should prevail. Here the defense summarizes the facts as presented in evidence using a "story line" or theme that absolves the client. At the same time, any weaknesses in the state's case may be highlighted, including, especially, references to support claims that the state has failed to prove its case beyond a reasonable doubt. The state, typically, makes its closing argument last, explaining why the jury or judge should find the defendant guilty.

In this courtroom battle, the judge functions as a referee. Judges generally do not directly question the witnesses or the defendant. That role, for the most part, belongs to the prosecutor and the defense counsel. Instead, the judge ensures that the rules of procedure are obeyed by affirming or denying challenges by the state and defense that they have been breached by the opposing side. In the case of jury trials, the jury decides questions of fact only and applies them to the law as provided by the judge. They are not to interpret the law but accept it as defined by the judge.

Sanctions

Sentencing alternatives include fines, probation, victim restitution, imprisonment, the death penalty (in 36 states and the federal system), a split sentence of imprisonment and subsequent probation/parole, community service, commitment to a mental health facility or treatment center for drug addiction or alcoholism, and suspended sentences. Sentencing alternatives tend to be grouped under one of two classifications: "determinate" or "indeterminate" sentences. Determinate sentences, as the term implies, are fixed by statute and associated with particular offenses. Here sentencing is routine and automatic. The judge has no discretion, and neither mitigating nor aggravating circumstances are considered. Deviations are not permitted. Everyone convicted of a particular crime in a given jurisdiction receives exactly the same sentence.

In reality, most determinate sentencing systems allow for some judicial discretion. There is often a range of sentences for each level of offense, and the judge has the discretionary power to choose a specific number of years within this range. The prosecutor may submit evidence of aggravating circumstances, such as the presence of a gun or irreparable injury to the victim, and request a more severe sanction. The defense, in turn, may submit evidence of mitigating circumstances, such as a positive motive for the crime or the defendant's cooperation in bringing the case to a close, and plead for a more lenient sentence. Thus, two persons found guilty of the same offense may receive different sentences.

Indeterminate sentences are those that by statute authorize the judge to impose a sanction that has both minimum and maximum limits. The extent of actual sanction, in turn, will depend upon the defendant's behavior in prison. His or her release at any point between the minimum and maximum sentence is determined by a parole board, which typically reviews the offender's prison adjustment history and considers the potential threat the defendant poses to the community if released. In this system, too, individuals convicted of similar crimes within the same jurisdiction may serve different lengths of time.

In addition, there are other noteworthy sentencing formats, including habitual offender statutes, mandatory sentencing laws, and hate crime statutes, aimed at the habitual, dangerous, and heinous offenders. These sentencing systems allow for the least amount of discretion and individualization. Even with these newer sentencing systems, uniformity of punishment does not prevail. In fact, because sentencing disparities have been the subject of much concern and debate within the criminal justice system, the federal government and 16 states in the 1990s incorporated sentencing guideline systems.

Appeals

All criminal trials allow for an appeal of the verdict and, where there are sentencing guidelines, the sentencing decision. Typical grounds for an appeal include (1) errors in trial procedure, (2) presence of inadmissible evidence at trial, (3) judicial bias or prejudice, (4) failure to allow exculpatory evidence, (5) allowing evidence that should have been suppressed, (6) the emergence of significant new evidence since the original trial, (7) the presence of an unqualified or prejudiced juror, or (8) being misled or lied to by the prosecutor or defense attorney. In most states, only the defense can appeal. Prosecutors cannot appeal either an acquittal verdict or a sentence that they feel is too lenient or inappropriate.

Appeals are generally heard by a panel of three judges. The procedure constitutes a formal review of written and oral arguments focusing on procedures relevant to the contended errors upon which the appeal is based. There is solely a legal argument made by the defense and responded to by the prosecution about procedures, not questions of fact. The appellate court determines whether or not the grounds cited in the appeal led to an error in the verdict or whether it was a harmless error, if it occurred at all. It can affirm the finding of the lower court, remand the case to the lower court for a new trial, set aside the verdict—a very rare finding—letting the defendant go free, or modify or reduce the sanction imposed.

FUTURE OF CRIME AND CRIME CONTROL

Projections for the future call for crime to escalate in scope and seriousness (Butterfield, 1995; Epstein, 1995, U.S. Department of Justice, 1995). Moreover, crime is undergoing a qualitative transformation. Many new forms of crime are anticipated. Most are economically motivated and technologically driven. These will include major disruptions of businesses, intellectual theft, malicious introduction of false information, tampering of medical records, confounding air traffic control activity, interference with national security systems, and the theft and/or distribution (sale) of nuclear devices (Moore, 1994).

Expectations are for the adaptation of new procedures for carrying out old forms of crime. Among these are computer-facilitated embezzlement, industrial sabotage, extortion, fraud, internal theft, blackmail, prescription drug law violations, and security law violations. There is also increasing concern that organized crime will operationalize their own satellite-assisted communications to commit crimes, avoid detection, and derail criminal investigations. Drug trafficking, international auto theft, gun smuggling, and money laundering are already profiting from such technology (Bennett, 1987).

Just as the forms and methods of crime will likely change, so, too, will the style of criminals and their venue. Criminals in the twenty-first century can expect to be better educated, computer literate, sophisticated, and less likely to confront their victims directly. As a consequence of these changes, criminals are more likely to be female and elderly. Furthermore, it is predicted that more crime will be found in small towns and rural areas, especially as industry moves out of the central cities and more people work out of their homes.

In terms of crime control, law enforcement will computerize and become even more technological. Community policing will likely continue to develop and spread nationwide. Moreover, police recruitment, selection, training, goal setting, budget requests, and related policy decisions are also more likely to incorporate community input—and possibly in the form of joint citizen-police ventures. At the same time, however, there will also be the continued development of paramilitary police units across America, introduced allegedly to fight terrorists but used primarily in such everyday policing as the war on drugs. Similarly, the police will likely be less involved in victimless crime operations and will concentrate more on tracking and investigating organized and white-collar criminality, probably led by specially constituted and trained units.

Also anticipated is improved collection and dissemination of information about offenders, offenses, criminal investigations, stolen property, crime victims, and so on. This will mean greater international cooperation in exchanging such information, especially with respect to increased numbers of criminals whose crimes affect the peace and security of more than one country (e.g., gun smuggling, terrorism). Invariably, this will entail enlisting the help of new computers and crime control software, as well as improved satellite communications.

Numerous changes in the criminal court system are likely to be instituted in the not-too-distant future. Its ability to cope with an increasingly sensitive multicultural theme in American society will improve by hiring more interpreters and multicultural staff. Court personnel are likely to become more representative of cultural diversity in their respective communities. Mediation and arbitration are also gaining salience as forms of dispute settlement in the United States. They might be adapted to such criminal offenses as fraud, domestic violence, public drunkenness, vandalism, as well as certain instances of theft, parental kidnapping, and petit theft (less than $250.00). Resolutions may entail restitution, counseling, community service, therapy, and halfway house residency.

Most likely to change in the future with respect to the criminal court system is the administrative mechanism through which criminal and civil justice is served. Among the possibilities are (1) a greater use of electronic surveillance in lieu of jail stays for those awaiting trial; (2) an expanded use of telecommunications to conduct arraignments; (3) more videotaping of witness testimony when they cannot be in court to testify personally; (4) electronic filing of all briefs, pleadings, motions, orders, and petitions, thereby saving time and expediting the dissemination of public information; (5) videotaping trials and editing out overruled objections, sidebars, inappropriate outbursts, and other extraneous or misleading information ancillary to their being presented to a jury; (6) use of computer graphics to reconstruct crime scenes; and (7) development of "kiosk jurisprudence," that is, court information stations located throughout the community where individuals could conduct court business such as filing complaints, paying fines, and receiving information about the status and outcomes of cases (Blowers, 1995).

With respect to punishment and corrections, most experts are pessimistic about the future. Projections anticipate a growing population of incarcerated offenders, as well as those under probation or some other form of community corrections. This means greater proportions of federal, state, and local budgets allocated for controlling convicted offenders. Given the high cost of public-run correctional facilities, there is a movement in progress that advocates privatizing such services. This has been done in a number of jurisdictions handling both adult and juvenile offenders.

Although many state and local governments are experimenting with privatizing corrections, it is a heatedly contested issue, one likely to continue well into the twenty-first century. Briefly, advocates claim that private companies are more economical, efficient, and effective than public agencies and reduce the number of escapes, riots, internal crime, and recidivism, as well as employee nonfeasance and malfeasance. Detractors contend that privatization will result in people doing longer prison sentences at public expense; inmates experiencing abuse and exploitation; a diminished public control over the use of correctional funds; and "net widening," that is, an increase in the number of persons being incarcerated as corporate owners press their vested interests and market their services.

In short, corrections in tandem with the police and courts will likely take advantage of computer technology and other electronic advances. In addition to greater use of electronic anklets worn by many offenders, which allow them to remain in the community as working adults and care providers for their families, it will become common to use heat registers and cameras to track prisoner movements and thus replace guards. Similarly, surgically implanted sensing devices will be able to monitor offenders returned to the community on probation or parole and shock them if they wander outside designated areas. The application of ultrasound to end violent and costly prison riots by temporarily rendering inmates unconscious is another strategy discussed. A major liability of such devices, apart from human rights concerns, is that they are costly to install and maintain.

In sum, the preference since at least the 1980s in the United States has been to punish criminals rather than to invest in reducing the socioeconomic causes of crime. Inequality, social poverty, underemployment, limited or negative educational histories, and other conditions related to criminality are frequently disavowed and disinherited. This will likely continue in the near future, aided by technologies that support a crime control model and expedite the administration of justice even at the expense of due process and individual rights.

REFERENCES

Abadinsky, Howard, and I. Thomas Winfree, Jr. 1992. *Crime and Justice: An Introduction*. 2nd ed. Chicago: Nelson-Hall.

Adler, Freda, Gerhard O. W. Mueller, and William S. Laufer. 1998. *Criminology*. 3rd ed. Westerville, OH: McGraw-Hill.

Beirne, Piers, and James Messerschmidt. 1991. *Criminology*. New York: Harper and Collins.

Bennett, Georgette. 1987. *Crime Warps: The Future of Crime in America*. New York: Anchor Books.

Blowers, Anita Neuberger. 1995. "The Future of American Courts." In B. McGuire and P. Radosh (eds.), *The Past, Present, and Future of American Criminal Justice*. New York: General Hall.

Bopp, William J., and Donald O. Schultz. 1972. *A Short History of American Law Enforcement*. Springfield, IL: Charles Thomas.

Browning, Frank, and John Gerassi. 1980. *The American Way of Crime*. New York: G. P. Putnam's Sons.

Butterfield, Fox. 1995. "Crime Continues to Deline, but Experts Warn of Coming 'Storm' of Juvenile Violence." *New York Times*, November 19, 12.

Cortese, Amy. 1995. "Warding Off the Cyberspace Invaders: Internet Crime Is Increasing. But There Are Ways to Reduce the Heat." *Business Week* (March 13): 92–93.

Davey, Joseph Dilan. 1994. "Crime in America Is Less Than You Think." *Human Rights* 21 (Spring): 1.

Ekirch, A. Roger. 1991. "Bound for America: A Profile of British Convicts Transported to the Colonies, 1718–1775." In Eric H. Monkkonen (ed.), *Crime and Justice in American History: Historical Articles on the Origins and Evolution of American Criminal Justice*. Westport, CT: Meckler, 88–106.

Epstein, Gail. 1995. "Juvenile Crime Wave Coming: Feds Report Arrests Expected to Double by 2021." *U.S. Department of Justice Report*. Washington, DC: Department of Justice.

Flaherty, David H. 1991a. "Crime and Social Control in Provincial Massachusetts." In Eric H. Monkkonen (ed.), *Crime and Justice in American History: Historical Articles on the Origins and Evolution of American Criminal Justice*. Westport, CT: Meckler, 231–63.

———. 1991b. "Law Enforcement of Morals in Early America." In Eric H. Monkkonen (ed.), *Crime and Justice in American History: Historical Articles on the Origins and Evolution of American Criminal Justice*. Westport, CT: Meckler, 127–76.

Gest, Ted, and Dorain Friedman. 1994. "The New Crime Wave." *U.S. News and World Report* (August 19): 28–29.

Greenberg, Douglas. 1991. "The Effectiveness of Law Enforcement in 18th Century New York." In Eric H. Monkkonen (ed.), *Crime and Justice in American History: Historical Articles on the Origins and Evolution of American Criminal Justice*. Westport, CT: Meckler, 264–98.

Hindelang, M. J., M. R. Gottfredson, and J. Garafolo. 1978. *Victims of Personal Crime: An Empirical Foundation for a Theory of Personal Victimization*. Cambridge, MA: Ballinger.

Knox, David, and Caroline Schacht. 1997. *Choices in Relationships: An Introduction to Marriage and Family*. 5th ed. Belmont, CA: Wadsworth.

Kornblum, William, and Joseph Julian. 1995. *Social Problems*. 7th ed. Englewood Cliffs, NJ: Prentice-Hall.

Lacaye, Richard. 1994. "Lock 'Em UP!: War on Crime." *Time* (February 7): 50–53.

"Less of It: About Crime." 1993. *Economist*. 329 (November 13): A33.

Moore, Richter, Jr. 1994. "Wiseguys: Smarter Criminals and Smarter Crime in the 21st Century." *The Futurist* 28 (September): 33.

"Public Opinion and Demographic Report." 1993. *Public Perspective* 3 (November–December): 18.

Reddy, Marlita (ed.). 1994. *Statistical Abstracts of the World*. New York: International Research Institute.

Reid, Sue Titus. 1987. *Crime and Criminology*. 4th ed. New York: Holt, Rinehart and Winston.

Sherman, Rorie. 1994. "Crime's Toll on the U.S.: Fear, Despair, and Guns: National Poll Finds Self Defense Replacing Reliance on Law Enforcement." *National Law Journal* 16 (April 19): 1.

Skogan, W. G., and M. G. Maxfield. 1981. *Coping with Crime: Individual and Neighborhood Reactions*. Beverly Hills, CA: Sage.

Staley, Joseph, and Cindy Ashkins. 1981. "Crime, Crime News, and Crime Views." *Public Opinion Quarterly* 45: 492–506.

U.S. Department of Commerce, Economics, and Statistics Administration. Bureau of the Census. 1995. *Statistical Abstract of the United States, 1995*. Washington, DC: Government Printing Office.

U.S. Department of Justice. 1992. *Criminal Victimization in the United States: 1973–1990 Trends*. A National Crime Victimization Survey Report. Washington, DC: Department of Justice.

———. 1995. *The Uniform Crime Report, 1993*. Washington, DC: Department of Justice.

U.S. Department of Justice. Bureau of Justice Statistics. 1998. *Census of State and Local Law Enforcement Agencies, 1996.* Washington, DC: Department of Justice.

Wagner, Stephen. 1995. "Cities That Satisfy: Urban Residents Value Low Crime Rates, Good Schools, Good Jobs, Strong Families, and Good Health." *American Demographics* 17 (September): 18–20.

Warr, W. 1985. "Fear of Rape among Urban Women." *Social Problems* 32 (February): 238–50.

INDEX

ABOUT THE EDITOR
AND CONTRIBUTORS

CHRIS ABOTCHIE is a Professor of Law and Social Sciences, University of Ghana at Legon.

HANS-JOERG ALBRECHT is Director of the Max-Planck Institute for Foreign and International Penal Law, Freiburg, Germany.

GREGG BARAK is a Professor and former Head of the Department of Sociology, Anthropology, and Criminology, Eastern Michigan University.

WOJCIECH CEBULAK is an Assistant Professor of Criminal Justice, Minot State University, North Dakota.

MAYLING MARIA CHU is an Assistant Professor in the Department of Social Work, California State University, Stanislaus.

EMILIO E. DELLASOPPA is Director, Program for the Study of Violence, Universidade do Estado do Rio de Janeiro (UERJ), Brazil.

OBI N. IGNATIUS EBBE is a Professor in the Department of Criminal Justice, State University of New York (SUNY), College at Brockport, New York.

GARY FEINBERG is an Associate Professor and Chair of the Department of Social Sciences and Counseling, St. Thomas University, Miami, Florida.

MARK S. GAYLORD is a former Associate Professor of Sociology at City University of Hong Kong, China.

NIC GROOMBRIDGE is Senior Lecturer in Criminology at St. Mary's University College, Strawberry Hill, a college of the University of Surrey, United Kingdom.

HAMID R. KUSHA is an Associate Professor, Department of Criminal Justice, History, and Political Science, Texas A & M International University.

INEKE HAEN MARSHALL is an Associate Professor, Department of Criminal Justice, University of Nebraska, Omaha.

JON'A F. MEYER is an Assistant Professor of Criminal Justice, Department of Sociology, Rutgers University, Camden, New Jersey.

GEORGE PAVLICH is a Professor of Criminology, University of Calgary, Canada.

EMIL PLYWACZEWSKI is a Professor, School of Law, University of Bialystok, Poland.

WILLIAM ALEX PRIDEMORE is at the Department of Sociology, University of Oklahoma.

RAYMOND TESKE is a Professor of Criminal Justice at Sam Houston State University, Huntsville, Texas.

HENK VAN DE BUNT is Director of Research and Documentation at the Centre of the Ministry of Justice, the Netherlands, and Professor of Empirical Criminology at the University of Amsterdam.

S. GEORGE VINCENTNATHAN is a Professor of Criminal Justice at Aurora University, Illinois.

JAMES ZION is the Solicitor to the Courts of the Navajo Nation and an Adjunct Professor of the Department of Criminal Justice, Northern Arizona University, Flagstaff.